CENSORED

The News
That Didn't
Make the News
—And Why

Carl Jensen

Shelburne Press

Library of Congress Cataloging-in-Publication Data
Jensen, Carl.
        Censored!

        Includes bibliographical references and index.
        1. Journalism–United States–Political aspects.
2. Television broadcasting of news–United States.
3. Freedom of the press–United States.   4. Censorship–
United States.   I. Title.
PN4888.P6J46 1993   323.44'5'0973   93-18837
ISBN 1-882680-00-6

Book design: Karen Wysocki
Cartoons: Tom Tomorrow
Cover design: Suzanne Anderson, Anderson-Carey Design
Desktop production: Midgard Computing
Index services: Mark Kmetzko
Editorial staff: Patricia Frederick, Marya Glass, Jesma Evans Reynolds, Pam Richardson
Production staff: Rhonda Angel, Karen Wysocki

First Edition 9 8 7 6 5 4 3 2 1
Printed in the United States of America

Project Censored Edition

Shelburne Press, Inc.
P.O. Box 2468
Chapel Hill, NC 27515
919/942-0220
FAX 919/942-1140

About the Author

Dr. Carl Jensen is a professor of Communication Studies at Sonoma State University and Director of Project Censored, an internationally recognized media research project. Founded by Jensen in 1976, Project Censored is America's oldest research project that annually explores news media censorship. Jensen also is editor and publisher of *America's CENSORED Newsletter*.

Jensen has been involved with the media for more than 40 years as a daily newspaper reporter, weekly newspaper publisher, public relations practitioner, advertising executive and educator. He spent 15 years with Batten, Barton, Durstine, and Osborn, the international advertising agency, where he was an award-winning copywriter, account supervisor and vice president.

Specializing in mass communications, Jensen received his B.A., M.A. and Ph.D. degrees in Sociology from the University of California, Santa Barbara, in 1971, 1972 and 1977, respectively.

Since 1973, he has been teaching media, sociology and journalism courses at Sonoma State University where he developed the university's B.A. degree in Communication Studies and the Journalism Certificate Program.

Jensen founded the Lincoln Steffens Journalism Award for Investigative Reporting in Northern California in 1981 and participated in the development of the Bay Area Censored awards program by the Media Alliance in San Francisco in 1989.

He has written and lectured extensively about press censorship, the First Amendment and the mass media.

Jensen has been cited by the National Association for Education in Journalism and Mass Communication for his "innovative approach to constructive media criticism and for providing a new model for media criticism." The Giraffe Project honored Jensen "for sticking his neck out for the common good" and for being a "role model for a caring society." Media Alliance presented Jensen with the Media Alliance Meritorious Achievement Award in the "Unimpeachable Source" category. The Society of Professional Journalists in Los Angeles awarded him its 1990 Freedom of Information Award.

In 1992, Jensen was named the outstanding university professor of journalism in California by the California Newspaper Publishers Association and was awarded the 1992 Hugh M. Hefner First Amendment Award in education from the Playboy Foundation for his achievement in defending the First Amendment.

He has been a guest on many radio/television news and talk shows including a PBS/Bill Moyers television documentary on Project Censored.

Jensen is married and has four children and three grandchildren. He and wife Sandra, his morgan-yellow Morgan and their great Great Dane Danske live in Cotati, California.

Acknowledgments

Many people have contributed to the success of Project Censored, starting of course, with those of you who have sent us nominated stories. We received more than 700 nominations of "Censored" stories for 1992 from journalists, educators, librarians and many others who are interested in the public's right to know. We truly are grateful to all of you who brought those stories to our attention.

Another group important to the project are the Sonoma State University students who participate as Censored researchers. It is their responsibility to analyze the hundreds of nominations received each year to determine whether they qualify as "Censored" stories of the year. Following are the SSU students who evaluated the "Censored" nominations of 1992.

Project Censored Researchers of 1992: Diane Albracht, Beverly Alexander, Peter Anderson, Judy Bailey, Jeannie Blake, Serge Chasson, Amy S. Cohen, Amy Doyle, G. John Faiola, Eric Fedel, Kimberly Kaido, Blake Kehler, Kenneth Lang, Therese Lipsey, Jennifer Makowsky, Stephanie Niebel, Nicole Novak, Valerie Quigley, Kimberly S. Anderson, Damon S. Van Hoesen

Many other groups and individuals have contributed to the success of Project Censored, not the least of which are the publications, mostly from the alternative media, that publish Project Censored's annual results, and the many radio and television news and talk show hosts who discuss the "Censored" stories each year.

We also wish to acknowledge the support we receive from Sonoma State University, particularly from Bill Babula, Dean of the School of Arts and Humanities; David Walls, General Manager of the SSU Academic Foundation; and Mark Resmer, Director of Computing, Media, and Telecommunications Services. I am grateful to Steve Rhode for giving us a crash cource in publishing law and to Jerry Greenberg for persuading Steve to work with us on a *pro bono* basis.

Two other organizations deserve special recognition. The interest, encouragement and financial support from the C.S. Fund, of Freestone, California, and Anita Roddick and the Body Shop Foundation, of England, contribute significantly to the successful outreach of Project Censored. Also, were it not for support from the C.S. Fund and the Body Shop Foundation, we would not have an assistant director, Mark Lowenthal, working with us. Among many other activities, Mark is directly responsible for responding to the thousands of letters and phone calls we receive from people throughout the country and abroad each year.

I also want to thank Joe Woodman, of Shelburne Press, for tracking us down and for having the faith and fortitude to publish this yearbook. It couldn't have been an easy decision. When I tried to find a publisher for an earlier version of this book, my agent was turned down by some 50 different publishing houses. The primary reason given was the sensitive and controversial nature of the subject matter. Thanks Joe for your faith in the First Amendment and for believing in us. And Joe isn't the only one at Shelburne who made this book possible. The TLC provided me by Elizabeth Woodman along with her sensitive editing and that by Pat Frederick makes this a more readable book. Pam Richardson deserves special recognition for coordinating the entire project. Others at Shelburne who have earned my gratitude include Diane Lennox (who spread the word about the book), Larry Levitsky, Joy Metelits, Fran Phillips, Laura Wenzel, Karen Wysocki and Ruffin Prevost. And a high-tech acknowledgment is due to America Online, the computer online service that provided us with instant coast-to-coast communications.

Finally, I want to thank my wife, Sandra Scott Jensen, for the many hours she spent reviewing early versions of this document, and for all the support and encouragement she has given me and Project Censored since its start in 1976.

About the Contributors

Tom Tomorrow is the "nom-de-cartoon" of Dan Perkins, whose weekly comic strip of social and political satire, "This Modern World," runs in 70 papers across the country. His work appears in many major weeklies, such as the *LA Reader* and the *Baltimore City Paper*, and a few forward-looking dailies, such as the *San Francisco Examiner* and the *Des Moines Register*. Perkins's work has also appeared in the *New York Times*, the *Washington Post* and the *Village Voice*. His first book, *Greetings From This Modern World*, was released in 1992 by St. Martin's Press. He lives in San Francisco with his girlfriend, his copier and an abundance of cats.

Marya Glass, who created the comprehensive resource guide in Appendix B, is a freelance writer and editor living in the San Francisco Bay Area. Her articles have appeared in various local publications; she also writes advertising copy while attempting to strike that delicate balance between earning a living as a writer and earning a living.

A Chicago native, she graduated with a degree in environmental studies and planning, as well as a journalism certificate, from Sonoma State University. As a student, she was involved in Project Censored 1990. She also received the Sonoma County Press Club's annual journalism scholarship for two articles she wrote about pornography in college curriculum, censorship and the arts.

Her journalistic interests are widespread, with special focus on media, the environment and social commentary. On her off-days, she has been seen reading supermarket tabloids in secretive corners of the laundromat.

How to Nominate a Censored Story

Some of the most interesting nominations Project Censored receives are from people who spot something in the back pages of their newspaper or in a small-circulation magazine and wonder why they haven't seen anything reported about it elsewhere. You, too, can help the public learn more about what is happening by nominating stories you feel should have received more coverage from the national news media. The story should be current and of national or international significance. It may have received no media attention at all, appeared in your local newspaper or some special interest trade magazine, or been the subject of a radio or television documentary that received little exposure or follow-up. Your nominations, input and suggestions are important to the success of Project Censored. To nominate a "Censored" story, just send us a copy of the story, including the source and date. The annual deadline is November 1. Please send nominations to:

NOMINATION
Project Censored
Sonoma State University
Rohnert Park, CA 94928

America's First Censored Newsletter

In 1992, Carl Jensen, founder and director of Project Censored, launched a national newsletter to report on censorship issues throughout the year. It now has subscribers throughout the United States and in more than a half dozen foreign countries. *America's CENSORED Newsletter* is published monthly (except in January). Readers learn about the latest Censored nominations; reports on censored books and films; profiles of censored investigative journalists; déjà vu updates on issues censored years ago; "junk food news" issues; tips on learning more about censorship and censored issues; and much more.

To subscribe to *America's CENSORED Newsletter*, please send $30 (U.S.) or $45 (international) to:

America's CENSORED Newsletter
P.O. Box 310
Cotati, CA 94931 USA

Project Censored Judges Acknowledgments

One of Project Censored's most difficult challenges is selecting the "Top Ten Censored" stories from the 25 top nominations. This responsibility falls to our distinguished national panel of judges who volunteer their efforts. Perhaps one of the greatest tributes to the project is that some of our judges, identified with asterisks below, have participated in Project Censored every year since selecting the first group of Censored stories of 1976. We are deeply indebted to the following judges who selected the top ten Censored stories of 1992.

Dr. Donna Allen, founding editor of *Media Report to Women*

Richard Barnet, senior fellow, Institute for Policy Studies

Noam Chomsky,* professor, Linguistics and Philosophy, MIT

Hugh Downs, host, ABC's "20/20"

Susan Faludi, journalist/author

Dr. George Gerbner, professor, Annenberg School of Communications, University of Pennsylvania

Nicholas Johnson,* professor, College of Law, University of Iowa

Rhoda H. Karpatkin, executive director, Consumers Union

Charles L. Klotzer, editor and publisher, *St. Louis Journalism Review*

Judith Krug, director, Office for Intellectual Freedom, American Library Association

William Lutz, professor, English, Rutgers University, and editor of *The Quarterly Review of Doublespeak*

Jack L. Nelson,* professor, Graduate School of Education, Rutgers University

Herbert I. Schiller, Professor Emeritus of Communication, University of California–San Diego

Sheila Rabb Weidenfeld,* president, D.C. Productions

Dedication

To Martin Jensen, my late father, who
taught me to honor truth in my personal life

&

To George Seldes, America's Journalist
Emeritus, who taught me to honor truth
in journalism

Contents

Preface

In response to growing national demand for news and information not published nor broadcast by the mainstream media in America, *CENSORED! The News That Didn't Make the News—And Why* is being published annually.

Formerly self-published as the *Project Censored Yearbook*, *CENSORED!* is published by Shelburne Press in Chapel Hill, North Carolina. As in the three previous *Yearbooks* (1989-1991), *CENSORED!* features background information about *Project Censored*, comments about the 25 Censored stories of 1992 by the original authors and others, brief synopses of each of the stories, and a chapter on the top "junk food news" stories of 1992, with comments by the news ombudsmen who selected them.

This edition also includes a special introduction by Hugh Downs; a déjà vu chapter of previously Censored stories that suddenly have been "discovered" by the mainstream media; an eclectic chronology of censorship since 605 BC that tends to put the whole issue into historical context; and a useful censored resource guide to alternative media organizations, electronic and print alternative media, as well as some selected mainstream media sources that we promise to keep current annually.

Also, *CENSORED!* fulfills a goal I've had since launching Project Censored in 1976–it contains reprints of the original censored articles wherever possible. For the first time, you'll be able to review the brief synopsis of the issue, see what the author has to say about the subject, and then read the original article in its entirety.

The synopses are originally written by Project Censored researchers participating in a seminar in news media censorship offered by the Communication Studies Department at Sonoma State University, a member of the California State University system. They are then edited for style and clarity. The synopses are not meant to replace the original articles upon which they are based, but rather to briefly summarize the major thrust of a longer article or, in some cases, a brochure or a book.

CENSORED! The News That Didn't Make The News–And Why is another effort by Project Censored to provide more information on important issues the public should know about. I hope you will learn more about issues that touch your life, your community and, in a larger context, the global village of which we are all citizens.

I also hope that it will disturb you to discover that all this information was available to the press and that you will wonder why your local and national news media haven't already told you about these subjects.

Finally, I would like to invite you to join Project Censored as a scout or source for stories that deserve more attention from the mainstream media. Please see "How to Nominate a Censored Story" for information on how to nominate stories for the "Best Censored of 1993."

– *Carl Jensen*

Introduction
By Hugh Downs

I n the same way that a fish is probably unaware that water exists, Americans take the rights of free speech and free press for granted. Many of us have a tendency not to think about those freedoms at all. How could we not be able to say anything we want in America? Or print anything we want?

These glorious rights, encompassed in the First Amendment, have uncovered malfeasance, foiled *coups d'état*, exposed extremism and kept a capitalist democracy on the rails for more than 200 years. Through it we have developed and preserved a political sense of humor.

Something in the American character tends to expel the grotesque. Aaron Burr's scheme for secession at Blennerhasset Island failed. Huey Long never quite emerged. And Senator Joseph McCarthy's reign-of-terror in the 1950s was destroyed. While it is true that as the late Willy Brandt told me in a TV interview, "There is a Nazi potential in every country," I have always felt that before such a faction could seize power in the U.S., it would be laughed out of the arena. Unless...

Unless we lost our freedoms of speech and press, and hate and fear could grow malignantly to the point where nothing was funny anymore. Consider the famous Jefferson statement that if he had to choose between government and no newspapers, or newspapers and no government, he would opt for the newspapers. This shows an awareness that a free people who can come into possession of true facts could, even in a condition of anarchy, forge a government that would be tolerable for them. But if a government existed which could keep truth from the people, it would be difficult, if not impossible, for them to establish justice and freedom.

If we have freedom of speech and the press, why is there talk about censorship here? No government agency screens the suitability of what is printed or broadcast. No official permission must be obtained to report a story or give a speech.

The reason for a growing concern about censorship is because it does exist, in both subtle and unsubtle forms: The mildest of these is what I would call Deference to Public Perception. If we report on a Mob hit, we feel no hint of restriction on exposing the facts. The public doesn't like gangsters. But if medical science were to discover that apple pie is bad for your health, we'd be inclined to put a spin on the story, deferring to the fact that the public would resist having such an American icon cast in a bad light. The story would be told with a hint of skepticism or given lower priority than it might deserve. Not everywhere, but in the more sedate and mainstream media.

For a specific example of this form of censorship, consider this: The Kennedy mystique has remained so strong in America that stories about President Kennedy's extramarital affairs, and the libidinous behavior of the whole clan, though long known, were reluctantly and tardily published in this country. An excellently researched and documented segment on the relationship between Marilyn Monroe and Jack and Bobby Kennedy was to be broadcast on "20/20" in 1985; but at the last minute the network quailed and we were not permitted to air it.

The network's stated reason was two-fold: The story needed more documentation. (It was better documented than any Watergate story I worked with.) The network also considered the story to be "sleazy" journalism. I could not agree with this. It was a sordid story; but unfortunately, we have to deal with these at times. If the subject of this piece were the owner of a home heating-oil company, I agree it would be sleazy. But, as I said then, a dead president belongs to history and to an accurate history, not a whitewash of any kind.

The substance of our censored Kennedy story was broadcast in England and later on cable in America, but by then there was no point in our seeking to follow. We lost some good people over that, including Sylvia Chase, one of TV's best journalists, who, I am happy to report, is back with the ABC Network as of this writing.

The second kind of censorship comes from Journalistic Fashion and Taste. President Roosevelt had polio and could not walk. But his paraplegia, although known and exploited for the March of Dimes, was never shown in pictures or described as part of a news event. No pictures of the wheelchair ever. It just was not done. There was no law about this, but the press simply didn't do it. Just as we never used the word "condom" until, several years into our battle with AIDS, Surgeon General C. Everett Koop saw that public squeamishness over the word was undermining an important health effort. (This, curiously, was a case in which a government official got rid of a taboo-type censorship.)

A third kind of censorship stems from a perverted Respect for the Office–at least where the presidency is concerned. Courtesy is nice. And the office deserves respect. But lately, out of public confusion about the office and the official, a good deal of the press, it seems to me, has been overly careful about looking discourteous. Maybe it's just a tendency to mirror public attitude, which I believe has been off-base for quite awhile in its perception of the presidency.

We have lost sight of the fact that anyone elected to that office is our servant. He is hired by us, paid by us and must answer to us. If his stewardship merits respect, we should pay it, but in the same way we reward any faithful servant. We seem tainted with a hat-in-hand attitude, bowing and scraping and knuckling our collective forelock. An invitation to the White House is regarded as a command to appear. I've seen people who couldn't attend a White House function worry about looking boorish or rebellious in declining. This is awful in a free country. Press reflection of this is mild, but it results in a form of censorship that manifests itself in overcautiousness.

The fourth type of censorship is overt: Government does have the power to block access to information, on several grounds–some possibly appropriate for the good of the whole nation but many not legitimate. Since the Nixon administration, the government has made several attempts to invoke prior restraint censorship, impose gag rules and bottle up documents for reasons that have nothing to do with national security. Instead, these actions are sanctioned by certain government officials who want to avoid embarrassment and/or preserve power. Even the Freedom of Information Act has been thwarted by administrations anxious to keep a lid on certain facts.

Obviously, this abuse of power threatens our freedom of press by not allowing reporters access to important information. Moreover, it delays justice and undermines democracy.

Some time ago my son, Hugh R. Downs, put me onto Carl Jensen's Project Censored, which he had discovered in preparing the radio commentaries I air on Bob Walker's "Perspectives" on ABC Talk Radio Network each Sunday. We've been covering the project ever since. As an indication of its importance, we get more mail on the Project Censored commentaries–more requests for transcripts–than on anything else I do.

American citizens seem to be increasingly athirst for answers that never come. And they seem to appreciate the efforts of anyone who can ferret out the truth about situations they see as mysterious.

A crusade against censorship is forming behind Carl's work. This book, like Project Censored, locates cans of worms and opens them. It creates an awareness where one is needed. *CENSORED!* will prove alternately enjoyable, alarming and infuriating. As you read of events and situations you may have heard of once, briefly, and then wondered why you never heard anything more, or why nothing was ever done about them, you will realize that the ability of those holding high office to stonewall, to lie, to coverup, is quite awesome. But as this book reveals, awesome too is our desire to know and to keep our press free. *CENSORED!* and Carl Jensen send a message that censorship will be exposed.

> "The only thing necessary for
> the triumph of evil is for good
> men to do nothing."
> —Edmund Burke

CENSORED

Chapter 1

Project Censored: Raking Muck, Raising Hell

The press is keeping a closely guarded secret from you and other Americans: despite your constitutional rights to free speech and a free press, you're only getting part of the information you need to be well informed about the world around you. This is true even if you happen to live in New York City, the so-called Media Mecca of the world. In fact, New Yorkers who depend on Dan Rather, the *New York Times* and Time-Warner for their news are often less well informed than residents of Podunk who turn to America's alternative press for their information.

Indeed, if the essence of communication is to transmit information from one location to another, and if a function of information is to provide knowledge to improve one's life, then we have succeeded greatly at the former and failed woefully at the latter. We may have a free press and the most sophisticated communications system in the world, but a free press and high technology don't guarantee a well-informed society.

As a society, we're exposed to more information now than ever before. Thanks to recent developments in communications technology and the growing diversity of news sources, the average citizen today is exposed to more up-to-the-minute news coverage from throughout the world than was available to our national leaders just a few years ago. CNN viewers in Keokuk, Iowa, were probably better and more quickly informed of events in the Gulf War than Lyndon Johnson was of Vietnam. Consequently, we're spending an ever-increasing amount of time with the information media. For example, TV news buffs can watch hourly updates on the networks, round-the-clock news on CNN and special coverage on channels like C-SPAN. In fact, in 1992 Richard Harwood, syndicated media columnist and former ombudsman for the *Washington Post*, reported that the average person spent some 3,256 hours a year, nearly nine hours a day, listening, watching and reading the media; more hours than were devoted to any other activity, including sleep and work.

We certainly can't complain about the quantity of information (indeed, it sometimes reaches overload). But what about its quality? Here we have an alarming situation. Despite the surfeit of news and information, you and 250 million other Americans aren't being told everything you need—and have a right—to know. The fact is, we are victims of subtle but pervasive forms of censorship.

Certainly, most of us believe the United States faces serious social and economic issues. But are we really fully aware of the scope of these problems? Do we have all the information we need to deal with them? The answer is no. And we cannot function as responsible citizens without being fully informed about primary social issues of the moment. Yet, it's unrealistic to expect anything to change, in Washington or in our communities, until enough people become fully aware of the status quo and vent their outrage.

For that to happen, we need someone out there raking muck and raising hell. This of course should be the role of a free press—but the media are selling us short.

Joseph Pulitzer once said, "We are a democracy, and there is only one way to get a democracy on its feet in the matter of its individual, its social, its municipal, its state, its national conduct, and that is by keeping the public informed about what is going on. There is not a crime, there is not a dodge, there is not a trick, there is not a swindle, there is not a vice which does not live by secrecy. Get these things out in the open, describe them, attack them, ridicule them in the press, and sooner or later public opinion will sweep them away...publicity may not be the only thing that is needed, but it is the one thing without which all other agencies will fail."

Yet, today the publicity and information of which Pulitzer spoke are not readily available to us. Why? Because our major media systematically omit news about significant issues, presenting instead a distorted picture of our society—the same mythical evocation of enduring prosperity that massaged us and deceived us throughout the 1980s. It's an image that a select segment of our society may wish to promote, but, in truth, it's an empty caricature that must be fleshed out and rendered realistically if we're to survive as a democracy.

To perceive how this situation has come about in a society with a much vaunted free press, we need to understand how the flow of information is manipulated.

Totalitarian societies practice outright, overt censorship. The state determines what can or cannot be said or printed by its monopolistic control over the media. The massive coverup of the 1986 Chernobyl nuclear power disaster by Soviet Communist leaders was a classic example of this form of censorship.

In 1991, a Russian parliamentary commission, chaired by Volodymyr Yavorivsky, revealed that Soviet authorities reacted to the Chernobyl disaster with "a total lie, falsehoods, cover-up and concealment" that led to thousands of deaths.

In democratic societies, we find economic pressures, a system that rewards journalists who go along and punishes those who rock the boat, and a less obvious, but nonetheless effective control of the media. The private sector owns and controls the newspapers and magazines, the radio and television stations—and it dictates what is reported. Consider the nuclear power issue, American-style. For more than 20 years, the failure of the press to widely report nuclear accidents and "incidents"— combined with the propagandistic promise of the "peaceful atom"—successfully lulled America into unquestioned acceptance of nuclear reactors in our neighbor-hoods. Then the Three Mile Island catastrophe in 1979 shattered the dream.

Whether by overt "Soviet-style" or covert "American-style" censorship, the efforts to cover up the hazards of nuclear power were successful.

The crucial difference is that citizens in a totalitarian society know their informa-tion is controlled and manipulated. Citizens of a free society, however, believe the mass media provide them with objective, uncensored information about world events and issues. Thus, we tend to be hoodwinked into believing we're well informed.

The control process starts with the need to gain ownership of the news- and information-producing media. In the United States, this already has happened. As media scholar Ben Bagdikian points out, fewer than 23 corporations now own and control the majority of the media in America.

Most Americans receive their news and information from one of the three television network evening news broadcasts. Others, who consider themselves better informed, have more diversified sources of news, including CNN and PBS television, local radio stations, one of the three weekly news magazines and, of course, the daily newspaper that arrives on their doorstep.

There are some 1,650 daily newspapers in the country today, fewer than in the late 19th century. And while some interpret this statistic as meaning we're privileged to have such a diversified, local source of information, the truth is that ownership control of these papers is becoming increasingly concentrated and their content increasingly standardized. Of all cities in the United States with daily newspapers, less than three percent now have competing papers. And a single wire service, the Associated Press, is the dominant source of non-local news.

The point is that our primary sources of news and information are increasingly being controlled by a small group of people.

To combat this lock on our right to know, I've conducted a national media research project since the mid-Seventies. It seeks to locate and publicize those dissonant messages; messages media monopolies don't want the rest of us to know.

Project Censored: An Early Warning System

Concerned about increasing social problems and public apathy, I launched Project Censored in 1976. Its charter was to explore and expose the systematic omission of certain issues from our national news media. My quest was specifically stimulated by personal bewilderment over how the American people could elect Richard Nixon by a landslide after Watergate, one of the most sensational political crimes of the century.

Now an international media research project in its seventeenth year, Project Censored ferrets out and publicizes stories of national importance on issues that have been overlooked or underreported by the mainstream news media. The project seeks to stimulate journalists and editors to provide more mass media coverage of those ignored issues, and hopes to encourage the public to seek out and demand more information on those and other matters.

Since its start, Project Censored has generated queries for more information about the project as well as about individual stories from journalists, scholars and concerned people throughout the world. It has been described variously as a tip sheet for investigative television programs such as "60 Minutes" and "20/20," as well as a distant early-warning system for society's problems. It has even been called a "moral force" in American media. In 1988, the National Association for Education in Journalism and Mass Communication cited the project for "providing a new model for media criticism for journalism education."

Despite its growing international recognition and influence, the project has largely been ignored by the major U.S. news media, not known for their inclination to accept and evaluate criticism. While the results of Project Censored have been published in major media outside the United States, including Canada, Mexico, England, Ireland, Sweden and Denmark, the results are regularly ignored by the leading newspapers in this country.

The Censored Research Process

For the last 17 years, researchers in the censorship seminar at Sonoma State University, in Rohnert Park, California, have reviewed thousands of stories that many Americans have not seen or heard about but should have. These underreported stories are nominated annually by journalists, scholars, librarians and the general public throughout the United States and abroad.

From the hundreds of stories submitted for consideration each year, the seminar researchers select the top 25 stories, according to a number of criteria, including the amount of coverage the story received, the national or international importance of the issue, the reliability of the source and the potential impact the story may have.

Next, the top 25 "Censored" stories are submitted in synopsis form to a panel of judges who then select the top ten stories of the year.

In addition to the individuals cited in "Project Censored Judges Acknowledgments" in the front of this book, judges who have participated in past projects include Hodding Carter, Shirley Chisholm, John Kenneth Galbraith, Charlayne Hunter-Gault, James J. Kilpatrick, Robert MacNeil, Mary McGrory, John McLaughlin, Jessica Mitford, Bill Moyers, George Seldes, Susan Sontag, Alvin Toffler and Mike Wallace.

Before examining why some issues are overlooked—what the Project considers "censored"—and why other issues are overcovered—what we call "junk food news"—let's define censorship.

Censorship Defined

Censorship has a long and scurrilous history, which dates back at least two millennia before the invention of the printing press. However, its longevity has not contributed to a universal understanding of what censorship is nor the various forms in which it is manifested. Definitions of censorship are as varied and numerous as there are scholars, politicians and lexicographers eager to address the subject. A brief review of definitions found in three authoritative sources provides insight into the problems surrounding censorship and people's attitudes toward it.

The *Encyclopedia of Library and Information Science* defines censorship as "an effort by a government, private organization, group, or individual to prevent people from reading, seeing, or hearing what may be considered as dangerous to government or harmful to public morality."

The *Encyclopedia of Social Sciences* offers the following definition of censorship: a "policy of restricting the public expression of ideas, opinions, conceptions and impulses which have or are believed to have the capacity to undermine the governing authority or the social and moral order which that authority considers itself bound to protect."

The *New Encyclopedia Britannica* calls censorship "the suppression or prohibition of speech or writing that is condemned as subversive of the common good."

The theme winding through these and most other definitions assumes that an elite group in society is almost forced to practice censorship in order to protect others from the dangers in a society. This thesis builds on the belief (shared by Plato, St. Augustine and Machiavelli, among others) that some individuals in society are best qualified to identify evil and therefore should be empowered to prevent its dissemination. Today's Schlaflys, Helmses, Wildmons, Buchanans and Robertsons are some contemporary proponents of this concept.

Conversely, I believe that a well-informed individual is better able to determine what is best for himself or herself. This belief—building on ideals such as those of Aristotle, Oliver Wendell Holmes, Jr., and John Dewey—provides the cornerstone of Project Censored. People are free only if they're able to make their own choice.

When I founded Project Censored in 1976, I expanded this definition of censorship. Rather than starting with the source of censorship as traditionally defined (the obligation of an elite to protect the masses), my definition begins at the other end—with the failure of information to reach the people.

First, Project Censored is founded upon the principle that real and meaningful public involvement in societal decisions is possible only if all ideas are allowed to compete daily in the media marketplace for public awareness, acceptance and understanding.

GOOD EVENING--I'M DAN RATHER. LEADING OFF THE NEWS TONIGHT, A MAJOR CONFLAGRATION THAT COULD HAVE DECIMATED NEW YORK CITY WAS NARROWLY AVOIDED THIS AFTERNOON!

"...IT WAS 4:00 P.M. IN THE CBS STUDIOS WHEN A TECHNICIAN LIGHTING A CIGARETTE ACCIDENTALLY DROPPED HIS MATCH!"

"HAD THERE BEEN A LARGE STACK OF OLD NEWSPAPERS NEARBY, OR A PILE OF GASOLINE-SOAKED RAGS, THERE MIGHT HAVE BEEN A FIRE WHICH COULD HAVE DESTROYED THE STUDIOS--AND, IN A WORST-CASE SCENARIO, POSSIBLY MUCH OF NEW YORK!

[ARTIST'S RENDITION]

Next, it recognizes that the mass media, particularly the network TV evening news programs, are the public's primary sources of information about world events. If, however, the public does not receive the information required to make informed decisions, then some form of news blackout or failure has occurred.

In brief, then, Project Censored defines censorship as the suppression of information, whether purposeful or not, by any method—including bias, omission, underreporting or self-censorship—that prevents the public from fully knowing what is happening in its society.

Another way to look at the conceptual differences is that definers of traditional censorship are concerned with controlling *dangerous expressions or ideas*; I prefer to suggest that a free flow of information is necessary to control or counteract *dangerous individuals or groups*.

Historically, censorship can be classified into three basic categories: religious censorship, political censorship and censorship of obscenities. Religion was the first major target of censorship, with non-believers and infidels punished for blasphemy and heresy. Next came the censorship of unacceptable political ideas, with the disloyal renegades who disagreed with the prevailing powers persecuted for treason. More recently, the controversial subject of sex has elicited punishment for those who utter obscenities, distribute pornography or even want to discuss safe sex.

We can now add a fourth important category—the censorship of news. In the mid-20th century, concurrent with the advent of television and the increasing value of information, news media censorship and self-censorship became such a powerful force it could no longer be ignored. For it is the free flow of news and information that warns a society of its problems. Without freedom of the press, we are grievously subject to and unaware of censorship of other forms, including religion, politics and morals. Redefining censorship has concerned many Project critics and even some of its participants. Ben Bagdikian, one of the first Project judges, voiced his criticism of the use of the term "censored" when the Project was first launched. After several years of reviewing the issues raised by the research effort, however, he withdrew his criticism, saying that we had finally "institutionalized the term."

Why Are Some Issues Overlooked?

One of the questions often asked is, Why doesn't the press cover the issues raised by Project Censored? The failure of the news media to cover critical and sometimes controversial issues consistently and in-depth is not, as some say, a conspiracy on the part of the media elite. News is too diverse, fast-breaking and unpredictable to be controlled by some sinister, conservative, eastern-establishment media cabal.

However, there are a variety of factors operating that, when combined, lead to the systematic failure of the news media to inform the public fully. While it is not an overt form of censorship, such as the kind we observe in some societies, it is nonetheless real and often equally dangerous.

The media's explanations for censorship are plentiful. Sometimes a source for a story isn't considered to be reliable; other times the story doesn't have an easily identifiable "beginning, middle and end"; some stories are considered to be "too complex" for the general public; on occasion stories are ignored because they haven't been "blessed" by the *New York Times* or the *Washington Post*. Reporters and editors at most of the other 1,650 daily newspapers know their news judgment isn't going to be challenged when they publish fashionable "follow-the-leader" stories, a practice that leads to the "pack" or "herd" behavior.

Another contributing factor to media self-censorship is the specter of libel suits. Long and costly jury trials, and sometimes large judgments against the media, have produced a massive chilling effect on the press and replaced copy editors with copy attorneys.

Nonetheless, the bottom-line explanation for much of the censorship found in the mainstream media is the media's own bottom line. Corporate media are too often driven by profit, not by a responsibility to inform the public. Many stories cited by Project Censored are not in the best financial interests of publishers, owners, stockholders or advertisers.

Equally important, investigative journalism is more expensive than the traditional public-stenographer school of journalism.

And, of course, the "don't rock the boat" mentality pervades corporate media boardrooms and filters down to the newsroom.

Jonathan Alter, media columnist for *Newsweek*, suggests an additional reason for the lack of coverage given some issues. According to Alter, some stories are not covered because they don't fit conventional definitions of news. This, of course, is why I suggest it's time for journalism to rethink these definitions. In a period of potential economic collapse, nuclear terrorism and environmental disaster, it's not news when a man bites a dog.

Real news is not repetitive, sensationalistic coverage of non-important events, such as the Murphy Brown-Dan Quayle episode that attracted so much media attention in 1992. That story is an example of "junk food news."

By contrast, real news is objective and reliable information about important events happening in a society. The widespread dissemination of such information helps people become better informed, and a better informed public can elect politicians who are more responsive to its needs.

Would It Make a Difference?

Finally, another question is often asked about the Project. Would it really make any difference if the press were to provide more coverage of the kinds of stories cited by Project Censored?

The answer is very simple: yes.

First, we must address the issue of a lack of public interest. Critics of Project Censored say that the media give the public what it wants; i.e., junk food news, because people aren't interested in reading about the issues raised by Project Censored. I counter this by saying that, unaware of alternatives, people will indeed read or watch what the mass media produce. However, I suggest it's the media's responsibility, as watchdogs of society, to explore, compile and present information people should know about in a way that draws their attention and relates to their everyday lives. People, indeed, have a genuine desire to know more about issues that affect them. Your interest in this book confirms that.

But then, the next question is, Would it make any difference if the people were better informed?

Hunger in Africa was consistently nominated as a Censored subject during the early 1980s. When I asked journalists why they didn't cover the tragedy unfolding there, they would reply: "It's not news," or "Everyone already knows about starving Africans," or "Nothing can be done about it anyway."

Early in 1984, an ABC-TV News correspondent in Rome came upon information that led him to believe that millions of Africans were being threatened by drought and famine. He requested permission from the home office in New York to take his crew to Africa to get the story. The answer was no. There's an ironic twist to this story. I subsequently discovered that the same ABC producer who refused to let the TV crew go to Africa killed a two-part "Nightline" series on Project Censored two years later that explored whether the news media ever overlook, undercover or censor important stories.

ABC was not the only, nor even the first, television network to reject the tragic story of starving children in Ethiopia. In October 1983, David Kline, a freelance journalist and news producer in San Francisco, shot film on assignment for CBS. The footage showed emaciated adults and some children near death. According to the *Columbia Journalism Review,* one of the children in Kline's footage was so thin that his heart could be seen beating through the chest wall. Nonetheless, Kline was told *the footage was not strong enough.* After being rejected by CBS, Kline offered the story to NBC and PBS; they both turned him down. Television networks weren't the only media to reject the story about millions of people facing death. Magazines such as *Life, Playboy,* the *New Yorker, Esquire, Harper's* and *Mother Jones* all rejected it. Only the *Christian Science Monitor* ran Kline's piece.

Later, a BBC television crew traveling through Ethiopia captured the stark reality of children starving to death. People throughout the world saw the coverage and responded. Overnight, it sparked a worldwide reaction that reportedly saved the lives of seven million Ethiopians.

Reflections on Censorship

Following are some additional insights into how Project Censored judges perceive "censorship" and the Project's critical role in identifying it.

Nicholas Johnson, a former member of the Federal Communications Commission and a founding member of the Censored panel of judges: "'Censorship' is defined by dictionaries, the general population, and the Supreme Court as something done by agents of governments. Although the First Amendment guarantees 'free speech' and 'free press,' it only protects those who wish to speak or write controversial information and ideas from suppression by governments.

"There is no First Amendment right to have your writing published in the local newspaper, even (or perhaps especially) if you are 'just are reporter'—not to mention a private citizen. The Supreme Court has said that publishers (and broadcasters) are free to keep out of their papers and programming ideas they don't like. As A.J. Liebling has said, freedom of the press is for those who own them.

"Ideas may be suppressed by private owners for any one of a number of reasons. They may run counter to their perception of their economic interests, their political inclinations, pressure from advertisers or their wealthy friends and neighbors, or their concept of 'patriotism' or 'decency.' They may be suppressed because owners deliberately hire repeaters rather than reporters, or because they don't provide good investigative reporters with the time and resources necessary to dig out the story.

"None of this is, technically speaking, 'censorship.'

"The reasons for the First Amendment are well known, among them: the more effective search for truth made possible by a 'marketplace of ideas,' its essential contribution to our capacity for self-governing, the check on abuses by government and other institutions, the 'safety valve' alternative it provides to violent strategies for change, and the self-actualization made possible through self-expression—an essential component of 'liberty.'

"Certainly suppression of information, ideas and opinion by governments— 'government censorship'—is something to be fought by a free people. Especially was this so in ages past when the greatest threats to free speech came from government.

"But is it not obvious that, from the perspective of the purposes of the First Amendment, it makes little difference whether the suppression is accomplished by government or private forces? Is it not obvious that the vigil of our forbearers over suppression by governments is one that, today, must be undertaken by our generation to be ever alert to suppression by media conglomerates and their advertisers?

"Recently a spokesperson for a major media conglomerate, on the occasion of a merger that would make it larger still, commented that someday there would be only five firms to control all the major media on planet earth. The corporation was simply positioning itself to be one of those five.

"Nothing such entities can do are defined by the Supreme Court as 'censorship,' because they are not governments. Carl Jensen knows better. And now, thanks to him, so do we all.

"I have been proud to lend my support to Project Censored virtually from its inception. And that is the primary reason why. Project Censored has actually redefined 'censorship' to give it a modern, late 20th-century definition. It is a definition that fits our times, and can carry forward the American dream for our grandchildren into the 21st century.

"But only if we understand it, and act accordingly."

Rhoda H. Karpatkin, president of the Consumers Union and a Censored judge since 1988: "If Americans can't get good information, they can't participate effectively in the political process. That means that when important news events are censored—concealed in one way or another from the public—citizen participation is undermined.

"In the formative days of our Republic, citizens relied on such publications as *The Federalist Papers* and Tom Paine's writings. Today, too, they rely on the press, and the press has to be reliable.

"The story may be hard to get, confused, complex, boring, repetitive, anathema to some constituency, or concealed by the government. But the citizen needs to know, and the press needs to reject the role of handmaiden to the censor.

"Project Censored shines a spotlight on news that an informed public must have, and on the ever present threat of censorship. It's a vital contribution to our democratic process."

Noam Chomsky, internationally renowned linguist, eminent commentator and scholar of politics and society, and Censored judge since 1976: "Censorship, broadly construed, comes in many varieties. The United States is unusually (perhaps uniquely) free of the most obvious form—direct state intervention to prevent publication or speech—though even here the record is far from perfect.

"Specifically, the statist reactionaries of the Reagan years (mislabelled 'conservatives,' in an Orwellian perversion) instituted new and sometimes unprecedented measures of censorship and secrecy to protect state power from public scrutiny and awareness.

"Nevertheless, the primary methods of control of thought and opinion in the United States lie elsewhere: in the fairly narrow control over wealth and resources. This concentrated power over investment and decision-making largely determines the character of the economy, and sets narrow conditions on the political system and the doctrinal institutions (media, publishers, schools and universities, etc.). The result is not usually called 'censorship,' but that is only because terminology itself is designed as an instrument of power and domination.

"As has been extensively documented, the effects of this concentration of power are to ensure that articulate opinion remains within a narrow spectrum supportive of the nexus of state-corporate power, and that the picture of the world that reaches the public is largely framed by the same interests.

"The system is not foolproof, and has a considerable range of 'statistical error' around the margins (as is also true, incidentally, even of most totalitarian systems). Furthermore, the limited evidence available suggests that educated sectors may well be more susceptible to indoctrination than the general public, which is more marginalized than strictly controlled and often has attitudes and opinions that depart dramatically from the doctrinal framework of the media and other ideological institutions.

"These comments are really truisms. In a free society, they would be taught in elementary schools, along with the huge mass of supporting evidence and analysis. In a well-controlled society, however, it is important to try to drive truisms about power and its exercise to the margins. As I understand 'Project Censored,' it is an effort to help the public appreciate such facts as these, which are of great importance in any society, particularly in one as free as ours, where an informed and organized public really could play a significant role in managing its own affairs."

George Gerbner, dean emeritus of the Annenberg School of Communications at the University of Pennsylvania and Censored judge since 1983: "The great value of Project Censored is that it calls attention to crucial but hidden events and issues that censorship tries to hide. But there is also a pattern behind much of what the project brings to light. That pattern reveals even more than facts and issues. It reflects an historic change in our culture.

"Most of the issues in 'The News That Didn't Make the News' are no longer deliberately suppressed. They just don't fit the unwritten rules by which most news (and other stories) are selected.

"Most of what we know, or think we know, we know from stories we tell. They weave a seamless web of the cultural environment that cultivates what we think, what we do, and how we conduct our affairs.

"That process used to be hand-crafted, home-made and community-inspired. It was designed to serve diverse interests and people who had something to tell.

"Now it is mostly mass-produced and policy-driven. It is the end result of a complex manufacturing and marketing process. It is supported by and serves the interests of a relative handful of global conglomerates that have something to sell.

"This condition did not emerge spontaneously or after thoughtful deliberation. It was a radical departure overriding significant public opposition little noted in our history books. But it has had far-reaching consequences.

"Ten-year-olds responding to a survey name more brands of beer than presidents. Nine out of ten six-year-olds recognize 'Old Joe,' the Camel cigarette ad. Global marketing strategies promote practices that drug, hurt, poison, and kill thousands every day; portrayals that dehumanize and stigmatize; cults of violence that desensitize, terrorize and brutalize.

"But the rules screen out news of the siege of our cities (except when riots erupt); the drift toward ecological suicide; the silent crumbling of our infrastructure; widening resource gaps and the most glaring inequalities in the industrial world; the costly neglect of vital institutions such as public education, health care, and the arts; and how make-believe image politics corrupts the electoral process.

"That is why we must resist the new censorship—both public and private—and extend the First Amendment beyond its use as a shield for the powerful. Project Censored is needed more than ever to expose the news that should be news but isn't, and the reasons why."

(PLEASE NOTE: George Gerbner is the chair of a newly organized citizen's group concerned with distortions of the democratic process such as those he cites above. For more information, please write Cultural Environment Movement, PO Box 31847, Philadelphia, PA 19104.)

Sheila Rabb Weidenfeld, former press secretary to First Lady Betty Ford and a founding member of the Censored panel of judges: "It is not surprising that there is such mistrust of the media today. Despite the vast numbers of journalists and media outlets in our society, major stories are overlooked, downplayed or trivialized. One need not be privy to the top stories selected by Project Censored each year to know something is amiss. What that something is has been defined by Carl Jensen as a form of censorship—self-censorship by the media.

"As a judge on Project Censored since its inception in 1976, I have seen many stories that deserve broad circulation. They deal with such issues as government abuse; illegal and dangerous products being dumped on the Third World; poisonous pesticides, pharmaceutical malfeasance or low-level radiation affecting an individual's health; violations of civil and human rights.

"Thanks to the recognition now coming to Project Censored, there is an increasing awareness of previously ignored important stories with some of them becoming today's headlines. This, at least, is a beginning."

Indeed, this is merely a beginning. But an important one. For in the final analysis, we must recognize the critical role a responsible press can play in our society.

The press has the power to stimulate people to clean up the environment; to prevent nuclear proliferation; to force crooked politicians out of office; to reduce poverty; to provide quality health care for all people; to create a truly equitable society; and, as we have seen, to literally save the lives of millions of human beings.

And this is why we must look to, prod and support a free, open and aggressive press. We have a constitutionally guaranteed free press in the United States, and we have the best communications technology in the world. Now let us seek a more responsible and responsive press, a press that earns its First Amendment rights. Then, and only then, will we all have the information we need to build a more enlightened, more engaged society.

> "Without criticism and reliable
> and intelligent reporting, the
> government cannot govern."
> — *Walter Lippmann*

CENSORED

Chapter 2

U.S. Censorship in 1992

In 1992, as in past presidential-election years, a number of politically relevant stories were overlooked, underreported or censored. The candidates and the media tried to hoodwink the voting public by sidetracking substantive issues and focusing instead on alleged infidelities and family values. Important issues were neither sufficiently investigated nor rigorously reported by broadcasters or publishers. Among the neglected stories were the following:

- The many unanswered questions about George Bush's involvement in and knowledge of the Iran/contra affair.
- The *quid pro quo* between the Bush administration and political contributors, exposed in a series of blockbuster articles in *Common Cause* Magazine.
- The disturbing report on homelessness, released by the National Conference of Mayors.
- The true reason-for-being behind Dan Quayle's Council on Competitiveness.
- The tragic death rate of Iraqi children after the Gulf War.
- Bill Clinton's knowledge of Iran/contra activities in Arkansas.

These are just five of the more commanding stories of 1992 that didn't get the attention they deserved. Some, like the Iraqgate issue, made our Top 25 Censored list. But many others—among 700 nominations in all—didn't end up on the list.

The Election-Year Media Milieu

For a presidential election year, it was not atypical for these political issues to go underreported. The 1991 *Censored Resource Book* revealed the same election-year bias toward similar stories since 1972.

Until 1990, when military matters dominated our Censored list, political/governmental topics were the leading underreported category since Ronald Reagan's election. (During the Carter years—1976 to 1980—the top-ranked undercovered subject was white collar/corporate crime.)

Interestingly, 1992 exhibited a noticeable shift: urgent but ignored environmental problems outnumbered political issues.

A look at the project's top-ranked Censored story of 1992 helps explain why many political, environmental and other important news items have difficulty reaching the American people. The #1 Censored story, the great media sell-out to Reaganism, revealed how the nation's major news broadcasters and publishers traded their traditional adversarial watchdog role for profits and deregulation during the Reagan/Bush era.

The story, written by nationally acclaimed media scholar and critic Ben Bagdikian, professor emeritus at UC Berkeley's Graduate School of Journalism, reported how the Reagan/Bush administrations gave print and electronic media owners in America "permission" to create giant, monopolistic empires. In return, Bagdikian reported, the media looked the other way while these administrations committed crimes and then lied about it.

The ongoing coverup of information about media monopolies is confirmed by three of our #1 Censored stories of the past five years: "The Information Monopoly" in 1987; "Global Media Lords" in 1989; and now, "The Great Media Sell-Out" in 1992. All were researched and written by Bagdikian.

The Top 25

Following are the major 25 stories of 1992 separated by category:

POLITICS:
3 — Censored Election-Year Issues
5 — Iraqgate and the Watergate Law
6 — The "Winning the War on Drugs" Lie
7 — Trashing Federal Regulations
8 — Government Secrecy

ENVIRONMENT:
11 — Solar Power
12 — What Happened to the EPA?
15 — Plutonium Is Forever
16 — America's Killing Ground
19 — Poison in the Pacific
21 — How to Sell Pollution for Profit
22 — Clearcutting the World's Rainforests

CORPORATE:
2 — Corporate Crime vs. Street Crime
18 — Censored Electric Automobiles
20 — Black Gold Conquistadors
23 — Censorship Through Bribery
24 — The No-Pest Shell Game

MEDIA:
  1 — The Great Media Sell-Out
  9 — Ad Pressure Corrupts Free Press
  14 — News Media Lose War With Pentagon

MILITARY:
  4 — U.S.–Leading Merchant of Death
  10 — Post-Cold War Black Budget

HEALTH:
  13 — The Specter of Sterility
  17 — Norplant: Birth or Social Control?

EDUCATION:
  25 — University of Arizona vs. Apaches

Comparing Lists

Let's compare Project Censored's top ten Censored stories of 1992 with the Associated Press's top ten "biggest" stories:

PROJECT CENSORED	ASSOCIATED PRESS
1. Media Sell-Out	1. Bill Clinton Wins Election
2. Corporate vs. Street Crime	2. Los Angeles Riots
3. Censored Election Issues	3. Hurricane Andrew
4. Weapons Merchant of Death	4. U.S. Troops to Somalia
5. Iraqgate and Watergate Law	5. Yugoslavia Civil War
6. War on Drugs Lie	6. U.S. Recession
7. Trashing Federal Regulations	7. Former Soviet Republics
8. Government Secrecy	8. Court's Abortion Ruling
9. Ad Pressure on News Media	9. Two Hostages Released
10. Post-Cold War Black Budget	10. Jeffrey Dahmer's Plea

In comparing the two lists, the news media's emphasis on reporting events *after* they occur versus the project's concern with the lack of coverage given issues *before* they become events is readily apparent. The coincidentally ranked #4 issue on both lists provides a striking insight into this comparison. For example, what impact did the sale of U.S. weapons to warlords in Somalia have on the tragic events in that country?

It's possible that had the American people known their government sold arms to despotic leaders in unstable areas—not only to Somalian warlords but also to Saddam Hussein in Iraq, Salvadoran death squads, the Nicaraguan contras—we might have been able to persuade our elected officials to stop the practice, just as a well-informed populace in a democracy should be able to do. And it's the watchdog role of journalism to provide people with that information.

Similarly, one has to wonder what price the public will pay in the future for the media's failure to reveal the "high crimes and misdemeanors" of 12 years of Reagan and Bush, as highlighted in the project's 1992 #1 story. How much more might we have done about drug abuse in America if we hadn't been told that we were conquering it, as cited in story #6? And how much long-range environmental destruction is due to the trashing of regulations by Bush and Quayle as featured in the #7 story?

In addition, one has to consider the degree to which the subjects on the Project Censored and AP lists directly affect the general public. It seems clear that issues raised by Project Censored have a greater potential impact than events on the AP list. For example, how important is it for the average citizen to know that serial killer Jeffrey Dahmer pleaded guilty, versus knowing how much money corporate crime takes out of his or her pocket?

Judging From Experience

The impact of a story on the public is but one of the variables Project Censored judges consider as they evaluate and select the top ten Censored stories of the year.

Following are reflections on this year's Censored selections by some of the judges who helped name the top ten stories of 1992:

Donna Allen, founding editor of *Media Report to Women* and a Censored judge since 1980, has long been concerned with the paucity of mainstream coverage of women's issues. Therefore she was pleased to see the Norplant controversy (is the contraceptive for birth control or social control) on this year's list:

"Censorship of women is so complete the public doesn't even know that we have information it needs to hear. How many Anita Hills will it take before the media begin reporting our health and safety (survival) information—not to mention the economic, political and still other information our half of the population has but that the whole public needs to know about? Project Censored is making a welcome start on focusing public (and media) attention on this serious shortcoming."

As a first-time judge, **Hugh Downs**, host of ABC-TV's "20/20" and longtime advocate of the public's right to know, addressed the difficulty of whittling the 25 most underreported stores down to a top ten:

"Surely I am not the only judge to have a hard time ranking these important stories. I doubt I am the only one who felt that about 17 of them belonged in the 'top ten,' or who agonized over whether two of them should change places. Juggling how important, how neglected, how accepted or understood by a public kept in the dark about them, and several other factors, put a strain on the computer aspects of my brain.

"'The Great Media Sell-Out' is probably the toughest sell—it tends to put the media's defenses up. Suing a lawyer or getting a doctor to testify against another one are somewhat the same challenge.

"It's hard to say whether threats to our freedoms or political safety are more important than threats to our physical well-being—pollution, armaments, food and drug—or whether stories about blatant injustice should rank above scandals involving our money.

"My personal bugbear remains government secrecy. Both the ease with which those in positions of power can black out what they don't want known (or stonewall if confronted with unwelcome facts) and the somnolence of the public about how much of this is going on alarm me.

"We don't seem to have an instinctive early warning system about this danger. There should be more concern about this than I find. Every now

and then I actually hear people talk about 'government rights' or say, 'well, the government should have secrets.' Some of these people wouldn't lend you 15 bucks without collateral, but they feel this secrecy is all right. I try to put across my view that government has no 'rights'—only responsibilities. If their eyes don't glaze over, I elaborate.

"So part of the job of the media is not only to expose improper secrecy on the part of government officials but to get the message across that our freedoms require openness.

"Finally, I wanted most of the stories in the top ten—maybe the top three. The job of picking 25 out of the 700 or so nominations must have been much more difficult than mine."

Susan Faludi, also a first-time judge, is author of *Backlash: The Undeclared War Against American Women* and a Pulitzer Prize-winning journalist:

"It struck me in reading over the nominations how many of them were, at bottom, about the failure of the press to follow its own basic mandate.

"Whether it was ignoring the real election-year stories or failing to cover Iraqgate, the media served so often as chief censor rather than whistle-blower. In the process, I think the media has had a real and damaging effect on political and public discourse this year—by sidetracking, misrepresenting and misframing the issues.

"Imagine how different the presidential campaign would have been if the press had refused to get derailed into endless and endlessly unilluminating examinations of Clinton's youthful behavior, and focused instead on the current national shame of homelessness.

"I ranked the media's sell-out to Reaganism first because it seems to me to be the most craven act of censorship on the part of the media—not just coverup, but coverup of one's own derrière.

"It seems fitting that 1992 was the year that the term 'muckraker' was redefined in the press (judging by the repeated misuse of this word in so many articles and columns in the past year) to mean a celebrity gossip and scandalmonger, rather than its real meaning—a socially responsible journalist who exposes scandal and corruption in government and business.

"The list of nominations is also depressing testament to the press's shorter and shorter attention span. Only a year ago, the environment was the hot trend story. Now, as the many cases of overlooked environmental disaster reports here demonstrate, the press has clearly decided that the worldwide ecological crisis is 'yesterday's story' and has moved on—or rather downward.

"I only hope that the list of Censored stories will inspire the few true remaining muckrakers to take up their notebooks and make any of these 25 undercovered events front-page news."

William Lutz, a professor of English at Rutgers University and editor of *The Quarterly Review of Doublespeak*, pillories inflated egos annually with his barbed (and well-deserved) revelations of Orwellian doublespeak:

"Thomas Jefferson agreed that only a fully informed electorate could make democracy work. Yet, as the stories nominated for the top ten Censored of 1992 reveal, information—substantive information—is very difficult to come by in our country.

"While on the one hand the public is inundated with 'trash' information (Madonna, the British royal family, George Bush's recreational activities, etc.), the public receives little real information, information necessary for citizens in a democracy to make informed decisions about the economic, political and social policies that affect their lives.

"Censorship takes many forms, and the withholding or deliberate downplaying of information is one of those forms of censorship. Project Censored is a small effort to combat this form of censorship. Project Censored is necessary to keep this democracy alive."

Jack L. Nelson, a professor in the Graduate School of Education at Rutgers University, has been a Project Censored judge since 1976:

"The 1992 nominations are heavily dominated by domestic examples of censorship in the media. About 80 percent of the Censored stories focus on the United States. That is surprising in an election year, when one would expect more media coverage of domestic news than international news.

"However, the heavy reportage of starvation, inept efforts at food provision, stalemates over attempted genocide in Serbia-Croatia-Bosnia, and Gulf War residue would suggest that international stories were generally better reported.

"As People for the American Way reported, there were more incidents of overt censorship in schools and libraries last year than during any of the previous ten years they have kept records. Efforts by Jesse Helms and responsive arts administrators have kept censorship healthy in that environment.

"Media censorship in the pooled coverage of the Gulf War and through advertiser and governmental influences over media representatives suggests no diminution in censoring there.

"The Supreme Court decision in *Hazelwood* has produced prior restraint and a chilling effect on school publications. And the resurgence of the religious right and the 'Politically Correct' left provide ample censorship on nearly every controversy.

"All in all, we may be in for a new McCarthyism without recognizing its dimensions."

Herbert I. Schiller, professor emeritus of communication at the University of California, San Diego, is an internationally recognized expert on global communications. Currently a Scholar in Residence at the American University in Washington, DC, Schiller has been a Project Censored judge for seven years. He summed up the reactions to this year's Censored nominations with this comment:

> "It was more difficult than ever to winnow the most egregious ten—all the reports deserve honorable mention and attention.
> "I am especially concerned with the degradation of the American information system [to which several of the selections referred].
> "Unless the course is reversed, we shall find ourselves with unlimited junk information and a frightening absence of vitally needed social (public) information."

Professor Schiller's fears concerning "junk information" are more than fulfilled by the citations in Chapter 4, "The Junk Food News Stories of 1992."

Media Heroes

In concluding this review of the media's performance in 1992, we should recognize that there are some noble "muckrakers" out there—the socially responsible journalists noted by Susan Faludi, for example, as well as a few fearless publishers. After all, each of the stories cited by Project Censored has been published *somewhere*, though most often in the alternative press.

Indeed, as Don Hazen, executive director of the Institute for Alternative Journalism (IAJ) in New York, reminds us, there are "individuals and groups that were and are especially brave at taking on powerful institutions and persistent about getting stories out." To substantiate this observation, Don sent along his selection of "Ten Media Heroes" of 1992 who are dedicated to fighting censorship and protecting the First Amendment:

MEDIA BIAS? SELF-CENSORSHIP? WHATEVER DO YOU *MEAN*? WHY, THE MAINSTREAM MEDIA *PRIDE* THEMSELVES ON THEIR BALANCED PRESENTATION OF *ALL* POINTS OF VIEW...THE *RIGHT WING*...

■ Deborah Chasnoff and INFACT, for making the documentary film *Deadly Deception: General Electric, Nuclear Weapons and Our Environment*, which exposed GE's connection to the nuclear industry, including its dismal safety record. In one of the system's sweetest ironies, Chasnoff urged viewers to boycott GE when she accepted an Academy Award for the film.

■ Cartoonist Dan Perkins, aka Tom Tomorrow, for his sharp and witty comic strip, "This Modern World," which reminds us of the absurdity of what often passes as political and public discourse. (Tom Tomorrow appears throughout this book, as well as in the monthly *America's CENSORED Newsletter*.)

■ "Murphy Brown" and her creator, Diane English, for kicking Dan Quayle's butt when he attacked Brown for scorning traditional "family values."

■ Barbara Trent and the Empowerment Project, for their documentary film *The Panama Deception*, which exposed the truth about the hidden motives, death toll and destruction associated with the Bush-ordered U.S. invasion of Panama.

■ Editor Linda Williams, reporter Andrea Ford and others at the *Los Angeles Times*, for exposing the *Times*'s hypocrisy in sending record numbers of black reporters to cover the LA riots, while the paper's hiring and promotional practices toward people of color remains unequal.

■ Herb Chao Gunth and the Public Media Center, the nation's foremost advocacy advertising agency, for effectively using advertising as a tool for social and political change.

■ Fred Clarkson and Skip Porteus of the Institute for First Amendment Studies, for understanding the Christian Right's recent strategy of stealth politics early on and for doggedly tracking its activities across the U.S.

■ Mark Weiss and the television series "P.O.V.," for showing the democratic potential of television amidst so much commercial fare, and for broadcasting *Color Adjustment*, Marlon Riggs's unflinching film on how blacks are represented on television.

■ *Adbusters* Magazine, for promoting media awareness and media literacy by countering the forces of consumerism with its anti-advertising spoofs.

■ James Danky and the Newspaper and Periodicals Division of the Historical Society of Wisconsin, for actively chronicling and preserving the small-circulation, alternative and underground presses.

(PLEASE NOTE: Ten Media Heroes was excerpted with permission from Don Hazen and the Alternet News Service.)

> "It is very difficult to have a free, fair and honest press anywhere in the world. In the first place, as a rule, papers are largely supported by advertising, and that immediately gives the advertisers a certain hold over the medium which they use."
> —Eleanor Roosevelt

CENSORED

Chapter 3

The Top 25 Censored News Stories of 1992

Following is a detailed analysis of each of the top 25 Censored subjects of 1992. Each segment starts with the title and the specific source data about the publication and author of the original article(s). An asterisk (*) following an article title indicates it is reprinted in full in Appendix A, "CENSORED Reprints." A brief synopsis of the article (or articles) originally nominated follows. The segment concludes with comments about the issue and article, in most cases by the author of the original source article.

CENSORED

The Great Media Sell-Out to Reaganism

Source: **Mother Jones**
1663 Mission Street, 2nd Fl.
San Francisco, CA 94103
Date: May/June 1992
Title: "Journalism of Joy" *
Author: Ben H. Bagdikian

SYNOPSIS: During the 1980s, the big media owners had reason to celebrate—Reaganism ushered in the era of giant, monopolistic media empires.

Take, for example, the big three networks—ABC, CBS and NBC. Each was acquired by corporations that might have been deemed unqualified under earlier FCC standards. In return, big media dispensed relentlessly positive news about Reaganism and the great trickle-down dream. The FCC also relieved broadcasters of traditional public service requirements, made it almost impossible for citizens' groups to challenge station license renewals and lifted limits on the number of stations a single corporation can acquire.

Newspapers enjoyed the Reagan era as well. In 98 percent of U.S. cities, the daily news business was already controlled by monopolies. But the administration further sedated anti-trust laws to permit the biggest newspaper chains to sweep up local monopolies. In addition, the National Labor Relations Board, stacked with promanagement members, gave the media giants permission to go on a ten-year union busting spree. And, like all big business, the broadcasters and print publishers benefited from Reagan's shifting of corporate taxes onto the middle class and the poor—but Americans did not see much coverage of that on television or in print media.

During this self-satisfied climate of comfort the normal restraint, traditionally exercised by most media owners, over inserting corporate propaganda into the news crumbled, leading to some startling changes in the industry. For example, top editors were made part of the business-management team, responsible for keeping up advertising lineage as well as overseeing editorial content. Many Time, Inc., editors received stock options; not surprisingly, many editors started to think more like stockbrokers than journalists.

Another disturbing management practice that evolved out of that era was the policy of conducting systematic screenings of new reporters to keep out journalists who might not readily comply with corporate wishes or who might join newsroom unions. Some major news companies, including Knight-Ridder (the nation's second largest newspaper chain), do such screening through mandatory, lengthy psychological questionnaires of potential new reporters. Others, including some papers in Gannett, the largest newspaper chain, order editors to be deliberately blunt in interviews so that applicants know the company wants only "team players" who won't rock the boat and who aren't in favor of unions. Hiring reporters who are not inclined to question authority is one sure way to control the news.

Ben Bagdikian observes, "During the degradation of the 1980s, government lying was too willingly supported by the media; high crimes and misdemeanors by the president of the United States became an acceptable public boast; looting the public treasury and cheating the citizens were treated by most editors as necessary for liberation of the marketplace. For almost ten years, the media remained silent on the obvious—that Reaganite politics were taking a frightful toll in human suffering and crippling the economy."

Ominously, Bagdikian warns, "From that kind of public morality neither the country nor journalism will soon recover."

SSU Censored Researcher: Amy Cohen

COMMENTS: This story about the capitulation of the nation's watchdog press during the Reagan/Bush administrations is the appropriate top Censored story of 1992 since it cuts to the core of Project Censored.

In brief, it confirms that the nation's major news media have overlooked, undercovered or censored information about high crimes and misdemeanors on the part of the administration, in return for "permission" to create giant, monopolistic media empires. In other words, news today is defined more with an eye on the bottom line than with a concern for the public's right to know.

This extraordinary charge can be traced back to 1982, when Ben Bagdikian completed research for his book, *The Media Monopoly*. At the time, he found that some 50 corporations controlled half or more of the media business in the U.S. By December 1986, when he finished a second edition of the book, the 50 corporations had shrunk to 29. By June 1987, when Bagdikian wrote an article for *EXTRA!*, the number was down to 26. In the fourth edition of *The Media Monopoly*, published in 1993, the number has dropped to 23.

"The Information Monopoly," by Bagdikian, was the top Censored story of 1987. It warned that the media's prevailing concern with the bottom line, coupled with traditional publishers' tendencies to avoid controversy, fosters widespread self-censorship among writers, journalists, editors and news directors.

The threat of a media monopoly took on global implications by 1989 when Bagdikian wrote "Lords of the Global Village" for *The Nation* (June 12, 1989). Selected as the #1 Censored story of 1989, it warned about the big five international media corporations that dominated information dissemination in the global village. The corporations cited by Bagdikian were Time Warner, Inc., the world's largest media corporation; the German-based Bertelsmann AG, owned by Reinhard Mohn; Rupert Murdoch's News Corporation, Ltd., of Australia; Hatchette SA, of France, the world's largest producer of magazines; and the U.S.-based Capital Cities/ABC Inc.

At the time, Bagdikian warned that the basis for all liberty—freedom of information—is in danger of being polluted by a new mutation of that familiar scourge of the free spirit: centrally controlled information.

And now, more than ten years after Bagdikian first tried to warn us about the dangers of monopolization, he's back with the top Censored story of 1992, revealing how some of those dangers have now taken their toll.

Bagdikian reports that his *Mother Jones* article was referred to or quoted or excerpted in some of the alternative media, and that the response there was fairly active for a time. But, he adds, "So far as I know it was neither quoted nor excerpted in any of the standard, mainstream media."

He also points out the dangers of ignoring the threats to a free flow of information: "If the flaws I pointed to had not occurred in the major media, we might have avoided the worst of the savings and loan disaster, the weakening of the rest of the banking system and the general self-destruction of corporate America, with its subsequent unemployment and recession."

Further, he says, "If the main media's blind eye toward the accumulating wreckage of Reaganite policies while he was in office had been broken during the 12 years of Reagan-Bush, it might have changed the political support of leaders who pushed these policies—Reagan and Bush themselves—and it would have shown the vulnerability of the media and of other large corporations to destructive greed."

Bagdikian notes that the limited coverage given his warnings benefited the "main media, whose corporations made unprecedented profits under the programs whose consequences on the economy they did not report accurately, all of corporate big business, and the politicians like Reagan and Bush who opened the floodgates to them."

PLEASE NOTE: Despite its criticism of publishing monopolies, the 4th Edition of Ben Bagdikian's The Media Monopoly, published in 1993 by Beacon Press, is now supposed to be in bookstores across the country. Or, as Ben says, at least in discriminating bookstores across the country. If all else fails, check a college bookstore or ask your local bookstore to order it.

2 CENSORED

Corporate Violators Dwarf Street Crime & Violence

Source: **Multinational Monitor**
PO Box 19405
Washington, DC 20036
Date: December 1991
Title: "Corporate Crime & Violence in Review" *
Author: Russell Mokhiber

SYNOPSIS: While the press continues to alarm the public with stories of street crime and violence, corporate violators run rampant. Writer Russell Mokhiber, in his analysis of ten of the worst corporations of 1991 for *Multinational Monitor*, reveals that public corruption, environmental degradation, financial fraud, procurement fraud and occupational homicide are on the rise.

The distortion of street crime is promulgated by comments such as those of *Washington Post* columnist Richard Cohen, who wrote that "Young black males commit most of the crime in Washington, DC." This statement ignores corporate criminology research revealing that corporate crime and violence inflict far greater damage on society than all street crimes combined.

As Mokhiber points out, Cohen doesn't acknowledge the criminal activities of Exxon, International Paper, United Technologies, Weyerhauser, Pillsbury, Ashland Oil, Texaco, Nabisco and Ralston-Purina, all convicted of environmental crimes in recent years. "All of these convicted corporations operate in Washington, DC. None of them are young black males," writes Mokhiber.

The Ten Worst Corporations of 1991, according to Mokhiber, are the following:

- *Alyeska*: for polluting Alaskan air and water and trying to silence whistleblowers.
- *American Home Products*: for closing its plant in Indiana and moving to Puerto Rico, committing numerous labor law violations in the process and resulting in a multimillion-dollar lawsuit.
- *Clorox*: for its "Crisis Management" public relations plan, which recommended dirty tricks to deal with the environmental movement.
- *Du Pont*: for running television commercials (set to Beethoven's "Ode to Joy") lauding its corporate concern for the environment, while earning the title The Nation's Number One Corporate Polluter, according to Mokhiber.
- *Ethyl Corporation*: for continuing to export a toxic lead gasoline additive—

banned in the U.S. for poisoning children—to Third World countries, where it poisons their children.

- *General Electric*: for continuing to sing it "brings good things to life," while heavily engaged in building weapons of mass destruction and bringing extensive pollution and contamination to the environment.

- *G. Heileman Brewing Co.*: for primarily marketing PowerMaster—a malt liquor that contained 31 percent more alcohol than other malt liquors—in minority neighborhoods already plagued by high rates of alcohol-related diseases.

- *Kellogg's*: for harassing an assistant attorney general in Texas who had charged the giant cereal maker with promoting misleading nutritional claims about a number of its products.

- *Hoffman La Roche*: for ignoring early warnings that Versed, a drug used as a sedative and an anethesiac, had deadly side effects if sold in a highly concentrated form. The drug has now been linked to about 80 deaths and many near fatalities.

- *Procter & Gamble*: for polluting a once pure Florida river; for mislabeling disposable diapers as degradable; and for selling coffee made from beans from El Salvador, home of the death squads.

While the press is always eager to hype some nonconsequential Ten Best or Ten Worst list, it was strangely silent about the "Ten Worst Corporations" list announced by the *Multinational Monitor*.

SSU Censored Researcher: Serge Chasson

COMMENTS: Since it started in 1976, Project Censored has cited a number of examples of underreported cases of corporate crime. The third-ranked Censored story that year reported how hundreds of thousands of people, most of them in Third World countries, were poisoned annually by drugs and pesticides banned in the United States but exported to foreign countries. Unfortunately, despite our efforts and those of others, this is a practice that continues to this day. (See, for example, the Ethyl Corporation entry in the preceding Ten Worst Corporations list.)

Writer Russell Mokhiber, editor of the *Corporate Crime Reporter* (CCR), says that his article received no mainstream media coverage, despite the fact a press release on the subject was widely distributed. He points out, "Most citizens, when they think of crime, think of street crime, not corporate crime. Yet many criminologists believe that corporate crime inflicts far more damage on society than all street crime combined." He concludes, "Yet, media emphasize street crime." Then Mokhiber rhetorically asks: "Why?"

One obvious reason is that street crime is much cheaper for the media to report than corporate crime. Street crime is handed to the media by law enforcement, often with sensational photo opportunities, and it requires little if any investigation. Corporate crime, on the other hand, requires some investigative initiative on the part of the media and rarely produces interesting visuals.

However, a more plausible answer is that the major media are sometimes part of the corporate criminal hierarchy; or they're allied with it through common interests or interlocking directorships, and thus not interested in rocking the boat. As Mokhiber points out, "No major newspaper in the U.S. has a reporter covering corporate crime full-time." We've all heard about the police beat; but how many of us have heard about the corporate crime beat?

PLEASE NOTE: Russell Mokhiber notes that he's been editing the Corporate Crime Reporter, a legal weekly based in Washington, DC, for seven years and that CCR is "the only weekly to cover white collar and corporate crime exclusively." For more information, write Corporate Crime Reporter, PO Box 18384, Washington, DC 20036.

3 CENSORED

Censored Election Year Issues

Sources:

(1) Common Cause Magazine
2030 M Street NW
Washington, DC 20036
Date: April/May/June 1992
Title: "George Bush's Ruling Class" *
Authors: Jeffrey Denny, Vicki Kemper, Viveca Novak, Peter Overby, Amy Young

(2) Washington Post
1150 15th Street NW
Washington, DC 20071
Date: January 9, 1992
Title: "A Profound Silence on Homelessness"
Author: Mary McGrory

(3) The Progressive
409 E. Main Street
Madison, WI 53703
Date: May 1992
Title: "Deregulatory Creep: Dan Quayle Clears the Way for Industry"
Author: Arthur E. Rowse

(4) "This World," San Francisco Examiner
110 Fifth Street
San Francisco, CA 94103
Date: October 11, 1992
Title: "46,900 Unspectacular Deaths"
Author: Mike Royko, *Chicago Tribune* Columnist

(5) Unclassified
2001 S Street NW, Ste. 740
Washington, DC 20009
Date: February/March 1992
Title: "The Mena, Arkansas, Story"
Author: David MacMichael

(Note: References to these articles are noted in bold face numbers in the following synopsis.)

SYNOPSIS: While the candidates and the media had us focusing on alleged infidelities, family values and rap-music lyrics, other far more important issues were ignored or underreported during the 1992 election year. Here are just some of the stories that played second fiddle to Gennifer Flowers, Sister Souljah and Murphy Brown:

■ George Bush and Iran/contra. Unanswered questions still lingering from the 1988 campaign remained unanswered and largely ignored by the mainstream media before election day. It was not until October 30, four days before the election, that Caspar Weinberger's "smoking gun" memo, implicating Bush in the arms for hostages intrigue, was widely publicized.

■ Bush's Team 100. A series of articles in *Common Cause* Magazine documented how major campaign contributors to George Bush were given ambassadorships and federal advisory committee appointments, and how federal regulatory issues that adversely affected members of "Team 100" were toned down. **(1)**

■ Homelessness. Despite a critical status report by the National Conference of Mayors that showed 25 cities suffer a serious problem with homelessness, and reporting an average 13 percent increase in requests for shelter, the presidential candidates barely mentioned it and the press did not pursue it. (2)

▪ Dan Quayle's Council on Competitiveness. Many a questionable (and unpublicized) action stemmed from this committee, whose intent was never really made clear. One of the most egregious dictates mandated in the Clean Air Act would allow polluters to increase emissions if the appropriate state agency did not object within seven days. After these revisions were enacted, it was discovered that 11 big air-polluting firms donated $788,270 to Bush and to Republican committees. The media muted the event. (3)

▪ An Unpublicized Result of the Iraq War. The death rate of Iraqi children rose dramatically in the months after the Gulf War, largely because of an outbreak of diarrhea caused by disabled water and sewage systems. In the first seven months of 1991, about 46,900 more children died than would have been expected, according to a study in the *New England Journal of Medicine*. (4)

▪ Where Was Bill? Covert operations run from a clandestine airfield at Mena, a small town in western Arkansas, included guns, drugs and other activities related to the Iran/contra travesty. Even though this trafficking occurred during Bill Clinton's administration as governor of Arkansas, and could not have happened without his knowledge, it attracted little attention from the mainstream media. (5)

SSU Censored Researchers: Blake Kehler, Kimberly S. Anderson, John Faiola, Kim Kaido

COMMENTS: If there is a cyclical pattern to Project Censored, it centers around the quadrennial spurt in censored political issues coinciding with presidential election years. *The Project Censored Yearbook* for 1991 documented two decades of critical issues that *might* have affected presidential elections but did *not* because of the lack of media coverage. Critical underreported presidential election-year issues cited included the following:

▪ 1972 Richard Nixon and Watergate
▪ 1976 Jimmy Carter and the Trilateral Commission
▪ 1980 Ronald Reagan and "The October Surprise"
▪ 1984 Ronald Reagan and Three Unreported Stories About Paul Laxalt, Edwin Meese and Charles Z. Wick
▪ 1988 George Bush and the News That Wasn't Fit to Print, a compilation of 15 serious questions about Bush's qualifications to be president that were not asked by the major news media during the campaign.

Thus, it is not surprising that a similar collection of issues went underreported during the 1992 election. As noted in the synopsis above, Project Censored focused on just five articles concerned with some of these issues. Here are comments by some of the authors:

Common Cause Magazine: Peter Overby responds on behalf of the authors of the potentially explosive *Common Cause* cover story about George Bush's campaign financing:

"'George Bush's Ruling Class' investigated favors bestowed by the Bush administration on members of Team 100, the 249 wealthy donors who gave at least $100,000 each in 'soft money' to the 1988

Bush-Quayle effort. Soft money—huge campaign contributions that are channeled through a legal loophole, in effect violating federal election law—has been perhaps the most underreported aspect of national politics during the past four years. In that time, few publications had the resources and time necessary to report on soft money donors and their influence on government."

Overby believes it is important for the public to be more aware of this issue:

"The $100,000 contributions and the influence we traced to their donors signal that government is for sale. Even Bush spokesman Marlin Fitzwater conceded, 'It's buying access to the system, yes.' Spotlighting such abuses will increase public pressure to close the soft money loophole."

The people who benefit from the lack of coverage given this issue, according to Overby, are the soft money players, both donors and recipients, who have "much to gain by keeping the public in the dark. George Bush, for one, vetoed a bill that would have banned soft money just days after the President's Dinner, which raked in some $9 million in soft money. He signed the veto statement on a Saturday night while White House reporters were being entertained at a semi-official dinner for the press corps."

Overby also notes that although Bill Clinton has expressed support for campaign finance reform, the Democrats raised more soft money than the Republicans during the last campaign.

The Progressive: Arthur E. Rowse, author of "Deregulatory Creep," which focused on the quid pro quo of campaign financing, provides an additional insight into the electoral abuses cited above:

"As the article pointed out, the mainstream media showed little interest in the way Quayle's Council on Competitiveness was assaulting the health and safety of Americans by blocking the implementation of federal laws. They were even less interested in correlating campaign contributions with companies benefiting from the regulatory slowdown. News coverage of the regulatory process—where laws are often negated after passing Congress—have routinely been minimal.

"A few of the larger newspapers occasionally tracked Council actions on wetlands and air pollution. But, true to form, it was a personal angle—when Quayle's top aide was caught feathering his own nest—that got the most attention. Quayle's own conflicts of interest stirred no journalistic follow-up of Congressional charges. Evening news programs dismissed almost everything. While campaign contributions to Congress were receiving broad coverage, the White House angle was ignored.

"When the article came out, I thought it might stir some further reporting in the major media, especially on the relationship of campaign contributions to regulatory relief. But nothing happened. After another small magazine showed interest in pursuing the topic, I tried to obtain copies of Vice President Quayle's detailed itinerary for leads on contributions that might be linked to specific regulatory actions. But the itinerary was not supplied, despite numerous calls to his office and many other likely sources. The possibility of finding incriminating quid-pro-quos was there, but the election killed the idea."

Ironically, despite the criticism of Rowse and many others, in mid-January 1993, Quayle, in a moment of extreme chutzpah, warned Bill Clinton that he would make a terrible mistake if he were to abolish the Council on Competitivenes.

Unclassified: David MacMichael, editor of *Unclassified,* published by the Association of National Security Alumni in Washington, says that the exposé of Iran/contra activities in Arkansas received practically no coverage except for investigative stories by Alex Cockburn in *The Nation* and a smear article in *Time.*

"This story illustrates how bipartisan involvement in U.S. government covert operations influences not only national but state and local politics, and corrupts law enforcement and the judicial process. There is a general conspiracy of silence that masks criminal activity under the guise of 'national security.'

"The Clinton campaign avoided hard questioning about Governor Clinton's tolerance of illegal contra support activities in the state of Arkansas—with accompanying possible narcotics trafficking during the 1980s. The Bush campaign was also spared questions about the activity in the district of one of Bush's key congressional supporters—John Paul Hammerschmidt.

"Information on this was provided to all Democratic primary candidates, but none used it. The Brown campaign said they would use it only if major media played it first."

MacMichael believes that the major media weren't interested, since they looked upon the issue as an Iran/contra leftover and basically went along with the Democratic campaign decision that Iran/contra was a dead issue.

Noting that "nobody wanted to touch this story with a pole," MacMichael says he received no calls from any major news media in the U.S. about the issue. Ironically, on December 29, 1992, he was contacted by a major media outlet—the French National Radio —for comments about the Caspar Weinberger pardon.

United States: the World's Leading Merchant of Death

Sources:
World Press Review
200 Madison Avenue, Ste. 2104
New York, NY 10016
Date: September 1992
Title: "The World's Top Arms Merchant" *
Author: Frederick Clairmonte

The Human Quest
1074-23rd Avenue N.
St. Petersburg, FL 33704
Date: July/August 1992
Title: "War 'Dividends'—Military Spending Out of Balance with Needy"
Author: Tristram Coffin

SYNOPSIS: In the 1980s, global arms-spending rocketed to nearly $1 trillion annually—or, about $2 million a minute. The two leading arms merchants were the United States and the former Soviet Union. Now the Soviet Union is gone, but its place has been taken by others, with the U.S. being the grand trafficker leading the pack.

With the end of the Cold War, some Americans held out hope that U.S. arms production and sales would be reduced and arms plants converted to civilian factories. This has not happened; instead, the

U.S. has kept its arms factories humming with exports. The *Defense Monitor*'s headline reads: "We Arm the World: U.S. Is Number One Weapons Dealer."

Some facts from the Center for Defense Information include the following:

▪ The U.S. is the world's top weapons supplier.

▪ The U.S. has provided over $128 billion in weaponry and military assistance to more than 125 of the world's 169 countries in the last decade.

▪ The U.S. continues to provide arms to a number of nations with chronic records of human rights violations.

▪ In Latin America, El Salvador's bloody regime garners the largest share of U.S. military sales.

Meanwhile, there are reports of increasingly hostile world opinion against militarization, which the U.S. appears to be ignoring. Critics say that the continued pathology of U.S. arms-spending, exacerbated by the decline in U.S. productivity in the Seventies and Eighties, can only further intensify the problems in America.

Former President Dwight Eisenhower tried to warn America of the dangers of this entrenched addiction and dependence on military production and sales:

"Every gun that is made, every warship launched, every rocket fired signifies in the final sense a theft from those who are cold and are not fed. This world in arms is not spending money alone. It is spending the wealth of its workers, the genius of its scientists, the hopes of its children."

As Frederick Clairmonte writes in the *World Press Review*:

"This was [Eisenhower's] warning against the menace of frantic proliferation that he branded 'the military-industrial complex,' a Frankenstein monstrosity whose growth in the decades to come Eisenhower could only dimly have conceived. In every year from 1951 to 1991, military outlays exceeded the combined net profits of all U.S. corporations."

While the world can take comfort from the exit of the Soviet Union from the first rank of death merchants, it is dismayed that the U.S. military-industrial complex has rushed to fill the vacuum.

Tristram Coffin, editor of the *Washington Spectator*, urges instead that "the U.S. should take the lead in organizing a cutback of arms shipments to small nations....The administration should prepare to repair the long-neglected infrastructure—bridges, roads, sewers, water supply systems. This would offer jobs to arms plant workers dismissed in cutbacks."

The American people should know that we alone are now the world's leading merchant of death and that the price to both America and the rest of the world is a costly one.

SSU Censored Researcher: Amy Cohen

COMMENTS: Linda Rogers, editor of the *World Press Review* responded to Project Censored on behalf of author Frederick Clairmonte, who resides in France.

"There is never enough coverage of what the United States is doing in this realm [international arms sales]. In 1992, when the Bush administration should have been using its considerable influence to promote peace, the U.S. was moving into position as the dominant arms merchant worldwide—as total world arms sales were declining.

"This development rated a few paragraphs in the major media, following a report from the Congressional Research Service, and then pretty much died as a story. But the foreign press was paying attention, so we put it on our cover.

"The public would benefit from wider exposure of this subject by being better informed about what the government, the military establishment and arms manufacturers are up to—and by translating the information into, for example, voting patterns.

"The Bush administration's promotion of overseas arms sales benefited by the limited media coverage. Bush was talking out of both sides of his mouth by challenging the Mideast to freeze its arms trade and reduce stockpiles (in the May 1991 "Middle East arms initiative") while preparing a huge arms transaction with Saudi Arabia. Our sources reported that more than $20 billion in U.S. weapons sales to the Mideast were arranged after Iraq invaded Kuwait—a large portion of it after the May 1991 arms initiative. Obviously, arms manufacturers also benefited from the scant media coverage."

5 CENSORED

Iraqgate and the Silent Death of the Watergate Law

Sources:
Covert Action Information Bulletin
1500 Massachusetts Avenue NW, Ste. 732
Washington, DC 20005
Date: Fall 1992
Title: "Bush Administration Uses CIA to Stonewall Iraqgate Investigation"
Author: Jack Colhoun

War & Peace Digest
32 Union Square E.
New York, NY 10003
Date: August 1992
Title: "BNL-Iraqgate Scandal"
Author: Kevin Sanders

The Paper of Sonoma County (CA)
540 Mendocino Avenue
Santa Rosa, CA 95401
Date: 10/22/92
Title: "Is Bush a Felon?" *
Author: Stephen P. Pizzo

New York Times
229 W. 43rd Street
New York, NY 10036
Date: 10/20/92
Title: "The Patsy Prosecutor"
Author: William Safire

SYNOPSIS: While some of the disturbing facts behind Iraqgate have started to appear in the press, the mainstream media all but ignored the story for more than a year.

Representative Henry B. Gonzales (D-TX), chair of the House Bank Committee, launched his intensive investigation into the scandal in 1990. Since February 1991, he has been regularly addressing a mostly empty House, and a loyal C-Span audience, about the role the Bush administration played in building up Iraq prior to the Gulf War. With the exception of conservative columnist William Safire, his revelations were basically ignored by the press.

But even without press attention, the scandal grew. Among Gonzales's allegations are several involving the Bush administration, which, he charges, did the following:

- Secretly sold nuclear, biological, chemical and missile-related weapons materials to Iraq.
- Blocked investigations into the use of the materials.
- Suppressed warnings of the dangers of such sales.
- Deliberately falsified documents on such sales submitted to Congress.
- Interfered illegally to halt investigations into the criminal activities of the Banca Nazionale del Lavoro (BNL), which was secretly diverting American agricultural loans to buy weapons for Iraq.

In an attempt to derail Gonzales, the CIA was enlisted to investigate him for revealing allegedly secret intelligence information. The CIA effort failed.

As the year 1992 drew to a close, the media seemed unconcerned with the Bush administration's covert, as well as overt, attempts to kill the Iraqgate investigation. These also involved the demise of the Watergate Law, which had assured independent investigations of criminal acts by top officials. The law, which provided for appointment of a special prosecutor to investigate top level members of the administration, expired on December 15, 1992.

In September 1992, Senate Republicans killed the legislation that would have renewed the law. To their everlasting discredit, Senate Democrats sat silently by in order to avoid an effort to have the law apply to members of Congress as well as to executive branch officials.

The key figure in the failure to appoint a special prosecutor to the scandal is Attorney General William P. Barr. CIA director Robert Gates accused the Justice Department, headed by Barr, of instructing the CIA to withhold documents critical to the investigation.

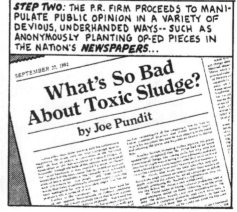

Columnist William Safire summarized the intrigue in his October 20 column: "In a last-ditch maneuver to block independent investigation into Iraqgate, Barr has hired a so-called 'special council.' But the man lending his good reputation to this subterfuge can be fired by the very attorney general he is supposed to investigate. Barr's strategy has been to stall past December 15.... No matter who is inaugurated in January, no autonomous prosecutor could then be named."

SSU Censored Researcher: Blake Kehler

COMMENTS: If there is a single issue future historians will use to evaluate George Bush's presidency, it probably will be Iraqgate. The secret sale of military materials to Iraq, the attempted coverup of the scandal, the demise of the Watergate Law on December 15, 1992, and the incredible efforts to intimidate a U.S. Congressman make Richard Nixon's involvement in Watergate pale in comparison.

Yet, while Henry Gonzalez started investigating Iraqgate in 1990, it was not until late in the election year of 1992 that the mainstream media started to provide the coverage the issue deserved. The administration was much quicker to recognize the potential impact of Gonzalez's efforts; as Congressman Gonzalez tells Project Censored:

"...the Bush administration has tried to thwart this investigation from the beginning. First they tried to ignore me, but I would not just 'go away.' They then tried to block my investigation by putting together a concerted effort—which I have called 'The Rostow Gang'—covering all of the departments that had anything to do with U.S. relations with Iraq, to try to keep me from having access to administration documents. However, the investigation continued to progress and the administration and apologists for the president in Congress have resorted to spurious charges of so-called 'national security.' The CIA has initiated a 'review' of my use of government documents in my Special Orders. Such efforts in Congress have been soundly defeated by a vote of the full House."

Authors of three of the key articles used in this nomination offer fascinating new insights into the issue and their efforts to get more media coverage of the scan-

...AS WELL AS SENDING OUT SLICKLY-PRODUCED "VIDEO NEWS RELEASES" WHICH MANY CASH-STRAPPED LOCAL NEWS DEPARTMENTS AIR VIRTUALLY *UNEDITED*... GIVING CORPORATE PROPAGANDA THE APPEARANCE OF OBJEC-TIVE *REPORTING*...

...AND SO YOU SEE, TOXIC SLUDGE IS ACTUALLY QUITE *GOOD* FOR YOU!

STEP THREE: PUBLIC OPINION IS *SWAYED* BY THIS ONSLAUGHT OF MEDIA MANIPULATION MASQUERADING AS *NEWS*...SINCE, AS P.R. FIRMS WELL UNDERSTAND, ANY LIE REPEATED *OFTEN* ENOUGH BECOMES *TRUE*...

I CAN'T IMAGINE *WHY* WE EVER WORRIED ABOUT *TOXIC SLUDGE!*

YES--HOW *SILLY* WE WERE!

dal. We start with investigative journalist **Stephen Pizzo**, who provides an overall look at the Iraqgate issue:

"Like most Americans I had never heard of the Banca Nazionale del Lavaro (BNL). I first learned of the bank and the role it played in the secret U.S. funding of Iraq when I reviewed testimony given during Special Orders by Rep. Henry Gonzalez. I made some inquiries, and by March 1992 had received about 100 still-classified documents from the departments of State, Commerce, Agriculture and Justice.

"The documents told a fascinating story, but maybe more so to me than to the handful of other journalists who also had them. During research in 1987 for our book, *Inside Job: The Looting of America's Savings and Loans*, my co-authors and I had found tantalizing evidence that some failed thrifts and banks had been bilked by covert operators to fund off-the-shelf operations during the 1980s. Many of these federally insured institutions later failed, leaving the taxpayers stuck with the tab. But like most alleged covert operations, there remained little solid proof of direct government involvement.

"For me the BNL documents represented the first solid evidence that the Reagan/Bush administrations had consciously misused banks to fund covert operations that would not have been favored by the American public or Congress. On that level alone, the story was an important one, particularly considering the mess left behind by failed thrifts and the tenuous condition of America's banks. If our own government shared responsibility for those losses along with the likes of Charles Keating, that was a hell of a story.

"But on another level the story raised questions similar to, and even more serious than Watergate. If the executive branch had engaged in such secret funding, the constitutional and legal questions raised by such a fact were enormous. First and most obvious were the legal questions. Consciously defrauding a federally insured bank by lying about the proposed use of the funds—and/or borrowing money with no intention of repaying it—is bank fraud—a federal felony. In the case of BNL, the loan fraud was compounded by the perversion of two federal loan-guarantee programs—$5.5 billion in all.

"Second, circumventing Congress, which has the constitutional duty to advise and consent, raises constitutional questions that make Watergate look like a minor matter. Either the constitution specifies clear separation of powers or it doesn't.

"When all the above are taken into consideration, it is remarkable that this story did not create a media firestorm. *Why didn't it?*

"There were several factors conspiring to keep this story in check. First of all, it involved banking. Journalists continue to shy away from considering banking as a serious or interesting 'beat.' We found this true in the mid-1980s as the S&L industry was being consumed in a financial holocaust—ignored by the press until too late. BNL was a bank—it made loans—and agricultural loans at that.

"Second, the story emerged at the beginning of the presidential election year. This hurt the story in two ways. First the election year 'soap opera'—Gennifer Flowers, Bush's mistress, Clinton's draft records, etc.—was a major distraction. But also the story itself held enormous political implications, which intimidated major papers. If the story had been handled in a manner consistent with its importance, it would have run on the front pages of major papers and would have supplied enough grist for weeks of follow-up pieces. But that concerned some editors. One of the few papers to run BNL stories during the election was the *Los Angeles Times*. Reporter Douglas Frantz had received some of the same documents I had and was running stories on BNL. But he complained in October, on National Public Radio, that his editors often buried his stories inside the paper because they feared that putting them on the front page could raise the story to such a level of importance that they could have an effect on the election, and they did not want to be accused of doing that.

"Ironically, the Clinton/Gore campaign also censored efforts to raise Iraqgate during the campaign. When I interviewed an official with the Democratic Party opposition research team, he told me that both Clinton and Gore had been fully briefed on the affair but that the campaign managers had decided that 'the matter is just too complicated to inject into a campaign. The public just won't get it and it will muddy our message about the economy.' The only mention it got was through Gore, who brushed it aside as 'a foreign policy blunder.'

"In fact, the documents show that the BNL operation was a conscious, well thought-out and executed plan to secretly finance Iraq's military. The facts imply that the choice of BNL as the bank that would be used for the scheme can be traced to BNL's involvement with Kissinger Associates (KA) and former KA employees

Scowcroft and Eagleburger. The matter may indeed have been a 'blunder' in that the administration did not foresee that Saddam Hussein would use U.S.-financed weapons to invade Kuwait. But it was not accident—as Gore's statement implied.

"The biggest problem with the reporting on BNL was that no one took the time to simply *tell* the story from beginning to end, putting its many players into their proper roles. Stories would break from time to time on the affair, but they tended to deal with a specific event, item or incident. But without an overall 'holistic' understanding of the story, readers were without mooring and had no way of judging or weighing the importance of the matter.

"I wrote my story ["Is Bush a Felon?"] the way I did because, unlike the Clinton/ Gore campaign handlers, I did not think it was too complicated for the American public to understand. I believed the public would come to the same conclusions I had if they simply had the same opportunity to judge them in the light cast by the original documents. After that they would be able to judge later developments for themselves as the case unfolded.

"The 'Iraqgate' case poses fundamental constitutional, moral and legal questions which, if left unexplored in the aftermath of the election, will also go unanswered. In a democracy, such unanswered questions represent nothing less than a toolbox for tyrants.

"With the change of administrations there is the danger that the press will now have a new reason to ignore the BNL affair. Looking back at the prior two administrations' misdeeds will be difficult at a time when a fresh administration is making sweeping changes. But if the press fails to fully expose the BNL affair—including the subsequent coverup by the White House and Department of Justice—that will allow high-ranking officials to escape responsibility for their actions. And, regardless of who is in the White House, if democracy is not about individual responsibility then it is about nothing at all."

Kevin Sanders investigated the "Chicago Connection" of the BNL-Iraqgate scandal for the *War & Peace Digest*, published by the War & Peace Foundation in New York:

"Although the BNL-Iraqgate story is now gaining intense international attention, the Chicago connection—the pivotal nexus of the whole scandal—remains completely unreported in mainstream media at this time.

"A full disclosure of the role played by the BNL bank of Chicago in secret international money transfers would link together holistically and coherently many unexplained elements in the Iraqgate, Inslaw, October Surprise and BCCI scandals, all of which seem to intersect in the Chicago branch of BNL.

"The vast, interlocking conspiracies that would probably be uncovered by an open investigation of the BNL bank would reveal hundreds of prominent political figures in several countries to be involved in criminal activities, ranging from treason to assassination. Many key figures of the Reagan-Bush years would be revealed in a particularly harsh light, since Reagan-Bush enterprises involving illegal arms deals—including October Surprise and Iraqgate—were financed through BNL bank transactions.

"Plato was once asked what he would ask to see if he were suddenly to be thrust into a future culture he knew nothing about

but wished to understand. He replied, 'That which is forbidden.' When the Chicago court refused to let Gonzalez see the documents on the Chicago branch of BNL, it immediately sparked my interest. What was being hidden and why? What would the forbidden knowledge reveal? These questions have still not yet been asked either by mainstream media or by government investigations.

"As Plato said, 'Ask the right questions and the universe will reveal all its secrets.'"

For his article in the *Covert Action Information Bulletin*, **Jack Colhoun** focused on the CIA connection and compared those implications with the Watergate CIA connection:

"The subject of my nominated article—the political implications of President George Bush's use of the CIA to stonewall Representative Henry Gonzalez's House Banking Committee investigation of the Iraqgate scandal—did not receive comment in the mass media last year.

"The public would greatly benefit from a wider public airing of my subject, because Bush broke a critical taboo of American politics when he involved the CIA in a domestic political controversy. The implications of CIA intervention in American politics is chilling, especially since Bush is the first former CIA director to serve as president.

"The CIA has not proved its case that Gonzalez's public investigation of the Iraqgate scandal has jeopardized U.S. national security interests. But it was revealed during the pre-trial hearing of Christopher Drougal, the manager of the Banca Nazionale del Lavoro-Atlanta branch, that the Agency withheld material evidence from U.S. District Judge Marvin Shoob, who presided over the hearing. The CIA withheld documents that indicated the CIA was aware that BNL-Atlanta was the financial cornerstone of an Iraqi arms technology procurement network in the United States.

"The CIA's withholding of evidence in the Drougal hearing was a great embarrassment for the Bush administration. The Justice Department suffered a major setback in its case against Drougal. But the mass media failed to draw the connection between the CIA's meddling in the BNL-Atlanta case to the CIA's effort to taint the Gonzalez investigation. The mass media have yet to explore the political implications of the CIA's intervention in the Iraqgate scandal.

"And the media have also failed to point out the relevance of the Watergate scandal to Iraqgate. A few days after it was disclosed in August 1974 that President Richard Nixon pressed the CIA to obstruct the FBI's investigation of the Watergate scandal, Nixon resigned. The public release of the so-called 'smoking gun' tape of Nixon instructing H.R. Haldeman, White House chief of staff, what to tell CIA Director Richard Helms sparked a firestorm of controversy because the CIA is barred by law from political operations in the United States."

Colhoun concludes that while George Bush and his administration were the chief beneficiaries of the mass media's failure to cover the CIA involvement in Iraqgate, the democratic process in the United States is the big loser.

As these three investigative authors reveal, Iraqgate deserved far more coverage than it received in 1992; further, the lack of coverage was not solely a function of the media's failure. In this case, the Clinton/Gore campaign also attempted to thwart further exposure of the scandal by hoping it would simply go away.

Finally, even at this writing, the Bush administration coverup of the Iraqgate scandal is ongoing and deserves the harsh glare of the media's spotlight. Iraqgate, one of our top ten Censored stories of 1992, should also be one of the top ten biggest news stories of 1993.

As Henry Gonzalez says, "The struggle for truth is never-ending, but it is essential if we are to have a chance at any semblance of representative or responsible government."

It is past time for the mainstream media to join authors like Pizzo, Sanders and Colhoun in the struggle for the truth about the Iraqgate issue and the coverup.

6

CENSORED

"We are Winning the War on Drugs" was a Lie

Sources:
In These Times
2040 N. Milwaukee Avenue, 2nd Fl.
Chicago, IL 60647-4002
Date: 5/20/92
Title: "Drug Deaths Rise as the War Continues"
Author: Mike Males

EXTRA!
130 W. 25th Street
New York, NY 10001
Date: September 1992
Title: "Don't Forget the Hype: Media, Drugs and Public Opinion" *
Author: Micah Fink

SYNOPSIS: When President George Bush went before the nation on September 6, 1989, to give a special address about the seriousness of the drug problem in the United States, the media and the public responded with alarm. By the end of that month, 64 percent of the public believed that drugs posed a greater threat than nuclear war, environmental degradation, toxic waste, AIDS, poverty or the national debt. The *New York Times* alone published 238 articles on drugs—more than seven articles a day—that month.

Fast-forward to 1992: The federal anti-drug budget has mushroomed to over $10 billion dollars; and the president proclaims, "We are winning the war on drugs." The problem with this proclamation is that it is a lie.

The sobering fact is that Americans are in greater danger from drugs today than ever before. In fact, despite "winning the war on drugs," drug deaths in the U.S. are skyrocketing at a much higher rate than drug arrests.

Before the Reagan/Bush administrations began their war on drugs, deaths from drug abuse and drug-related murders had declined from a peak of 8,500 per year in the early 1970s to 7,700 in 1982. Since 1982 the numbers have steadily climbed. Drug abuse deaths have risen by 50 percent and drug-related murders have tripled—to more than 13,000 in 1990. *This is the steepest increase and highest level in history.*

Today's drug statistics are startling:

▪ During a single week of the present-day drug war (as opposed to the "pre-drug-war era"), there are 15,000 more arrests, 5,000 more pounds of cocaine seized, 10,000 more people sent to drug treatment and 100 more drug-related deaths.

▪ Street drugs (marijuana, LSD, cocaine, heroin) are not the main killers, as they are portrayed. Rather, prescription drugs (barbiturates, stimulants) are most lethal, accounting for more than 8,000 deaths annually, while street drugs account for 3,000 deaths. (Also overlooked is the "legal-drug" death toll: 400,000 annually from tobacco, 100,000 from alcohol.)

▪ Teenagers are often portrayed as the most at-risk group for drug abuse. However, of the 13,000-plus drug-abuse deaths in 1990, adults aged 20 to 59 accounted for 11,000 of those fatalities.

▪ Marijuana, LSD and other hallucinogens account for fewer than five deaths a year but make up more than half of all drug arrests.

▪ Prescription drugs cause more than half of all drug deaths but comprise only 10 percent of all drug arrests.

- White adults over the age of 25 account for two-thirds of all drug deaths but account for only one-third of all drug arrests.

It is more than ironic that the mainstream media that helped Reagan/Bush create a drug war hysteria remain silent or ignorant of the real problems that exist today.

SSU Censored Researcher: Nicole Novak

COMMENTS: The sincerity of the Reagan/ Bush administrations' war on drugs was first questioned by Project Censored in the #4 Censored Story of 1989, which asked, "Does the administration really want to win the war on drugs?" The answer, based on the experiences of one of the nation's top federal narcotics prosecutors, Richard Gregorie, was "no."

Gregorie's aggressive and successful eight-year assault on big-time cocaine bosses and drug-corrupted officials from Miami to Medellin was stopped by the State Department, and in January 1989 Gregorie quit in disgust to go into law practice in Miami.

The same issue resurfaced as the #5 Censored Story of 1990. Titled, "Continued Media Blackout of Drug War Fraud," the nomination revealed the experiences of Michael Levine, a retired undercover agent from the Drug Enforcement Agency. His critical exposé of the DEA closely parallels the experiences of Gregorie.

And now the American public is learning about the tragic results of the war that never was. Mike Males's article about rising drug deaths clearly contradicts President George Bush's optimistic "We are winning the war on drugs" statement.

At the same time, the mainstream media—once so eager to herald the War on Drugs—are less eager to confess its failure and the toll it has taken in human lives.

Investigative author Males says his article in *In These Times* sparked additional coverage only in the alternative press and not in the mainstream media. He notes that while there has now been some sporadic coverage of various experts who feel we're "losing" the war, there has been "nothing on the spectacular rise in drug deaths."

Males feels the public "needs to be informed that despite rosy claims of officials, the single biggest tragedy—drug death increases—is provable by a solid outcome measure that shows the drug war is a disaster."

7

CENSORED

Trashing Federal Regulations for Profit

Sources:
The Nation
72 Fifth Avenue
New York, NY 10011
Date: March 23, 1992
Title: "Bush's Regulatory Chill: Immoral, Illegal, and Deadly" *
Authors: Christine Triano and Nancy Watzman

The Progressive
409 E. Main Street
Madison, WI 53703
Date: May 1992
Title: "Deregulatory Creep"
Author: Arthur E. Rowse

SYNOPSIS: In his State of the Union address on January 28, 1992, President George Bush declared a 90-day "moratorium" on new federal regulations as a way to help the economy out of the recession that began in the summer of 1990.

Shortly thereafter, Public Citizen and OMB Watch compiled a list of affected regulations. Some of them would have done the following:

1. Prevented worker exposure to toxic chemicals: a 90-day delay could cost an estimated 289 workers' lives.

2. Forced manufacturers and hospitals to report adverse effects associated with medical devices to the FDA; would keep the public up to date on hazards such as those associated with silicone breast implants.

3. Prevented a replay of the S&L fiasco: a regulation pending at the FDIC would require banks, not the taxpayers, to pay for their own bailout.

4. Protected farm workers from exposure to dangerous pesticides.

By optimistic White House calculations, deregulation could save consumers up to $20 billion a year, but the public sees it differently. In fact, polls show the general public firmly opposes deregulation of business, especially when the purity of air, water, food, drugs and other necessities is involved. One survey shows that people rated "reduced safety and environmental regulations" last among 16 ways of helping the economy. Professional economists are also skeptical.

Well then, given no viable political or economic reason, what inspired the Bush administration to pursue deregulation so zealously? Consider these coincidences between contributions to the Bush-Quayle campaign/Republican National Committee and some federal decisions:

Developers contribute $2,277,490: wetland protection acreage reduced.

Food industry contributes $1,352,000: nutrition guidelines pulled back; nutrition labeling delayed a year.

Oil and gas industry contributes $1,150,360: stripper-well fees reduced; rules on natural gas usage relaxed; limits on hazardous air blocked.

Air polluters contribute $788,270: emission standards delayed.

Insurance industry contributes $450,000: product-liability limits pushed.

Airlines contribute $315,700: limits on noisy engines reduced.

Pharmaceutical industry contributes $185,002: drug-approval process speeded up; "orphan drug" competition bill vetoed.

Auto industry contributes $156,250: proposal for gas-tank canister dropped; stricter auto efficiency opposed.

Investigative writer Arthur E. Rowse says that when Public Citizen's Congress Watch cited the coincidence between the auto/petroleum contributions and the regulatory concessions, the news was ignored by the *Washington Post*, the *New York Times* and the *Los Angeles Times*. And when OMB Watch pointed out how many workers could die if workplace rules were delayed, leading reporters yawned.

The benefits of coincidental contributions and deregulation were not lost on George Bush. On April 29, he extended his original 90-day moratorium on new federal regulations for another 120 days.

SSU Censored Researcher: Beverly Alexander

COMMENTS: While the press has come to recognize the detrimental impact of deregulation on our financial institutions, particularly on savings and loans, it has yet to recognize a similar impact on other parts of society. Were it not for watchdog groups, such as Public Citizen and OMB Watch, and the nation's alternative press—in this case *The Nation* and *The Progressive*—it is doubtful anyone would be aware of the Bush/Quayle deregulatory quid pro quo program.

Investigative authors Christine Triano of OMB Watch and Nancy Watzman of Public Citizen report:

"President Bush's moratorium on federal regulation—which started as a 90-day freeze, was then extended for another 90 days, and finally extended for an entire year—received only scattered media coverage, and most of that in the print media. Network television didn't cover it, falling back on the excuse that the topic of federal regulation didn't make 'good pictures.'

"When the media *did* report on the moratorium, they tended to rely heavily on White House sources that did not provide complete information on the topic. There was also a tendency to cover just a small piece of the moratorium—for example, to write a story about one particular environmental regulation that was stalled. Few reporters were willing to dig through the administration's doublespeak to find out how the moratorium was damaging health, safety and environmental regulations *overall*, at all the federal agencies. When Public Citizen and OMB Watch set out to answer that very question, they found themselves pretty much alone in the effort.

"President Bush's announcement of the rule freeze during his 1992 State of the Union address consisted of just a couple of sentences in a long speech. He followed up with a memo to federal agency heads, giving instructions about how to carry out the moratorium, but those memos were not for general release to the public.

"Given the dearth of media attention to the rule freeze, it was terribly difficult for a curious citizen to obtain any substantive information about the moratorium. Yet the moratorium had very real effects on programs that the American public cares about. The victims of delay or weakening included nutrition-labeling regulations for meat and poultry, nursing home safety-enforcement regulations, and a pesticide record-keeping requirement designed to help minimize danger from spills and other accidents. If the public had had more information about this sort of moratorium-caused damage, there would have been a groundswell of concern about it—and perhaps Congress more strongly would have felt the mandate to do something about it.

"The mainstream media's limited coverage of the regulatory moratorium was based on more than the fact that regulation is a less than sexy issue. Uncovering the links between corporate America, campaign finance, and the startling consolidation of power in the executive branch is a near impossible task.

"Bush's rules-freeze neatly illustrates how the Bush and Reagan administrations have paid back their corporate supporters over the past twelve years by doling out regulatory favors. While these supporters no doubt enjoyed the benefits of the media's limited coverage of the moratorium, it is the Bush administration whose interests were overwhelmingly served by keeping the public from too closely scrutinizing its actions. By proclaiming the moratorium at various times a recession-buster, a boost for small business and a shot to overzealous regulators, Bush successfully managed to divert most others from calling it what it really was: an election-year sop to big-business contributors.

"Bush's regulatory moratorium was extended several times after our article was published, the last time being at the Republican convention in Houston, when Bush pledged to extend it for another year if elected. In various cases where the freeze was challenged, federal agencies were found to have improperly delayed vital consumer and environmental protections. Still, the exact toll of calling the federal regulatory agencies to a halt for nearly 12 months is yet to be fully assessed."

Author Arthur Rowse, whose article appeared in *The Progressive*, says that wider reporting of the quid pro quo between deregulation and campaign financing would bring direct benefits to many people by exposing the efforts of the Bush/Quayle administration, and the Reagan administration before it, to impede the implementation of federal laws affecting health and safety:

"Such attention would also better alert the public to how campaign funds are traded for political favors, would build public pressure for making campaign laws more democratic, and would force elected officials to respond better to general public interests.

"Poor coverage of these topics directly benefits wealthy special interests—including large media firms—that already control the government and the country, no matter which political party is in power. The poorer the coverage, the greater the success of such groups in grabbing special privileges, a process that would be defeated by exposure. With media firms more and more occupied with maximizing profits rather than maximizing coverage, it may not be long before democracy and freedom—including press freedom—will be weakened to the point of no return."

Rowse feels that federal regulation is still a "journalistic backwater and consequently a source of public ignorance and confusion. The news media have done little to find out why the public seems to be so anti-Washington while demanding (in poll after poll) more government protection for public health, safety and consumer rights. Here is an area where journalists, by doing their job, could help make democracy work and even score some points with press bashers."

8 CENSORED

Government Secrecy Makes a Mockery of Democracy

Source: **Issues in Science and Technology**
307 Massachusetts Avenue NE
Washington, DC 20002
Date: Summer 1992
Title: "The Perils of Government Secrecy" *
Author: Steven Aftergood

SYNOPSIS: In 1991 some 6,500 U.S. government employees classified 7,107,017 documents, an average of more than 19,000 documents per day. Steven Aftergood, a senior research analyst at the Federation of American Scientists (FAS) in Washington, DC, says our information policy is in disarray, with widespread over-classification and an inefficient and costly information system. Further, the classified files are overflowing with records of policy decisions, historical and budget documents, and reams of environmental data that could not possibly compromise our national security. Some examples:

Secret historical documents: As of last year, the oldest classified military document in the National Archives was dated April 15, 1917, and concerns U.S. troop movements in Europe during World War I.

National Security Directives (NSD): These secret presidential directives withhold basic policy documents concerning space, telecommunications, counternarcotics, etc., from Congress as well as the public. Until May 1992, not a single Bush administration NSD had ever been made public; at that time, President Bush, under pressure, partially declassified his directive concerning U.S. policy on Iraq.

The Black Budget: About 15 percent of the Defense Department's budget for weapons acquisition has been classified in recent years, keeping the cost of a program, its purpose, even its existence a secret from Congress. Often the excessive secrecy leads to abuse involving program failures, cost overruns and fraud.

Secret environmental impact data: The Department of Energy has withheld data on the health effects of its nuclear weapons production facilities. No matter how potentially dangerous a proposed project may be to the public, information about its hazards can be concealed.

Intelligence information: There are more than a dozen intelligence agencies within the government, including the National Reconnaissance Office (NRO), responsible for satellite reconnaissance. Ironically, the very name and existence of the NRO are classified. Further, the combined budget for these agencies is secret because it is felt that official disclosure of such a number, estimated to be about $30 billion a year, would jeopardize American agents or sensitive technologies. Concerned with an ever-increasing criticism of its secrecy, the CIA last year prepared a report on how the agency might achieve greater openness—and then classified the report.

While governments require some degree of secrecy, it was only with the start of the Cold War that it went beyond military information and became an institutionalized part of the U.S. bureaucracy. In 1951, President Truman established a classification system that included civilian as well as military agencies. The system has been revised a number of times since and reached a peak of openness under the Carter administration. This trend toward openness was reversed by President Reagan, who, in 1983, issued an executive order that said, in essence, when in doubt, classify. And if there is a question of what level of classification, the higher level is to be adopted. Now the system is totally out of control.

As Aftergood concludes, "Openness in government is not a threat to national security...it is the foundation of the nation's political way of life and the source of much of its strength."

SSU Censored Researcher: Kimberly S. Anderson

COMMENTS: The millions of documents now being classified annually, as author Steven Aftergood points out, can be traced to Friday, March 11, 1983, when President Ronald Reagan issued an executive order to "stem the flow of leaks of classified government information."

At the time, Anthony Lewis, columnist with the *New York Times*, warned that this was "the most dangerous executive order in many years: dangerous to the American system of democratic control over public policy. It is also, so far, dangerously misunderstood."

Aftergood offers some further points:

"Considering its importance in determining the boundaries of permitted public knowledge, the government secrecy system has not been closely scrutinized or even widely recognized.

"Even when the news media report the eruption of scandals such as Iraqgate, they have rarely stopped to examine the structural factors that make such scandals possible. One of these factors is certainly the arbitrary exercise of classification authority, which all too often allows political misconduct to be concealed in the name of national security.

"Wider exposure of the systemic abuse of government secrecy would finally make it politically possible to reform the secrecy system and to challenge it when warranted. Government officials quite naturally tend to conceal information they deem sensitive. It is incumbent on an informed electorate to assert its right to know and to demand government accountability. The necessary first step is to acknowledge the problem.

"It is hard to say that anyone benefits by ignoring the explosive growth of government secrecy, except of course those who have secrets they wish to maintain. But if there is in fact a core body of information that truly must be protected in the interests of national security, as I believe, then that information too may become less secure when classification authority is invoked for bureaucratic or political advantage, and the credibility of the classification system declines.

"It is easier to say who is harmed by ignoring secrecy, and that is almost everyone, to some degree. Excessive secrecy has not only become a hindrance in science and technology, it has infected much of government information policy, frustrating public debate on a range of crucial subjects from foreign policy to the environment, and subverting the operation of our political institutions."

Aftergood also has a tip for the Clinton administration:

"Since the national security classification system is based on Executive Order, not statutory law, it can be unilaterally altered by the president. One may hope that the Clinton administration will finally see fit to reverse at least some of the abuses of the Cold War secrecy system, and especially the excesses of the Reagan/Bush years."

9 CENSORED

How Advertising Pressure Can Corrupt a Free Press

Source: **Center for the Study of Commercialism**
1875 Connecticut Avenue NW, Ste. 300
Washington, DC 20009-5728
Date: March 1992
Title: "Dictating Content: How Advertising Pressure Can Corrupt a Free Press" *
Author: Ronald K.L. Collins (Foreword by Todd Gitlin)

SYNOPSIS: The free press in America isn't free at all—at least from the influence of advertisers on the content of the news. While people fear governmental control of the media, a far more subtle yet pervasive influence comes from advertiser pressure. "Dictating Content: How Advertising Pressure Can Corrupt a Free Press," a report by the Center for the Study of Commercialism, documents dozens of examples of advertiser censorship in the media.

One of the crudest forms of censorship is defined as "direct economic censorship," which occurs when an advertiser overtly dictates to the mass media what the public shall or shall not hear. Examples include the impact on consumer reporting on the automotive industry, which throws around its weight with huge advertising budgets. "We don't even bother with auto-related stories anymore," says Seattle reporter Herb Weisbaum. "Even a simple consumer education story on how to buy a new car can draw the wrath of local car dealers." He adds, "Stories are being killed...watered down; and saddest of all, stories are not even being attempted because reporters know they'll never make it on the air."

Similarly, the major ad revenues spent on the local level by realtors and retail stores influence coverage of their industries. The extraordinary influence of tobacco advertisers on the coverage of smoking and its connection with cancer is also documented.

Other forms of media bias include reporter self-censorship (when the specter of an advertiser's reaction dissuades a reporter from even suggesting a particular story); reporting fake news (advertiser-created reports or news segments presented as legitimate, unbiased news accounts); using stories as bait (stories that purposefully flatter current or potential advertisers); using puff pieces to increase ad revenues.

Achieving editorial independence is difficult, given the pressure for advertising income. And those who try to maintain journalistic integrity often face a real threat to their livelihood. According to the journalists responsible for the "Dictating Content" report, "When interviewed for this report, reporters caught in the crossfire between advertisers and editors requested anonymity for fear of losing their jobs or being blacklisted." One editor confirmed he was fired after clashing with his publisher over advertiser influence; the publisher added that he would jeopardize his future in the industry if he talked for the record. One long-time reporter was fired for apparently embarrassing his publisher when quoted about his paper's "sensitivity to car advertisers."

The Center for the Study of Commercialism invited 200 media outlets to a press conference in Washington, DC, on March 11, 1992, to announce the results of its study. Not a single radio or television station or network sent a reporter, and only two newspapers, the *Washington Post* and the *Washington Times*, bothered to attend. The *Post* didn't run a story at all; the *Times* ran one but didn't name the advertisers cited in the study. The press conference, designed to show how advertisers suppress the news, made its point.

SSU Censored Researcher: Amy Cohen

COMMENTS: Many media critics have accused the press of being vulnerable to advertiser pressure in the past. Until now, however, there hasn't been broad evidence of how that dynamic works. Thanks to the Center for the Study of Commercialism, in Washington, DC, such evidence is available, albeit still ignored by the press itself. Author Ronald K.L. Collins describes the study and how it was received by the news media:

"To the best of our knowledge, 'Dictating Content' was the *First* report of its kind addressing the topic of how advertis-

ing pressure may affect editorial content in the print and electronic media. The report cited more than 60 specific instances of print and/or electronic media, advertising-related censorship, including over two dozen never before revealed. ('A remarkable achievement, considering how terrorized are most newsrooms when the question is broached,' wrote Doug Ireland of the *Village Voice*, 3/24/92.)

"For the first time, the report told Americans—particularly consumers—how the content of the media information may be influenced by direct or indirect advertising pressure. Such information may have a significant impact on some of the most important decisions Americans make, from the homes and the cars they buy to the pharmaceutical drugs they may need. Moreover, public knowledge of advertising pressure connected to alcohol and tobacco is vital to the public health and safety.

"Some media (the *Washington Post*, for one) did not cover the story of our report because, according to one reporter, the problem was purportedly 'well known' within the journalism community (i.e., in the newsrooms, in the scholarly journals, etc.). Even if true, such arguments overlook an important fact: the public has been kept in the dark about this form of private censorship affecting freedom of the press.

"In short, information of the kind set out in 'Dictating Content' is a crucial part of the public's Right To Know, without which the high goals of the First Amendment are unattainable.

"Over 200 print and electronic media news organizations received press releases and press conference invitations concerning our report, 'Dictating Content.' While the report received limited to fair coverage in newspapers, it received absolutely no coverage by network TV and no coverage in any major magazine. The only TV coverage was a short March 12, 1992, Fox Morning TV News (Washington, DC) report. All major networks and magazines were sent advance press releases and/or copies of the report. Still, no network TV or major magazine reporters were assigned to cover the story—and none did.

"The total network TV and major magazine blackout surrounding the release of 'Dictating Content' was perhaps predictable given that our report surmised that the problem of advertising pressure is probably most acute in the network and magazine media.

"Unless the sunlight of the media is shed brightly on the topic of advertising pressure affecting the press, then the problem is likely to continue and will probably grow worse. Too many editors and producers will remain timid in the face of ad pressure; too many reporters will remain reticent about doing stories that may be killed or may result in their firing; and all too often the public will be denied information vital to informed decision-making in the marketplace. Meanwhile, a vicious cycle of censorship will continue, trading the short-term gains of commerce for the long-term gains of uninhibited communication.

"The Center for the Study of Commercialism is continuing its efforts in this field. Currently we have embarked on a study of the major college textbooks used in journalism and communication departments to determine to what extent, if any, the topic of advertising pressure and editorial integrity are addressed. Similarly, the Center is attempting to organize groups such as the Society of Professional Journalists and the American Society of Newspaper Editors to take some long needed action in this area by way of establishing some code of voluntary guidelines.

"Still, the problem continues. For example, in a recent study conducted by the Society of American Business Editors & Writers, 75 percent of those editors and reporters polled said they were aware of increasing pressure by advertisers to influence the content of business sections. Almost half responded that advertising pressure has affected the way their publications edited or reported the news. Worst of all, such important information about this form of censorship goes largely unreported, especially on network TV and in major magazines.

"In a highly commercial culture such as ours, the First American metaphor of a marketplace of ideas can only be realized where there is some critical distance between the forces of the marketplace and the freedom of press, especially ideas critical of the marketplace. Unfortunately, quiet though powerful censorial forces have prevented that message from making its mark."

10 CENSORED

The Pentagon's Post-Cold War Black Budget is Alive and Prospering

Source: **Mother Jones**
1663 Mission Street, 2nd Fl.
San Francisco, CA 94103
Date: March/April 1992
Title: "The Pentagon's Secret Stash" *
Author: Tim Weiner

SYNOPSIS: Today, and every day, close to $100 million flows through underground pipelines from the U.S. Treasury to the Pentagon to fuel the national-security machinery of the United States. The black budget ("black" in the sense of being unseen, covert, hidden from light) is the secret treasury of the nation's military and intelligence agencies. It is appropriated and spent with only the scantest public debate or media scrutiny.

Of the roughly $36 billion in the secret budget today, about $5 billion goes to build and develop weapons programs, many of which remain so highly classified that only the two most senior members of the congressional armed services and appropriations committees know anything about them.

Robert Costello, in charge of buying weapons at the Pentagon during the last years of the Reagan administration, said, "Inside the Pentagon the mind-set is, 'I'm going to use secrecy to build my nice, isolated little cocoon.'" And when resident skeptics criticized such secrecy, "They

fired the bastards who wanted to put the screws on them."

Why isn't there more publicity? After all, public pressure and congressional anger forced the lid off the now famous B-2 bomber. And reporters and public-policy advocates uncovered strange programs with eerie names such as Timberwind (a Star Wars program to build a nuclear-powered rocket engine for missiles designed to shoot down incoming Soviet nukes), MILSTAR (a network of space satellites and blast-hardened ground stations that would endure a six-month nuclear war) and Island Sun (involving a convoy of generals hurtling down highways in lead-laced tractor-trailer trucks, dodging nuclear detonations and barking commands through scramblers—a Dr. Strangelove-style operation).

The realization that the Cold War has ended apparently has not yet penetrated the inner catacombs of the Pentagon nor stilled projects such as these. After a half-century of lucrative and unchecked black budgets, starting with the Manhattan Project that brought us Hiroshima, the secret cache largely remains inviolate. The wall surrounding the black budget has proven more durable than the one that divided Berlin. Iran/contra exposed the inherent dangers of unexamined secrecy; the congressional investigation of Iran/contra revealed that the whole fiasco never could have happened without the machinery and cloak of the secret budget.

The solution is not difficult. Congress could demand disclosure of data on the cost and character of secret programs but has only done so on a piecemeal basis; nor has Congress ever confronted the underlying fact that the secrecy system itself defies the Constitution, which requires the government to publish a complete and accurate account of all federal spending.

"The fault lies with the Congress," says Representative Pat Schroeder of Colorado. "If we forced the release of this information, there would be no issue. As long as the Congress goes along with the Pentagon's secrecy program, we have no (legitimate) complaint."

The "Pentagon's Secret Billion-Dollar Black Budget," also by Tim Weiner, was Project Censored's #7 story of 1990. Weiner's latest investigation reveals that the official end of the Cold War did not end the Pentagon's secretive Cold War mentality.

SSU Censored Researcher: Damon S. Van Hoesen

COMMENTS: Tim Weiner, Washington correspondent for the *Philadelphia Inquirer*, has written extensively on the issue of the Pentagon's black budget. However, he feels that the subject is still undercovered. Weiner's work on the black budget won him the Pulitzer Prize for national reporting in 1988; his book, *Blank Check: The Pentagon's Black Budget*, was published in 1990.

Weiner believes that the press has a responsibility to warn the public about the dangers inherent in the secrecy surrounding the Pentagon's black budget, but there are reasons why it doesn't fulfill that responsibility. "The black budget is an arcane, obscure issue that takes a lot of time to explain," Weiner says. "Further, it requires expertise in several different areas including espionage, government secrecy and large sums of money."

Weiner is not optimistic about any substantial change that might occur in Pentagon secrecy regulations under the Clinton administration. "I don't think we'll see much change," Weiner predicts. "Secrecy in government is seductive, a shield, and all governments use it."

CENSORED

Solar Power Eclipsed by Oil, Gas and Nuclear Interests

Sources:
Multinational Monitor
PO Box 19405
Washington, DC 20036
Date: April 1992
Title: "Solar Eclipsed"
Author: Julie Gozan

The Christian Science Monitor
One Norway Street
Boston, MA 02115
Date: 3/12/92
Title: "Unbind Solar Energy From Washington's Red Tape"
Author: James Weinstein

SYNOPSIS: On November 27, 1991, the California-based solar energy firm Luz International Limited announced that it had filed for bankruptcy. Luz designed, built and operated the world's nine largest Solar Electric Generating Systems (SEGS), which generated 95 percent of the world's solar electricity.

Luz's collapse reflects the problems faced by a solar power industry shackled by hostile government policies and the protection of natural gas and oil interests. While the Department of Energy (DOE) claims to be committed to the development of solar energy, the facts reveal that while the cost of generating solar power has decreased 73 percent from 1980 to 1990, federal research and development (R&D) spending on solar energy has decreased 90 percent.

Presently, the nuclear industry receives more than 70 percent of the DOE's funding outlays for technology-specific development. According to the DOE's R&D budget, the total administration request for nuclear fission and fusion for fiscal 1993 is $1,377 billion, an increase of $100 million from 1992. However, the total request for conservation R&D, renewable energy and state and local conservation, combined, is just $768 million, down $100 million from 1992.

Investigative author Julie Gozan reports that if it weren't for government subsidies, nuclear power would be priced out of the market. Gozan notes that while the cost of solar is down to 8 cents per kilowatt hour, the cost of producing nuclear energy is nearly 13 cents per kilowatt hour.

According to an article in the *Christian Science Monitor*, the next generation of solar plants, which had been planned for construction by Luz in 1994-95, would have brought costs down to 6 to 6.5 cents per kilowatt hour—*less than the cost of natural-gas electric generation.*

Government obstacles to safer, cleaner energy go beyond fiscal favors for nuclear power and the oil and gas industry. Lawmakers set a cap of 80 megawatts on the amount of energy that a solar plant can generate and sell. Luz, which had the capacity to build SEGS that would generate 200 megawatts, or enough energy to meet the electricity needs of 200,000 homes daily, was forced to build plants below this optimum usage and had to "dump" solar energy rather than use it.

Author Gozan also reports that in order to compete with oil and gas, solar power must somehow match hidden government subsidies given to conventional fuels. Oil and gas receive the equivalent of a 25 percent tax credit. These include an immediate tax write-off for drilling costs and "percentage depletion" for the cost of pipes, pumps and tanks used to complete a well.

As Luz International Chairman Newton Becker observed when the company filed for bankruptcy, Luz's demise was not attributable to technical or economic failure; it was simply the result of our not having a national energy policy. Meanwhile, environmentally sound solutions fall victim to money and politics.

SSU Censored Researcher: Blake Kehler

COMMENTS: "In the early Seventies someone said we wouldn't have solar power until the oil companies get a monopoly on the sun. Now it appears that this is happening." That was the lead paragraph to the #9 Censored story synopsis of 1980. It continued, "Within the last five years, a powerful elite of multinational oil companies, aerospace firms, utilities and other large corporations has been quietly buying into the solar industry. The group's aim appears to be to squeeze out smaller competitors and control development so that alternative energy sources will never threaten its massive investments in fossil fuels and nuclear power."

Sources for the 1980 nomination were *New West*, now defunct, and *Mother Jones*. But that was then and this is now. And while the sources for the #11 Censored story of 1992 have changed, the subject matter hasn't. In fact, the current story bears witness to the prescience of the 1980 nomination. It told how the big boys were buying out the smaller competitors to control the fledgling solar industry; the 1992 story reveals how the big boys finally have forced Luz International Limited, the world's leading solar energy company, out of business.

Investigative author Julie Gozan reported that the plight of the solar industry has received no coverage in the mass media. "Although the Luz bankruptcy was widely reported in newspapers and financial journals," says Gozan, "these contained no analysis of the solar industry and its obstacles." Gozan believes the public would benefit from greater exposure of this issue. "As the public is exposed to the viability of solar energy as a safe, effective and potentially inexpensive source of energy, more pressure will be placed on the federal government to provide equal incentives for the solar and other renewable energy industries with those for nuclear and fossil fuels. As solar becomes competitive and widely available, the U.S. public will be able to access alternatives to non-renewable, polluting and dangerous energy sources.

"The nuclear and fossil fuel industries bank on the current lack of public awareness of solar and other renewable energy technologies. It is in the interest of those industries to suppress information about safe and clean energy alternatives."

Investigative author James Weinstein, whose article on solar energy appeared in the *Christian Science Monitor*, concurs with Gozan on the lack of coverage given this issue. Solar energy receives "little or no attention," Weinstein states, "or is treated like an exotic or unrealistic alternative, for obvious commercial reasons."

The public would benefit from wider coverage of the solar issue, Weinstein adds, because "it would accelerate the pace of ultimately unavoidable transfer of energy dependence from oil, coal and nuclear to solar and biomass."

Unfortunately, however, the news media have been more than cooperative in the suppression of information that would accelerate that transfer. The nation's leading newspaper, the *New York Times*, which prides itself for printing "all the news that's fit to print," is known for its support of nuclear power. One of the top 25 Censored stories of 1988, "The New York Times: America's Pro-nuke Newspaper of Record," reported an investigation by *EXTRA!* that revealed the *Times'* long-standing pro-nuclear editorial policy.

What Happened to the EPA?

Source: **In These Times**
2040 N. Milwaukee Avenue, 2nd Fl.
Chicago, IL 60647-4002
Date: 4/22/92
Title: "Wasting Away at EPA"
Author: Joel Bleifuss

SYNOPSIS: The Environmental Protection Agency (EPA), created by Richard Nixon in 1970, has been the watchdog agency protecting our air, our water, our resources and our ecology for more than two decades. But some of its critics believe our environment would be in better shape today if the EPA hadn't been around.

William Sanjour, a longtime EPA whistle-blower, is one of those not satisfied with the EPA's performance. In early 1992, he came up with a series of proposals that would thoroughly reform the agency.

Sanjour's proposal titled, "Why EPA is like it is and what can be done about it," was prepared for and published by the Environmental Research Foundation, in Washington, DC. He addresses the question, "Why is EPA so often on the wrong side of environmental issues when the EPA is chartered to protect the environment?"

Sanjour has had a lot of time to ponder this question: For the past three years, he has had a desk at EPA but nothing to do since his superiors have refused to assign him any work.

In his report, Sanjour charges that when the EPA does act to protect the environment, it is only because the agency 'was forced or coerced into taking action.' He mentions three points: 1) The EPA, more often than not, opposes congressional attempts to pass tough environmental laws; 2) The EPA spends more time and money figuring out how to exempt corporations from regulations than it does enforcing them; and 3) The EPA's will to regulate is so weak that a proposed regulation must be under a court-ordered deadline (brought by an environmental group) before it will even be considered for the EPA administrator's signature.

According to Sanjour, the problems at EPA are shared by all regulatory agencies (i.e., they are more concerned with protecting the interests of the party they are supposed to regulate than in protecting the public's interests).

EPA administrators are also concerned with protecting their own interests. Sanjour lists 20 high-ranking EPA officials who left the agency and went on to prosperous careers in the hazardous waste management industry. Most of the former EPA administrators are now millionaire waste industry executives, and ten of them are now employed by the world's largest waste management corporation—Waste Management, Inc., and its subsidiary, Chemical Waste Management.

Sanjour cites a number of disturbing conflicts of interest resulting from the revolving door system between the EPA and the corporate waste industry; he also suggests 14 proposals for cleaning up the EPA.

In These Times author Joel Bleifuss concludes that Sanjour has come up with a number of workable solutions to the crisis at EPA and hopes the nation's environmental organizations will pressure Congress to implement them.

In addition, the nation's media should have put William Sanjour and his comprehensive report on the national agenda so that the public could learn why our environment is the way it is and what can be done about it.

SSU Censored Researcher: Jennifer Makowsky

COMMENTS: "What happened to the EPA?" is an appropriate question to ask at the end of the Reagan/Bush era, particularly since it now appears that the agency, designed to protect our environment, defected and joined our environment enemies.

Joel Bleifuss, in his story of an EPA whistle-blower, documents the final battle in the Reagan/Bush war against the agency. He notes that while "specific instances of regulatory abuse at the EPA are occasionally covered by the mass media, the structural problems at the EPA have been totally ignored."

Bleifuss adds that if information about the close ties between waste industry officials and senior environmental regulators in the government were made public, it would undermine the public's trust in the waste industry. And since the waste industry is one of the most corrupt industries in the world, Bleifuss says it should be exposed as such.

Events leading up to the demise of the EPA as a regulatory watchdog were cited in several recent censored nominations.

In the #2 ranked story of 1988, Jim Sibbison, former EPA publicist turned investigative environmental reporter, exposed Reagan administration overt efforts to soft-pedal pollution stories. Sibbison also revealed how executives from industry met secretly with officials of the White House's Office of Management and Budget to discuss pending new EPA regulations; the OMB allowed the executives to suggest revisions in those regulations and the EPA subsequently made the necessary changes.

In one of the top 25 Censored stories of 1989, Sibbison, in yet another expose, documented how public employees were leaving the EPA for high salaries in the very corporation they formerly were supposed to regulate. The synopsis was titled, "The Revolving Door Between EPA and Polluters."

And, in the #8 Censored story of 1991, investigative journalist Eve Pell revealed how American corporations, no longer concerned with toothless EPA regulations, had gone on the offensive to retaliate against the environmental movement with a wide assortment of dirty tricks and attack strategies.

Nonetheless, like the Phoenix, the EPA may rise again. As noted in the synopsis, William Sanjour, the scorned EPA whistle-blower, has developed a number of workable solutions to the crisis at EPA which, with the support of a new administration and Congress, could help the agency fulfill its original charge.

13 CENSORED

The Specter of Sterility

Sources:
British Medical Journal
B.M.A. House
Tavistock Square
London WC1H 9JR
England
Date: 9/12/92
Title: "Evidence for Decreasing Quality of Semen During Past 50 Years"
Author: Niels E. Skakkebaek

New York Times
229 W. 43rd Street
New York, NY 10036
Date: 1/1/91
Title: "Research on Birth Defects Turns to Flaws in Sperm"
Author: Sandra Blakeslee

USA Today
1000 Wilson Boulevard
Arlington, VA 22229
Date: 3/8/92
Title: "Sperm Count Slid"

San Francisco Examiner
110 Fifth Street
San Francisco, CA 94103
Date: 9/11/92
Title: "Scientists Note Dramatic Decline in Sperm Count"
Author: Steve Connor

SYNOPSIS: Picture this: Civilization as we know it today, destroyed—not by nuclear holocaust nor by fouling our environment, but by the inability to produce children.

A new study, published in the *British Medical Journal*, by a Danish research team, details a drastic decline in the volume of ejaculations and the concentration of sperm within them. This review of available studies shows sperm density halved and semen quantity decreased by nearly 25 percent since 1940.

The Danish team leader, Professor Niels E. Skakkebaek, said he could not give a firm explanation for the decline, but there were signs the results of toxin build-ups in the environment were disrupting the function of the testes. The implications of these findings are that more and more Western men are incapable of fathering children.

This issue was first nominated as a Project Censored story in 1978 because of reports of sterility among workers at a chemical plant in Lathrop, CA. After investigating, the EPA suggested that chemicals similar to DBCP "have worked their way up through the food chain and are finally poisoning man." Dr. Kenneth Bridbord surmised the declining birth rates in the Fifties and Sixties may have been caused by the effects of toxins on male fertility. According to the more recent Danish study, a corresponding dramatic increase in male genito-urinary abnormalities and testicular cancer supports the theory that environmental factors are to blame for the declines in sperm counts.

Environmental pollution doesn't only affect human fertility. In a study by the International Joint Commission (IJC), animals living in the Great Lakes basin were found to be exhibiting abnormalities in sexual functions—including a blurring of male and female reproductive roles and genitals decreasing in size. The researchers blamed substances such as dioxins, lead and PCBs, which disrupt the animals' endocrine systems that produce hormones governing behavior, growth and sexual development. In one conclusion, the IJC report said contaminant levels in humans are approaching the same levels that have caused adverse effects in wildlife populations. "Most troubling is the experts' conclusions that humans are being affected as well," states the report.

And even if fertility is not affected, the resulting children might be. A study by Dr. Devra Lee Davis, a scholar at the National Academy of Sciences, found that certain genetic mutations or other alterations in sperm can lead to permanent defects in children. Sperm is now known to be vulnerable to toxins, and can produce familiar birth defects like heart abnormalities and mental retardation, as well as lesser known sperm-caused defects.

This was an important story when first cited by Project Censored in 1978; 14 years have passed without major media attention. New studies now confirm that this is not an issue that is going to go away and is one that deserves to be put on the national news agenda.

SSU Censored Researcher: Valerie Quigley

COMMENTS: Sandra Blakeslee, science writer for the *New York Times*, says that the issue surrounding sperm is underfunded and ignored. "The problem is not a traditional case of censorship," Blakeslee says, "but rather it appears to be a cultural bias in medicine. Research on reproductive medicine generally focuses on women. There's a stunning ignorance about sperm in our society." Blakeslee, concerned with the limited coverage given an issue as important as this, says she definitely plans to write more on the subject.

Meanwhile, the need for more research and coverage on the issue was clearly evident some time ago, as noted by Dr. Kenneth Bridbord of the Office of Extramural Coordination and Special Projects at the National Institute for Occupational Safety and Health (NIOSH) in Washington, DC.:

"There is no question in my mind but that this is a major problem facing the nation. I would not be surprised, based on the evidence we have looked at so far, to find that the declining sperm count represents a potential sterility threat to the entire male population. We do not know the seriousness of the threat at this time, but the DBCP (pesticide) findings may be just the beginning of it.

"What the government must do is reexamine everything we know about spermatogenesis and toxicity. If you look at fertility in America, it shows a decline in the latest Fifties and Sixties which we have always assumed social and economic changes in American life were responsible for. But if our worst fears about the effects of toxins on male fertility are true, it isn't too far afield to assume that the birth rate dropped then because of chemical interference with testicular functioning.

"Had we asked the right kind of questions then, we mightn't be in the fix we're in today."

Ironically, Dr. Bridbord, issued that dire warning in an article by Raymond M. Lane that appeared in *Esquire* Magazine in April 1978. The above statement by Dr. Bridbord was excerpted from the #7 synopsis of Censored stories of 1978, titled "The Specter of Sterility."

His warning was clear and ominous: a major problem faced the nation and we failed to ask the right questions.

But even now, 15 years later, as Sandra Blakeslee confirms, we are still not asking the right questions. The primary source for this Censored nomination of 1992 was a major study by Danish research scientists published in a British medical journal.

CENSORED

News Media Lose the War With the Pentagon

Source: **The Nation**
72 Fifth Avenue
New York, NY 10011
Date: 5/11/92
Title: "The Media's War"
Author: Jacqueline E. Sharkey

SYNOPSIS: In the wake of protests over press restrictions and censorship during the Gulf War, the Pentagon and major media representatives have negotiated guidelines for coverage of future conflicts. However, the agreement, hailed as a positive step in the relationship between the military and the media, appears to be worthless.

Supported by Washington bureau chiefs, the American Society of Newspaper Editors and high-level executives from electronic and print media, the agreement is designed to prevent the Pentagon from controlling the media as it did in the Persian Gulf, where journalists were confined to pools that had limited access to the battlefield.

A major flaw in the agreement is that no consensus was reached on "security reviews," which deal with the critical prior restraint aspect of censorship. More important, however, is the fact that the Pentagon has a well-documented history of violating media coverage agreements such as those drawn up in the wake of both the Grenada and Panama invasions, where journalists were prevented from covering much of the fighting. In fact, the only sig-

nificant change to previous coverage agreements is *the inclusion of more restrictive measures.*

Under the proposed agreement, reporters who violate the Pentagon's guidelines for protecting military secrecy and U.S. troops can have their combat credentials suspended and be expelled from battle zones. Ironically, these guidelines have not been written yet, and the Pentagon is not required to consult with journalists before writing them.

"What the Pentagon is doing is giving itself a club to use over journalists," says Scripps-Howard reporter Joan Lowy, who covered the Gulf War. "They're going to write these ground rules, but we don't know what they are yet. And then if you don't go by their interpretation...as they interpret them under security review, they'll kick you out. It's a very effective form of censorship."

Jane Kirtley, executive director of the Reporters Committee for Freedom of the Press, believes the very existence of the proposed agreement is an admission of how weak the media's position is now. She says that endorsing the agreement is "writing your own death warrant."

In the meantime, major media executives proudly proclaim the agreement as "a victory for common sense that few predicted a year ago." Others perceive it as merely additional evidence of the great media sellout to the administration, as noted in the synopsis "The Great Media Sell-Out to Reaganism."

SSU Censored Researcher: Amy Cohen

COMMENTS: Jacqueline E. Sharkey is author of *Under Fire—U.S. Military Restrictions on the Media from Grenada to the Persian Gulf.* Published by the Center for

Public Integrity, a public-interest organization founded by investigative reporters to promote in-depth coverage of federal government activities, *Under Fire* was the first book to document the disastrous effects of the Defense Department's media regulations in the Gulf War. Sharkey's article for *The Nation* grew out of the book.

Sharkey reports that the revision of the Pentagon's wartime media-coverage rules received little major media exposure.

"The *New York Times* and the *Washington Post* ran short stories buried inside the A section," Sharkey says, "but network news programs and the news weeklies largely ignored the issue.

"This is especially serious in light of the fact that the media had acknowledged (albeit late and reluctantly) that they had been manipulated by the Pentagon and the White House during the Gulf War and had presented a misleading and highly sanitized view of the conflict and its consequences to the American people. Nevertheless, just 14 months after the war ended (and the *mea culpas* about the media's poor performance had begun) news executives agreed to 'revised' rules that will enable the Pentagon to impose the same type of de facto censorship of images and information during the next U.S. military operation.

"Committing troops to military operations abroad is one of the most serious decisions a democratic government can make. This has become a crucial issue in the United States during the past 10 years as the Reagan and Bush administrations have used 'limited wars'—in Grenada, Panama and the Gulf as a foreign policy tool that also has bolstered their approval ratings in the polls. In each of these wars, the press was increasingly controlled, and the information increasingly sanitized.

"Retired Army Col. David Hackworth—America's most-decorated living soldier, who covered the Gulf conflict for *Newsweek*—has pointed out that this situation, combined with low U.S. casualties, has given the public a distorted picture of war and its consequences. This could have serious repercussions for the country during the next conflict, when American casualties could be much higher.

"What people need to evaluate whether their government should send its troops to war—and whether that decision was worth the price that had to be paid—is independent, objective information. That is exactly what they will not get the next time the United States engages in a military operation, because the 'revised' wartime-coverage rules will enable the Pentagon and White House to control images and information once again. People have a right—and a need—to know that their ability to obtain enough information to evaluate elected leaders and their policies adequately has been seriously compromised by the media's surrender to the Pentagon.

"During the U.S. military operations in Grenada, Panama and the Gulf, the White House and Pentagon restricted press access and controlled information not for national security purposes, but for political purposes, to protect the image and priorities of the Defense Department and its civilian leaders, including those of the president, the commander-in-chief. White House and Pentagon officials benefit greatly from lack of exposure about the ways in which the 'revised' rules for covering future operations will allow the government to control perceptions, and therefore public opinion, about decisions to go to war.

"The major media also benefit from lack of coverage about this issue. At a time when public confidence in the media has fallen significantly, news executives have to be concerned about what would happen if the American people realized that the press had sacrificed their interests—and their need for first-hand, objective information in wartime—because of pressure from the very political institutions with which the press is supposed to have an adversarial relationship."

Research material from *Under Fire* has been used by various news agencies for follow-up stories and the book is being used in political science and journalism classes in Washington, DC, Texas and Colorado. Following *The Nation* article, Sharkey debated Assistant Secretary of Defense for Public Affairs Pete Williams about the revised rules, and previous versions used in Grenada, Panama and the Gulf, during a session for media and military personnel arranged by the Freedom Forum and shown on C-SPAN, and on a CBS-Radio talk show.

While other journalists now have criticized the media for going along with these new rules, Sharkey points out that much of this debate has not been reported in major media. "The public remains uninformed about what these rules represent," she concludes, "or the repercussions they will have on the American people's ability to obtain in-depth information about the causes and consequences of future wars."

PLEASE NOTE: For more information about Under Fire—U.S. Military Restrictions on the Media from Grenada to the Persian Gulf, *write The Center for Public Integrity, 1910 K Street NW, Suite 802, Washington, DC 20006.*

15 CENSORED
Plutonium is Forever

Sources:
Utne Reader
1624 Harmon Place, Ste. 330
Minneapolis, MN 55403
Date: July/August 1992
Title: "Plutonium Is Forever"
Author: Monika Bauerlein

Harper's Magazine
666 Broadway, 11th Fl.
New York, NY 10012-2317
Date: August 1992
Title: "The Last Cold-War Monument"
Author: Alan Burdick

Los Angeles Times
Times-Mirror Square
Los Angeles, CA 90053
Date: 7/26/92
Title: "All Shook Up"
Author: Jennifer Warren

SYNOPSIS: In the 1950s, a nuclear energy critic warned "nuclear waste is like getting on a plane, and in mid-air you ask the pilot, how are we going to land? He says, we don't know—but we'll figure it out by the time we get there." Well, 40 years later, we're ready to land our nuclear plane, and we still haven't figured out how to do it.

Each year, the nuclear industry produces tons of high- and low-level waste not knowing what to do with it. Nicholas Lenssen, a researcher at the Washington-based Worldwatch Institute, estimates the worldwide volume of high-level nuclear waste at more than 80,000 tons. In 1990, the world's 413 commercial reactors produced 9,500 tons. And that's not counting the tens of thousands of tons from weapons programs, and medical and industrial uses. In 1989, U.S. reactors alone produced 67 times the plutonium it would take to give everyone on earth lung cancer.

There have been two great hopes for nuclear waste disposal—Yucca Mountain in Nevada and the Waste Isolation Pilot Plant (WIPP) in New Mexico.

Yucca Mountain was selected by the Department of Energy (DOE) as the national "permanent repository for high level nuclear waste." But after ten years of research and $6.7 billion spent by industry, including $2 billion in taxpayer funds, not a single hole has been dug in the mountain. The primary obstacle to the Yucca Mountain site is public opposition. In June 1992, a 5.6 tremor confirmed fears in Nevadans already leery of their state becoming the permanent home for tons of waste which remains dangerous for hundreds of thousands of years. It now appears that this repository will evolve no further.

Unlike Yucca, WIPP is not intended to house high-level waste but rather low-level nuclear garbage—radiation contaminated rags, rubber gloves, test tubes, pipes, etc. Nonetheless, the dangers of radioactivity in this waste make it imperative that WIPP not leak (appreciably) for the next 10,000 years.

Incredibly, the site selected for WIPP is in a stratum of salt thought to contain significant amounts of brine. The DOE itself estimates that within 20 years of burial, the thousands of soft-steel drums containing the waste will corrode and their contents will be exposed. Despite the potential hazard, however, WIPP seems destined to open. It is the only existing repository and, with the apparent demise of the Yucca repository, the pressure for a dump site is building. In any event, critics say that WIPP is only a partial solution. To contain the volume of plutonium-contaminated waste currently in retrieval storage across the country would require three WIPPs; to hold the entire backlog of military and commercial waste, ten WIPPs would be needed.

Yet another hurdle must be jumped—what kind of a sign do you put up to warn whoever may be inhabiting the earth in 10,000 years to "Keep Out" of WIPP? The simple "keep out" sign probably would not suffice. As Alan Burdick, senior editor of *Sciences*, asks, "Who knows whether humans will speak English ten millennia hence—or whether the term 'human' will still apply?" As Burdick reminds us, of the original Seven Wonders of the World, only one—Khufu's pyramid in Egypt—still stands, a mere 4,500 years old; Stonehenge is a thousand years its junior. And remember, plutonium is forever.

SSU Censored Researcher: Blake Kehler

COMMENTS: Monika Bauerlein, managing editor of *City Pages*, an alternative weekly in Minneapolis, says that, except for some coverage in the alternative press, the issue of nuclear waste hasn't received much attention anywhere for as long as she can remember.

"Mainstream coverage has been largely limited to: a) post-Gulf War stories about whether nuclear energy could be our salvation after all; and b) local stories in areas with a specific interest—towns near a potential waste repository, etc.

"From what I have seen covering this issue over the years, the U.S.—and the world—is at a crossroads on the question of nuclear energy. The nuclear industry, having laid low for most of the past decade, is beginning a major push for a 'new, safe' generation of reactors that are supposed to not only generate power, but also help us save the ozone layer. The Bush administration's National Energy Strategy calls for at least doubling the number of reactors in the next 20 years, and there's no indication that the Clinton team would change those plans at least in the immediate future.

"During the debate on this strategy before Congress in 1991 and 1992, there was practically no media coverage of the nuclear waste aspect; instead, most stories revolved around fuel-efficiency standards and the Arctic National Wildlife Refuge. Consequently, major decisions were made with little or no public input—decisions which can and probably will affect not just us, but countless generations to come.

"This is particularly frustrating because, despite the official line that disposal plans are perfectly on track, government and industry officials admit that a solution (including a 'permanent repository') appears further and further away, rather than closer at hand. As a result, even people who are normally nuclear-energy boosters—some utility executives, for example—are beginning to say that building any more plants is simply not cost-efficient.

"In other words, this issue is overripe for public debate and decision-making. Even assuming that the question of reactor safety has been solved (and it hasn't), what will make or break the nuclear program are 'front-and-back end' matters including uranium mining and processing (another vastly undercovered story) and nuclear waste. And we only know one thing for certain: the longer we take to address these things, the bigger a problem we have on our hands."

Monika Bauerlein has one final comment and warning:

"I clearly remember Chernobyl—I still treasure a radioactive sweater I was wearing the night it rained nuclides in Germany—and the resulting rash of stories about nuclear safety. The story died down after a while, which, unfortunately, tends to make people think that the issue must have gone away. Of course it hasn't. And in some ways, I find it astonishing that there hasn't been more attention—from the media, but also from activists.

"This is a question that divides the establishment (nuclear-power boosters vs. skeptics) and affects local communities, opening unlimited possibilities for vigorous arguments and grassroots interests. It also bridges the gap between areas too often separated, like economics (how long can we afford to ignore a problem if it's starting to cost us?), environmental protection, race (why are so many of the tentative sites on or near Native American lands?), etc.

"In a word, it's one of those issues that virtually scream for a *real* public debate—not only over the future of the nuclear program, but over the future of this society as a whole."

America's Killing Ground

16 CENSORED

Sources:

Multinational Monitor
PO Box 19405
Washington, DC 20036
Date: September 1992
Title: "America's Killing Ground"
Author: Julie Gozan

SF Weekly
425 Brannan Street
San Francisco, CA 94107
Date: 9/23/92
Title: "How the Feds Push Nuclear Waste Onto Indian Land"
Author: Juan A. Avila Hernandez

SYNOPSIS: Corporate waste brokers and the U.S. federal government believe they have discovered a solution to the nation's rapidly growing garbage disposal problem—dump industrial and household waste, and perhaps even nuclear waste, on Native American lands. Because of their sovereign status, Native American reservations are not subject to state, county, municipal and many federal waste-facility operating standards, a potential boon for waste companies.

The corporate salespeople attempt to entice tribal leaders by presenting their disposal plants as unique opportunities for "economic development" and increased employment on impoverished Native American reservations. But they fail to mention the serious health threats posed by the hazardous wastes.

Since 1990, toxic waste disposal companies have contacted more than 50 U.S. indigenous groups, offering millions of dollars in exchange for the right to dump U.S. trash on Native American grounds.

Meanwhile, the federal government, which has "trustee" responsibility to protect Native American lands is also promoting the disposal of waste, including nuclear waste, on the reservations.

At a conference of the National Congress of American Indians (NCAI) in San Francisco, David Leroy, head of the federal Office of the Nuclear Waste Negotiator, tried to persuade Indian leaders to store hundreds of canisters of highly radioactive waste on their reservations; he promised each tribe $100,000, no strings attached, just to consider the deal.

One of the government's largest nuclear waste proposals calls for the Department of Energy to spend $32.5 billion on the Yucca Mountain Nuclear Waste repository planned for the Western Shoshone reservation in Nevada. DOE hopes to convert Yucca Mountain into a receptacle for 70,000 metric tons of high-level nuclear waste. But, as noted in the "Plutonium Is Forever" nomination, it is increasingly doubtful this will happen.

Native Americans are not simply turning their lands over to the waste promoters without a fight. But one critic, columnist Elmer Savilla, who criticized David Leroy's speech at the NCAI conference as a condescending sales pitch, warns that the "tribes' lack of political power and urgent need for development leave American

Indian communities vulnerable and at risk." He adds, "Mr. Deep Pockets carries a bag full of goodies, including school assistance, health care programs and employment programs. Could this be called bribery?"

The media should be informing the public that non-native U.S. citizens can support Native American's rights to self-determination and a clean environment by demanding that their tax dollars not be used to peddle nuclear and other toxic waste to Native Americans.

In the meantime, as the *Multinational Monitor* points out, each incinerator, landfill or toxic storage facility built on a reservation poisons thousands of Native Americans and their lands.

SSU Censored Researcher: Pete Anderson

COMMENTS: Author Julie Gozan charges that "there has been no coverage of corporate waste dumping on Native American land in the mass media in 1992.

"As the practice of dumping toxic and hazardous waste on Native American land comes to light, public awareness will be fostered about the issues of environmental racism in the United States, hopefully fighting the 'not in my backyard' attitude that allows waste storage facilities to be built on reservations and in African-American and Latino neighborhoods disproportionate to white and upper-income neighborhoods.

"As corporations are held increasingly accountable to consumers, companies will be able to get away with fewer such dangerous waste schemes in the United States, to the health benefit of the entire U.S. public. Support will increase for source reduction and recycling as a means of eliminating the 'garbage problem.'

"As federal accountability to indigenous people in the United States and awareness of the continued exploitation of Native Americans grows within the U.S. public, hopefully there will be greater support for indigenous economic and community development plans and for grassroots organizations, such as CARE, that are campaigning against dumping on Native American land.

"The primary beneficiaries of this subject being 'censored' are the waste management companies such as Waste Tech and O&G that are looking to profit by getting around federal regulation of waste dumping. The federal agencies with complicity in the waste deals also benefit because their officials are able to rely on an 'easy' solution to the country's waste problem—at the expense of Native American health and lives."

Juan A. Avila Hernandez, a journalist with the Center for Investigative Reporters, whose article was published by *SF Weekly* and distributed by Alternet, agrees that the issue is being ignored by the major news media: "The subject of my article—the way the federal government has funded tribal organizations to help site nuclear waste on Indian reservations—has received little attention in the national media. While local newspapers write stories almost every time a nuclear waste site or landfill proposal is announced by a nearby tribe, rarely do reporters place the subject in proper context. The story, 'How the Feds Push Nuclear Waste onto Indian Land,' examines the paper and money trails that show the federal government has used millions of dollars in grants and contracts to target tribes, using national Indian organizations that have become increasingly dependent on federal dollars for their budgets.

"Both the general public and the Native American community would benefit from wider exposure of the federal plan to use Indian reservations as temporary nuclear waste sites and the way the plan is being administered. Like all Americans, Native Americans are concerned for the future of their families and communities. Few reservation residents are aware, however, that their lands are being considered to solve the national problem of nuclear waste storage—in some cases, tribal leaders have already agreed to accept large grants to consider storing waste before other tribal members even hear of the proposal. Such decisions have caused splits among Indian families and tribes, with at least some tribal dissenters experiencing harassment, assaults and even death threats. Communities near reservations also would benefit from better exposure of this issue.

"The limited coverage of this subject most benefits the federal government and the nuclear industry. Nuclear waste has long been the Achilles' heel of the nuclear industry and its supporters in Congress. According to the Nuclear Waste Policy Act of 1982, the federal government has the responsibility of storing spent fuel from nuclear reactors. Yet there is no process that guarantees the safe storage of nuclear waste, and in recent years, no community in the U.S. will agree to take it. Successfully placing a temporary nuclear site on an Indian reservation would give both the nuclear industry and its Congressional supporters much-needed time to lobby for the approval of more nuclear reactors."

While the mainstream media have shown no interest in Hernandez's extraordinary charges of official government bribery, his article has been distributed to members of the Native American Journalist Association; also, Native American environmentalist groups have informally distributed the story to many reservations in the country.

17 CENSORED

Norplant: Birth Control or Social Control?

Source: **EXTRA!**
130 W. 25th Street
New York, NY 10001
Date: July/August 1992
Title: "Norplant: Birth Control or Control of Poor Women?"
Authors: Ethel Long-Scott and Judy Southworth

SYNOPSIS: If we are to believe the national mainstream media and some politicians, Norplant, the implantable birth control device of the Nineties, is quickly becoming society's cure-all birth control solution. With the media touting effectiveness and safety and politicians proposing giveaways and mandatory implantation as a solution to unwanted pregnancy, welfare and child abuse, Norplant seems to be a perfect solution for personal convenience and social control.

Norplant is produced in the form of birth control capsules that are implanted for five years in a woman's upper arm. Promoted as a safe and effective method of birth control, Norplant was approved by the Food and Drug Administration in December 1990.

The appeal of easy, no-maintenance birth control was ballyhooed in the press with such approving headlines as "A Sound Implant" (*San Francisco Chronicle*) and "A Matter of Choice" (*Newsday*). The press has for the most part ignored questions posed by doctors and women's organizations and instead touted pharmaceutical promotional statements of "effectiveness and choice," while safety and sterilization considerations went unexplored.

Joyce Mills, chair of the Health Care Committee of the Women's Economic Agenda Project (WEAP), charges that Norplant is unsafe and not adequately tested. "Women using Norplant in Brazil suffered central nervous system damage, prolonged menstrual bleeding and other serious side effects," she reports.

The device is even more controversial since the dangers go beyond health risks. Legislators in Hawaii, Kansas, Louisiana, Ohio, South Carolina and California are advocating mandatory implantation for some drug abusers and welfare mothers. California Governor Pete Wilson has proposed providing free Norplant to women receiving Medi-Cal, that state's low-income health program. WEAP called these proposals "a throwback to the days when California led the country in performing forced sterilization on poor women."

While the American Medical Association (AMA) condemned the court-ordered use of Norplant for women convicted of child abuse and questioned state proposals to pay women on welfare to use

Norplant, its criticism has been ignored by the press.

The National Black Women's Health Project warns that "with the availability of Norplant, we are witnessing the aggressive imposition of punitive birth control measures on poor women and women of color, just as sterilization and other so-called population control measures have been forced upon African-American women and new immigrants in this country historically, and continue to be imposed on women of color in developing or so-called Third World countries around the world."

In denouncing court-imposed use of Norplant, the AMA points out that for more than 200 years, the "common law has considered any medical treatment performed without a patient's consent to constitute a battery."

Nonetheless, the media continue to promote the drug's effectiveness while downplaying its potentially dangerous side effects and ignoring its human rights implications.

SSU Censored Researcher: Judy Bailey

COMMENTS: Investigative author Ethel Long-Scott says the mass media did not give "sufficient or appropriate exposure to a surgically implanted birth control drug with unknown long-term side effects and with such incredible potential for social control. All the news coverage not only gave the pharmaceutical industry's view that it was safe, but implied through tone and choice of comments that it could be a solution to the growing problem of increasing numbers of poor children. They also implied that because it might curb the birth rate of poor women, which the media sees as a great social problem, we needn't be as critical about its safety. The media generally didn't bring up the widespread negative experience of women in Brazil, who found Norplant caused such great suffering and harm that they repulsed it.

"One of the most responsible things the media can do is alert people to what is really going on, beneath the surface of public policy. Norplant and its predecessors like just-approved Depo Provera, are being publicly cloaked in the mantle of an advance in reproductive rights. In playing up that one aspect of these drugs above all others, the media pushes them as 'good' tools to carry out forced sterilization and restrict the reproductive rights of poor women. The *Philadelphia Inquirer* editorial suggesting Norplant as a solution to poverty is just the most blatant example of the attitude that underlies most media coverage. History gives us horrible examples of the havoc wreaked by societies that try to fix problems by eliminating the people they affect, rather than eliminating the causes of the problems.

"The context in which the media place their discussions of Norplant restricts societal choices and the seeking of truth because it sends the following sinister message: 'Poor people are not functioning in a responsible manner. They are to blame for their own plight, as well as for some of our problems, like taxes that are too high, and we must make better decisions for them. If our economic system is not able to provide full employment, feed its people and keep its women and children safe and sheltered, out of doorways and away from random violence, it is not society's fault. We as a society do not have an obligation to make sure that women and children are able to have a roof over their heads, mini-

mal nutrition, decent health care and the basics for a dignified life. It is not up to society to make sure its benefits and protections work for the poor as well as for the rich. That is the responsibility of these impoverished individuals and their families, and if they can't do the job, we should keep them from bringing into the world more people who might possibly turn out like themselves.'

"Put most directly, the interests being served (by the limited coverage given the dangers of Norplant) are those of the middle, upper and ruling classes. The pharmaceutical industry obviously benefits in no small way from the media focus on the potential benefits of its products, rather than the harm they do, both demonstrated and potential. The people in power benefit from this attitude of, 'if there's a problem, blame the victims.' There is a lack of sharp questioning about why the richest society the world has ever known must tolerate millions of unemployed, unconscionable lawlessness in the name of law enforcement, the criminal rape of low income neighborhoods by all sorts of unchecked predatory interests and rampant and escalating poverty. And that lack of sharp questioning, even where examples make this obvious, as with Norplant, prevents us as a society from debating and putting into place real corrections for the problems.

"In the United States and all over the world we are facing cataclysmic changes. Huge new societal questions are presented by the increasing replacement of workers by computerized machines and the structural unemployment that results. If the media, by refusing to dig deeply enough into important issues, continue to promote rationalities and ideologies that support throwing people away, that support lying about or ignoring the mounting numbers of homeless and hungry souls in every city and town throughout our country, we will go down in history a nation that never understood why our economic system failed us, just as the leaders of the former Soviet Union never understood why their economic system failed them. It's no accident that eugenics and sterilization had important roles in Nazi Germany. Why aren't people who see that issue in Norplant getting into the media? In the 1990s, will the media continue to play the role of a half-blind cheerleader for people in positions of money and power who would rather settle the issue by regulating the behavior of the poor, even if it takes the imposition of a police state, instead of attacking the real problems?

"The big issue here, which the mass U.S. media almost universally fail to understand, is that our country's ideology says the poor, as well as the rich, are capable of seeing what they need to improve their lot in life, and going for it. But the way our society functions today—with the generous help of the media—the poor are seen as too ignorant and undisciplined to know that they need."

Finally, even as this is being written in early 1993, it appears that, despite the eloquent pleas and warnings of journalists like Ethel Long-Scott, Norplant is well on its way to becoming America's cure-all birth control solution for the 1990s.

Despite serious questions concerning its testing procedures and safety, not to mention the ominous implications for social control, Norplant is now offered as a form of birth control by California's Medi-Cal; and on January 10, 1993, CBS News reported that a low-income Chicago high

school has been selected as an experimental study site for the Norplant device.

Nonetheless, the nation's news media have yet to put the issue on the national agenda for discussion.

18 CENSORED

The Censored News About Electric Automobiles

Source: **Earth Island Journal**
300 Broadway, Ste. 28
San Francisco, CA 94133-3312
Date: Fall 1992
Title: "The Suppression of Ideas By the Oil and Auto Industries"
Author: Ed Schilling

Title: "When America Made Electric Cars"
Author: Robert G. Beaumont

SYNOPSIS: The conventional wisdom on transportation of the future envisions a world without gas-guzzling and polluting cars...a world where electric cars are the norm. To the surprise of many, however, the potential for mass-produced electric cars is already here and has been present for some time.

Over the last 40 years, tens of thousands of electric vehicles have been built, sold and put on the road. They've been designed and manufactured by small, independent companies, while Detroit's "Big Three" automakers apparently never got beyond the tinkering stage. Instead, the auto industry has been more adept at subverting any threat to the money-making infernal combustion engine.

In the 1930s, General Motors conspired with Standard Oil of California, Phillips Petroleum, Firestone Tire and Rubber and others to secretly dismantle the nation's energy-efficient, electrified mass-rail system. They bought and then destroyed trolley lines in cities, including Sacramento, Salt Lake City, Portland, Tampa, Baltimore, El Paso and Long Beach. The companies were subsequently convicted of violating the Sherman Anti-Trust Act and fined $5,000 each; their executives were each ordered to pay a $1 fine.

Meanwhile, others continued to explore the benefits of electric-powered transportation. In one 24-month period, from May 1974 through April 1976, Sebring-Vanguard, Inc., produced over 2,250 small, electric-powered CitiCars and marketed them for more than $6 million. To date these vehicles have accumulated more than 20 million miles without a fatality or single injury. Unfortunately, though, Sebring-Vanguard lacked the capital to mass-produce and soon went out of business. Now, according to Sebring-Vanguard founder Robert G. Beaumont, a marketable, useful electric car could be produced and sold for under $8,000.

Early in 1990, prompted by strict new laws requiring "emission free" vehicles for the Los Angeles market by 1995, GM rushed to unveil its electric-powered Impact. Able to go 125 miles between two-hour charges, the 2,000 pound Impact claims a top speed of 110 miles per hour. So, here are a couple of questions for GM: What took you so long? And why aren't these cars on the market by now?

In the U.S. today, where one out of five jobs depends on the auto industry, Detroit's car makers continue to test, rather than mass-produce, new electric engines. Some experts predict that the nations that invent, produce and profit from the imminent boom market for electric autos and advanced batteries will be Germany, Britain and Japan, which forged ahead in the 1980s while the Reagan administration was ripping the solar panels off the White House and slashing funds for conservation and alternative energy programs. In Europe, electric rechargers already have been installed at some city parking meters.

One would think that the major media would recognize the importance of this issue to our economic and environmental survival, and give the electric car the coverage. But, hey, our economic and environmental survival doesn't have an advertising budget.

SSU Censored Researcher: Kenneth Lang

COMMENTS: Investigative author Ed Schilling reports there has been little press coverage of this subject; and that coverage generally consists of prototype photos with short captions in the business section of newspapers. He adds, "No one has explored the historical development of electric cars, electric hybrids or Sterling engines in any real depth."

"The mass media seldom, if ever, question the monopolistic practices of the 'Big 3' automakers, or their continuous shelving of viable prototypes, or their long history of creating an almost total reliance on the private car. The relationship between these factors and America's increased dependence on foreign oil continues to be overlooked.

"The general public would benefit greatly as informed consumers. They would come to realize to what degree their choices have been limited by the suppression of viable transportation alternatives. The average city commuter, stuck in traffic for hours a day and forced to inhale sickly levels of polluted air, may become angered to find out that viable automobile alternatives existed 25 years ago, but were never produced. If he knew more about the transportation conspiracy, he may become outraged enough to take action. The American people have a right to know, to affect change and to translate knowledge into power."

19 CENSORED
Poison in the Pacific

Source: **The Progressive**
409 E. Main Street
Wisconsin, WI 53703
Date: July 1992
Title: "Poison in the Pacific"
Author: Robert Walters

SYNOPSIS: In 1962, Johnston Island, a once idyllic atoll in the mid-Pacific, became the site of one of man's most destructive experiments—the atmospheric nuclear tests conducted by the United States. Today, it is once again the site of a potentially catastrophic event—the dismantling and destruction of more than 60 million pounds of aging but increasingly deadly chemical weapons. The Johnston Atoll Chemical Agent Disposal System is a massive incinerator complex built by the

Army at a cost of $240 million. This will serve as the prototype for similar facilities to be built at eight designated sites in the United States.

The 400,000 chemical weapons to be destroyed on Johnston Island were fabricated for use in World Wars I and II and then for deployment against the Soviet Union during the Cold War. Because they're increasingly unstable, military experts fear that if not soon neutralized, they could explode or ignite spontaneously—possibly causing a catastrophic accident.

Equally worrisome, the testing has not gone well. Originally, the test period was to last about 16 months, from mid-1990 through late 1991. But as investigative journalist Robert Walters discovered, "Work had to be halted on 65 of the first 85 days of scheduled operations in 1990 because gas-leak monitors sounded false alarms, conveyor belts melted, the incinerator overheated and mechanical equipment failed. Last year, major repairs and modifications required a protracted shutdown."

Meanwhile, given the anxiety and hostility among residents of communities adjacent to almost all of the eight mainland Army bases where decommissioning is scheduled to occur in the future, serious questions have arisen about whether those facilities should ever by built in the U.S. Now, thought is being given to dismantling the entire U.S. operation and moving it to Johnston Island. Not surprisingly, this prospect has made Pacific Island residents and public officials, including those in Hawaii, increasingly fearful that the region's air, land and water will be poisoned by seepage of lethal dioxins and furans produced during the incineration process.

However, the Army is not overly concerned with the feelings of the 1,200 residents of Johnston Island: 900 of them are employees of companies holding Defense Department contracts and the other 300 are Army personnel.

When President George Bush flew to Hawaii on a political trip in 1990, he held a little-publicized meeting with the leaders of 11 small mid-Pacific nations to discuss their concern that the Johnston Island testing operation would become the sole disposal site. He assured the leaders that the U.S. planned to dispose of "only the chemical munitions...found in the Pacific Islands and those relatively small quantities shipped from Germany." (One hundred thousand chemical artillery shells, originally stored in West Germany, were shipped to Johnston Island in late 1990.) Despite the President's reassurances, there is still concern among the islanders.

SSU Censored Researcher: Pete Anderson

COMMENTS: Investigative author Robert Walters charges that "Nothing—absolutely nothing—that occurs in the interior Pacific 'receives sufficient exposure in the media' in any given year. The article in question was about environmental perils in the region, but other issues are equally well ignored. That's ironic at a time when the 'Pacific Basin' supposedly has become so important to the rest of the world.

"In fact, all of that region's highly publicized growth is occurring in the nations along the ocean's rim. The interior island jurisdictions, scattered across a vast expanse of water that covers one-third of the planet's surface, have been consigned to the status of 'fly-over country.' For those traveling between Seattle, Los Angeles or Chicago and Tokyo, Taipei or Hong Kong, island countries such as Nauru and Niue have become the region's counterparts of Kansas and Nebraska—not suitable for viewing at an altitude of less than 35,000 feet.

"Understanding what occurs in the insular Pacific is especially important for citizens of the United States, which defeated Japan in World War II for rights to exercise military, economic, and cultural control over the single largest geographic feature on the face of the Earth.

"In the ensuing decades, this country has abused its position of power. It has conducted atmospheric nuclear tests that still contaminate the homes—and bodies—of innocent indigenous people, established debilitating welfare economies through the islands and now tests a discredited 'Star Wars' system by firing missiles from a California military base into an atoll in the Marshall Islands.

"There's almost certainly a correlation between the lack of press coverage and the growing popularity of the insular Pacific as a venue to dump the 'civilized world's' industrial, commercial and residential garbage. The physically remote location minimizes the likelihood that the news media (or others who might engage in oversight) will be on hand to report on what is occurring."

As Walters said in his article: "Entrepreneurs from outside the region prefer to do business in the remote locations of the interior Pacific, where they're unlikely to encounter aggressive regulators, environmentalists, curious journalists or others who might cramp their style."

CENSORED

Black Gold Conquistadors Invade Ecuador

Sources:
National Catholic Reporter
115 E. Armour Boulevard
Kansas City, MO 64111
Date: May 1, 1992
Title: "Oil Companies Invade Ecuador for 'Black Gold'"
Author: Leslie Wirpsa

Urgent Action Bulletin
Survival International
310 Edgeware Road
London W2 1DY
England
Date: July 1992
Title: "Dallas Oil Company to Invade Waorani Land"
Authors: Survival International—Jonathon Mazower and Charlotte Sankey

SYNOPSIS: "Five hundred years ago, the Spanish came with mirrors, Bibles and swords, dominated with bloody force and the fear of God," writes Leslie Wirpsa, Latin American Affairs reporter for the *National Catholic Reporter*. But today, Wirpsa continues, "in their relentless search for black gold, the oil companies are bringing [to Ecuador] sweets, tacky dresses, sports shorts and T-shirts, along with their monstrous machines. And, like the Spanish, the oil companies continue to disrupt the culture, communal economies and social fabric of the indigenous communities. In addition, they are ravaging Ecuador's Amazon ecosystem, one of the most biologically diverse in the world.

"In terms of exploitation, there are

indexes and then there are indexes," says Bishop Gonzalo Lopez Maranon, Carmelite bishop for Ecuador's eastern Amazon forest. "It seems to me the exploitation by the multinational companies is incomparably more oppressive, more exploitative, more destructive than the system used 500 years ago."

Texaco Petroleum Co. drilled the first oil well in Amazon territory in 1969. Today, oil drilling occurs in 10 percent of Ecuador's 32 million acres of the Upper Amazon Basin. Texaco sold its drill sites to Petroecuador, an Ecuadorian company, in 1991. The destruction left behind by Texaco, and now continued by Petroecuador, was so great that the Amsterdam-based International Water Tribunal morally condemned the two companies for spoiling Amazon water systems.

In her book *Amazon Crude*, environmental writer Judith Kimerling, working for the Natural Resources Defense Council, documented the damage done to Ecuador's Amazon by the oil company. She revealed that 16.8 million gallons of oil have been poured into the fragile environment over the past 18 years as a result of pipeline cracks and spills. And about 4.3 million gallons of "toxic production wastes" are flushed into the region's lagoons, rivers, streams and groundwater tables each day.

Carlos Luzuriaga, former subsecretary for Petroecuadors's Environmental Division, estimated that 50 percent of the water systems in the eastern oil-producing area are contaminated. Carlos Esquetini, former Ecuadoran deputy secretary of energy, said that "Texaco has been in this country for 20 years. Texaco was our professor. They taught us how to produce and pollute. They never taught us how to clean up the mess."

Responding to criticism, Petroecuador recently promised to clean up the poisonous pools of waste materials located by its oil wells. But "Primer Plano," a popular Ecuadorian news documentary program, revealed the company merely covered the sites with dirt; the toxic muck continues to seep into the soil, contaminating Amazon groundwater aquifers. Shortly after denouncing the dirty practices of the oil companies, "Primer Plano" was taken off the air.

And the invasion of the black gold conquistadors continues. The July 1992 *Urgent Action Bulletin*, issued by Survival International, the worldwide movement to support tribal people, warned that the Maxus Energy Corporation, a Texas-based oil company, was starting construction of a road and an oil pipeline into the land of the Waorani, the most vulnerable of the Indian peoples in Ecuador.

The United States continues to import half of the 300,000 barrels of crude pumped from the Ecuadorian Amazon each day.

SSU Censored Researcher: Pete Anderson

COMMENTS: Survival International authors Jonathon Mazower and Charlotte Sankey report that the Ecuadorian invasion by oil companies received no coverage in the mainstream media: "The media see the very real, life-threatening problems faced by indigenous peoples daily as completely marginal—and, even if worthy of attention, not the substance of stories to sell the papers. This in 1992, the year of the Columbus anniversary, when indigenous peoples were at least a little higher up the news agenda than its usual rock bottom!

"The public should be informed of the consequences of the overriding belief in *growth* as the mainstay of progress.

When U.S. companies reach further and further into ever more remote corners of the earth for their oil supply, with no regard for the people, the Western public needs to be told the real story behind the oil they use in their homes and cars. The general public can then see a clear link between their daily lives and human rights abuses and feel empowered by using their influence as consumers.

"The oil company, Maxus [cited in the article] will clearly be happy for as long as it can continue its operations unhindered by negative publicity."

The authors point out that this article, while focusing on Ecuador, is part of a long-standing and ongoing campaign by Survival International to publicize the plight of indigenous people, the most marginal of all peoples: "[The article] is a tool in our letter-writing campaign, where thousands of our members worldwide read the piece, and then follow the instructions as to how to write to the Ecuadorian president (for example). This is a very effective way of campaigning: a) as South American governments seem to be becoming more concerned about their international image; and b) politicians often see one letter from a member of the public to represent the views of several hundred other people who do not write.

"The extreme vulnerability of the Waorani people is made clear in the text. Any extra publicity Project Censored can give them is very much welcomed."

PLEASE NOTE: For more information about Survival International and its letter-writing campaign, please write Urgent Action Bulletin, Survival International, at the above address.

21 CENSORED

How to Sell Pollution for Profit

Sources:

Multinational Monitor
PO Box 19405
Washington, DC 20036
Date: June 1992
Title: "Selling Pollution"
Author: Holley Knaus

Associated Press
50 Rockefeller Plaza
New York, NY 10020
Date: November 5, 1992
Title: "L.A. Incentives to Clean Air; Credits Traded for Less Pollution"
Source: *Santa Rosa* (CA) *Press Democrat*

SYNOPSIS: In early May 1992, the Wisconsin Power and Light company sold "pollution credits" to the Tennessee Valley Authority (TVA) for about $3 million. In effect, this deal gave TVA permission to spew into the air an additional 10,000 tons of sulfur dioxide, the primary source of acid rain.

The sale, the first to be implemented under the pollution credit trading system, authorized by the misnamed 1990 "Clean Air Act," was hyped by the media as an example of using market forces to control pollution. Outside of environmental groups, few questioned the dangerous precedent set by this deal.

The act sets ceilings on the amount of sulfur that polluters will be allowed to emit after 1995; then, incredibly, if a plant reduces its emissions more than required, it can sell its "extra" emissions reductions to another plant that fails to reduce its emissions to the required level.

Critics say the pollution credit program is based on the fundamentally flawed premise that a certain level of pollution is acceptable. "Clean air should be protected, not traded and sold like a used car," says Chris Blythe of Wisconsin's Citizens Utility Board.

Pollution credits serve the interest of polluters, at the expense of consumers, the environment and public health, in several ways:

1. Pollution credits undermine positive effects of straight regulation; under this system, instead of buying smoke scrubbers, companies buy the right to pollute.

2. Since allowances are based on past fuel use and emission rates, companies that polluted excessively received the biggest allowances. It is thus possible for these companies to profit the most by selling credits.

3. Since the right to emit pollution has been turned into a commodity, the federal government, in effect, has handed over valuable assets to polluters.

4. The system allows companies who are doing well financially to buy the right to pollute indefinitely, forcing the public to keep breathing the toxic fumes.

Unfortunately, the idea is spreading. Canada is considering pollution trading for air and water emissions, and the United Nations has considered a global market for greenhouse gas credits to be bought and sold. And in November, Southern California officials announced they were considering the incentive program for the nation's smoggiest region—a four-county area (Los Angeles, Orange, Riverside and parts of San Bernardino) involving more than 2,000 pollution sources.

As the *Multinational Monitor* points out, "The value of human health and the environment cannot be determined by market forces.... U.S. citizens should demand strict limits on polluting sources, much stronger emphasis on pollution prevention, moves toward a total elimination of emissions and the abandonment of a system that turns harmful sulfur fumes into valuable assets."

However, the citizens will not know what to demand if the media don't explain to them that creating a market in pollution, such as the "clean air act" has done, will never clean the air.

SSU Censored Researcher: Kenneth Lang

COMMENTS: The concept of issuing pollution credits to promote clean air—allowing polluters to buy and sell pollution—is one you could expect only from an administration that believed a "trickle-down" theory of economics would work. The only aspect less credible was the media's failure to explain this environmental outrage to the public.

Investigative author Holley Knaus says, "While the subject was covered in the mainstream press, most of the reporting was uncritical of the concept of 'pollution credits' and failed to express the views of those opposed to the idea. The implications behind the idea of pollution markets went unexplored. I am also unaware of any editorial in the mass media that argued against pollution credits.

"The public receives far too little information on benefits given to corporations at the expense of the environment and human health.

"Pollution credits undermine the efforts of those environmentalists working for pollution prevention and emission reductions—critical reporting on this issue should make clear the opposition of most of the environmental community to this idea pushed by the Environmental Defense Fund. Exposure to the arguments against pollution credits would inform citizens' responses to the idea."

Knaus also points out that utilities—particularly those that are buying credits rather than cleaning up their pollution—are the ones who benefit from the flawed "pollution credits" concept and the limited coverage given it by the press.

CENSORED

Clearcutting the World's Rainforests

Sources:
Multinational Monitor
PO Box 19405
Washington, DC 20036
Date: September 1992
Title: "The Scramble for African Timber"
Authors: Virginia Luling and Damien Lewis

Environmental Impact Reporter
PO Box 1834
Sebastopol, CA 95473
Date: September 1992
Title: "Alert: Clearcutting in Far East Russia"
Author: Juliana Doms

SF Weekly
425 Brannan Street
San Francisco, CA 94107
Date: June 24, 1992
Title: "The Killing Forests"
Authors: Angela Gennino and Sara Colm

SYNOPSIS: After years of uncontrolled devastation, the plight of South America's Amazon rainforests was finally put on the international media agenda, and the world's environmentalists heaved a sigh of relief. However, the timber industry has taken its clearcutting machines to areas of the world not in the media spotlight. For example, there is a myth that the African rainforests and their inhabitants remain isolated and secure from the timber interests. As a result, the ongoing destruction of Africa's equivalent of the Amazon continues to escape the attention of the Western world.

The forests of Zaire, which contain half of Africa's and 13 percent of the world's rainforest, an acreage surpassed only by Brazil, are now under siege. Ninety per-cent of Zaire's forest has been parceled out, mostly to the powerful elite—President Mobutu and his political and military allies. The situation in Zaire is typical of that in the rest of Central Africa; 90 percent of the Central African Republic's rainforest has been allocated to European compa-nies, and European aid agencies are fund-ing new roads to speed up the timber extraction. Africa's forest people have only recently begun to oppose actively the log-ging companies and are now taking their case to the world's media in hopes of attracting support.

At the same time, large pristine forests in Far East Russia are faced with the same threat of clearcutting. Two major timber projects are working through the Russian bureaucracy—one is spearheaded by a U.S. lumber company, Weyerhauser, and the other by the South Korean automobile corporation Hyundai. They both have their eyes on the Siberian Forest. The vast, untouched Siberian Forest is home to a unique blend of forest ecosystems, many endangered plant and animal species (in-cluding the Siberian tiger) and thousands of indigenous people who subsist on for-ests and rivers that would be directly af-fected by clearcutting. Weyerhauser plans to clearcut in the Botcha River Basin area upon completion of a joint venture agree-ment with the local forest industry, which has the right to log in the basin.

Meanwhile, ink on the United Nations' peace treaty for Cambodia was hardly dry before chainsaws were roaring through that nation's forests. Ironically, the treaty that was to bring peace sparked a new deforestation craze in Cambodia that could turn into one of the world's great ecologi-cal disasters. Investigative authors Angela Gennino and Sara Colm report, "Decades of war have already taken a heavy toll on Cambodia's forests—the country had lost nearly 40 percent of its forest cover before the peace accords. But this new round of logging might boost the annual rate of deforestation by as much as three to four times the previous levels. At this frenzied pace, warns the United Nations Development Programme, the loggers could devour what little is left of the country's forests within the next 10 years—and destroy Cambodia's ability to feed itself."

While world public opinion may have prevented the timber companies from totally destroying the South American rainforests, media attention should now follow their clearcutting machines to other parts of the world.

SSU Censored Researcher: Diane Albracht

COMMENTS: While the media can take some satisfaction in finally putting the destruction of South America's Amazon rainforests on the international agenda (to the point where a California group called Rainforest Products, Inc., now markets a breakfast cereal named "Rainforest Crisp"), a comparable, and possibly even worse, destruction of rainforests is quietly taking place in other locations throughout the world.

Damien Lewis, an environmental research photojournalist from London, with his co-author Virginia Luling, has investigated the environmental disaster occurring in Africa.

Lewis decries the lack of media attention on what's happening in tropical Africa. "Between the sensational newsfriendly stories of the drought and famine in sub-Saharan Northern Africa, and especially Somalia at present, and the breaking up of apartheid in South Africa, Central (tropical) Africa receives very little media and news coverage at all.

"The story of the rape of the African rainforests has received little if any coverage on TV (both news and documentary), and has suffered from a dearth of coverage in the print media, whether it be the dailies or newsweeklies.

"The story published in *Multinational Monitor* (which has also been published in the UK and Europe) is the result of a considerable amount of investigative research both in Africa and the U.S., trying to piece together which companies from which (Northern) countries are operating in which areas of Africa's rainforests, and to whom they are exporting their timber—and at what economic and ecological cost to the African countries themselves.

"The destruction of the world's rainforests is one of the greatest human and environmental crises facing humankind. Unfortunately, the real culprits for the destruction of this vital natural resource are often not identified, and the blame all too often is placed upon 'the poor rural farmer' clearing the forests, or the 'irresponsible Third World governments liquidating a priceless global asset.' The reality in Africa tells a far different story, and one noticeably absent from the global media.

"It tells of vast, highly destructive logging carried out by almost exclusively northern transnationals, for export to 'First World' markets in Europe and the U.S., to satisfy First World demand for tropical timber and the loo-seats, tables and doors made from it. It tells of the wanton destruction of a priceless resource, the profits from which are made predominantly in the north. It shows that rather than blaming the developing world for the loss of these forests, the blame lies fairly and squarely with ourselves. Only by recognizing this will we even start to solve the problem.

"A conspiracy of silence seems to surround the whole issue of the destruction of Africa's rainforests. If you consider how much coverage the burning of the Amazon or the logging in Malaysia receives, there is a glaring lack of coverage of this issue. Africa is one of the only sources of raw (i.e., not processed into sawn timber or products) logs, and hence one of the few remaining areas where enormous profits can be made by foreign companies. As the logging is carried out by European and U.S. logging companies, and the market for the timber is the U.S. and Europe, it is clear who profits from the silence surrounding this issue. Certainly, the UK government earns more than five times as much for the VAT (value added tax) it charges on tropical timber imported into the UK than all the aid it gives to the tropical countries.

"It has been extremely difficult to secure publication of this article on this subject. One major UK magazine actually commissioned and then turned down this article, because it didn't want to stick its neck out. However, it has now secured publication in the *Multinational Monitor*, in Norway's *Natur e Miljo* Magazine and in the UK's *BBC-Wildlife* Magazine."

Co-author Virginia Luling, also of London, added, "Compared with the relatively wide coverage given to the destruction of the rainforest in South America and Southeast Asia, that of the African forests is almost unknown. Yet, if deforestation rates are expressed as a percentage of original forest area, then it is Africa that has suffered the highest level of deforestation in the last decade. Those who suffer most from this are the Pygmies and other forest-dwelling people. Survival International (the international movement to support tribal people) will not slacken its efforts to publicize their plight."

Investigative writer Juliana Doms, who explored forest clearcutting in Far East Russia, notes that little is published on international forestry activities, especially in a consistent manner that would expose the magnitude of the problem worldwide.

Doms also points out that more media coverage would generate a stronger urgency to develop specific international forestry policies and to implement the Forest Principles developed at the Earth Summit last year.

Doms believes that the issue of "clearcutting the Siberian forests should be used as a test case for the Clinton/Gore administration in forcing international cooperation in protecting the environment." But she also recognizes that the economic fragility of the world market—especially in Russia—will make it difficult to demand protection of those forests, particularly since "the multinational timber giants have the hard currency that Russia needs."

23 CENSORED

Censorship Through Bribery

Source: **The Progressive**
409 E. Main Street
Madison, WI 53703
Date: August 1992
Title: "Buying Silence"
Author: Geoffrey Aronson

SYNOPSIS: Many companies, especially within the nuclear power industry, frequently attempt to muzzle whistle-blowers with so-called "money-for-silence" agreements. Some would-be whistle-blowers, in fear of jeopardizing their job security, pledge not to reveal safety violations in return for token cash settlements.

Investigative reporter Geoffrey Aronson warned how tragic such agreements could be: "A confidential report, titled 'Secret Money for Silence Agreements in the Nuclear Industry,' compiled in May 1989 by the staff of the U.S. Senate's subcommittee on nuclear regulation, warned, 'If management hadn't suppressed safety information from Morton-Thiokol's engineers, the *Challenger* disaster could have been avoided. It is frightening to think that we may be dealing with multiple nuclear equivalents of the *Challenger* disaster.'"

Joe Macktal, a worker at the Comanche Peak nuclear power plant in Texas, settled with his employers, Brown & Root, Inc., for $35,000 (of which $20,000 went to legal fees). Macktal had been fired after he discovered potential construction problems at the plant. The company promised not to blacklist him (in an industry where news of "trouble-makers" travels fast), in exchange for a pledge not to appear voluntarily in any administrative or judicial proceedings regarding the safe operation of Comanche Peak. Grudgingly, he agreed to this and also to taking reasonable steps to resist any subpoena requiring his testimony at such proceedings.

Macktal later revealed the agreement anyway, but the Nuclear Regulatory Commission (NRC) ruled that the restrictions imposed on Macktal's ability to communicate with federal agencies did not constitute "a violation of Federal law or NRC regulation." Later, bowing to pressure, the NRC reversed its position. "Yet whether through ignorance or guile, corporate attorneys representing the nuclear power industry are still attempting to peddle hush money settlement agreements," Aronson reports. "One draft settlement written in January 1992, for example, would require the whistle-blower 'not to cooperate in any investigation of the company by the NRC.'"

Although the NRC and the Secretary of Labor have decided to outlaw future attempts to muzzle nuclear whistle-blowers with "money-for-silence" agreements, no such protection for prospective informers and the public exists outside the nuclear industry. According to Aronson, the Toxic Substances Act, the Occupational Safety and Health Act, Superfund and laws regulating mine safety, clean air and clean water, can all be undermined by money-for-silence agreements.

In September 1991, the National Whistle-Blower Center petitioned the EPA to adopt regulations that would explicitly outlaw restrictive agreements. The EPA declined. "Without EPA action," explains Steven M. Kohn, an attorney who chairs the Whistle-Blower Center, "environmental whistle-blowers will remain without protection. Many will be gagged by outrageous hush-money restrictions."

SSU Censored Researcher: Blake Kehler

COMMENTS: Author Geoffrey Aronson feels that the subject of secret settlement agreements to squelch further inquiry or publicity has rarely been a topic of media inquiry. Instead, Aronson said, "Concern has centered on the issue of public access to court proceedings generally, and the desire to unseal court-ordered sealed documents used in specific cases; Agent Orange and auto liability cases come to mind.

"When actions against the Comanche Peak nuclear plant were settled in the summer of 1988, there was coverage in the Texas press and an article that I wrote for the *Nation* in late 1989. Subsequent hearings on Capitol Hill were episodically covered in the *Washington Post*. To my knowledge, however, there has been no inquiry into the use of these types of settlement agreements in the other environmental arena which I discussed in my *Progressive* article.

"The public should be aware of the tension that exists, and the conflicts that arise in the nuclear power and other environmentally related areas when issues of public health and safety compete with corporate and private interests. Public safety may well be compromised by a legal and bureaucratic system that 'privatizes' disputes relating to violations of statutes aimed at protecting the public good. I feel it is also important to illuminate the conflicts that arise when 'public interest' lawyers serve masters whose interests are not necessarily coincident—the 'public' and

their individual client whistle-blowers.

"Those best served by current practices (such as secret settlements) are corporate interests and government regulatory bodies with a stake in minimizing the public impact of health and safety concerns raised by whistle-blowers."

Aronson also wanted to acknowledge his appreciation to the Fund for Investigative Journalism for supporting both *The Nation* and *The Progressive* articles.

24 CENSORED

The No-Pest Shell Game

Source: **E Magazine**
PO Box 5098
Westport, CT 06881
Date: November/December 1992
Title: "The Shell Game"
Author: Diana Hembree and William Kistner

SYNOPSIS: It wasn't long after the original Shell No-Pest Strip, sold by the Shell Chemical Company (a division of Shell Oil Company), became a popular household item in 1966 that serious scientific questions were raised about its safety. By 1971, every Shell pest strip manufactured in the U.S. bore a label warning buyers not to hang the strips in a room occupied by babies, the elderly or the infirm; it also warned consumers not to use the strips in kitchens, hospitals, nurseries or restaurants.

Finally, in 1987, an Environmental Protection Agency (EPA) study officially linked the active chemical in pest strips—

dichloros, or DDVP—to an unusually high cancer risk. By then the controversial device had all but disappeared from stores and homes in the United States.

This was not the case in Mexico. To find the strips widely marketed today, as revealed in an investigation by journalists Diana Hembree and William Kistner, all you have to do is go across the border to Mexico. There, in many drugstores and supermarkets, you can buy the DDVP-laced pest strips (called Shelltox Matavoladores—"flying-insect killer") from Shell Mexico. However, the popular product does not carry a label warning Mexican consumers of possible cancer risk from exposure to DDVP. Even worse, for more than 20 years, Shell Mexico's instructions for using the pest strips contradicted the safety warning labels required in the U.S. In fact, the packaging advised buyers to hang them in kitchens, bedrooms and just above baby cribs. This now discontinued label has not been recalled and is still found on shelves in popular supermarkets.

Dr. Joseph Ross, professor emeritus at the UCLA School of Medicine, describes Shell Mexico's pest strip instructions as "appalling." Noting that infants are more sensitive than adults, Ross stresses that hanging a pest strip above a baby's crib "is potentially extremely hazardous. The [instructions] are unconscionable. They're just heartless. It's shocking to me that great corporations with reputable people would allow this to happen."

Shell Mexico and Shell Oil Company are both wholly owned subsidiaries of the Netherlands-based Royal Dutch Shell.

This story, of 1992 vintage, is reminiscent of Project Censored stories dating back to 1976 when the #3 Censored story

revealed how major corporations were selling banned pesticides and drugs to Third World countries. A conservative World Health Organization study estimated that some 500,000 people, the majority of them in Third World countries, were poisoned annually by banned pesticides and drugs at the time.

It also reveals that unethical and immoral marketing practices by multinational corporations, applying inadequate standards to Third World countries, continue to endanger foreign consumers to this day.

SSU Censored Researcher: Mark Lowenthal

COMMENTS: Speaking on behalf of herself and co-author William Kistner, author Diana Hembree, of the Center for Investigative Reporting, reports, "The subject of 'The Shell Game'—the multinational's questionable marketing practices in the Third World—received little or no media attention last year.

"Our story examined the flaws in Royal Dutch Shell's regulation and oversight of one of its popular household pesticide products, No-Pest Strips (whose active ingredient, DDVP, is linked to cancer, blood disorders, nerve damage and genetic damage) in Mexico. Shell Mexico advised consumers to use the pest strips around infants and in kitchens, thus completely contradicting health and safety warnings required on Shell pest strips in the U.S. This is the first time, to our knowledge, that a story has ever exposed the difference in Shell's marketing standards. (Searches through *Nexis, Dialog* and *Journal Graphics* data files failed to turn up any stories on the subject).

"Although the dumping of banned or dangerous U.S. products in other countries has received some publicity over the years, less attention has been paid when a hazardous product developed here is manufactured and sold by local subsidiaries in another country—without safety warnings.

"Millions of consumers in the United States, Mexico and other countries would benefit from wider exposure of this subject in the mass media by being more wary of DDVP pest strips, which expose people to a suspected carcinogen 24 hours a day. Although Shell stopped making its controversial pest strips years ago, other U.S.-made pest strips containing DDVP have quietly made their way onto the market in recent years; if the American public realized that medical reports have linked DDVP with leukemia and fatal blood disorders in children, they would be better able to protect themselves from exposure to pest strips and popular bug sprays containing DDVP.

"Consumers in Mexico, Nicaragua and Bolivia, where Shell Mexico strips are found, would also be able to make an informed choice when considering whether to buy a DDVP pest strip, and where to hang it. At the very least, they would know that Shell pest strips sold in the U.S. warned consumers *not* to hang the pest strips around infants, the elderly, in kitchens, hospitals, or the sick and infirm.

"Pest strips containing DDVP are also reportedly sold in Australia and Japan, where the public would also benefit from a greater knowledge of DDVP hazards. Finally, wider exposure of the flawed testing and regulation of pesticides like DDVP might stir more calls for reform.

"The parent company—in this case, the Netherlands-based Royal Dutch Shell—benefits from the limited coverage [given this issue] because its wholly owned subsidiaries can likely sell more pesticide products if marketing standards are looser in poorer countries. Also, without media scrutiny, the multinational's regulatory staff has little incentive to promote the same marketing standards for pesticide safety in a developing country as those used, for example, in the United States.

"Although Royal Dutch Shell officials told us that the parent corporation always shared the latest in scientific studies on the safety of DDVP and other pesticides with Shell subsidiaries, this was apparently not the case with Shell Mexico.

"In addition, a Royal Dutch regulator's assertion that DDVP is 'not hazardous to humans, but specifically hazardous to flies' contradicts data from the EPA and National Center for Toxicological Research as well as medical studies from the U.S. and other countries; such a statement suggests that, in the absence of media attention, the multinational has little incentive to amass up-to-date health and safety research on the pesticides used in its products.

"We mailed 'The Shell Game' to various environmental groups and pesticides companies as well as to sources in the article, some of whom responded with calls or letters. Alternet has distributed the story as published in *E Magazine*; in this way, we hope to reach a larger audience in the United States. We are also considering translating the story into Spanish for distribution through newspapers such as *Excelsior* or *La Jornada*, or helping with a short news story for Univision News, broadcast to households throughout Mexico and much of Central and Latin America."

David R. Ellison, an attorney with Ellison, Hinkle & Bayer, in Ventura, California, who represented a family in a little-publicized law suit filed against the Shell Chemical Company over the original Shell No-Pest strip, expressed his feeling about the issue raised by Hembree and Kistner: "It is incredible what corporate greed will drive people to do—it is unfortunate there are not more whistle-blowers, but at least we have competent and capable investigative reporting that can function within the atmosphere of a free press.

"Though sometimes I feel like an ant on the beach with a 40-foot tidal wave coming, it is still nice to stand up for what you know is right and to fight for the truth of those principles."

25 CENSORED
University of Arizona Desecrates Sacred Native American Site

Sources:
Action for Cultural Survival
Cultural Survival, Inc.
215 First Street
Cambridge, MA 02142
Date: July/August 1992
Title: "Apaches Protest Observatory"
Author: Jennifer Rathaus

Huracan
PO Box 7591
Minneapolis, MN 55407
Date: Summer 1992
Title: "Vatican Denies Sacred Ancestry of Mt. Graham"
Author: Sal Salerno

Northern Sun News
PO Box 581487
Minneapolis, MN 55458-1487
Date: Fall 1992
Title: "Native American Sacred Lands in Crisis"
Author: Sal Salerno

National Catholic Reporter
115 E. Armour Boulevard
Kansas City, MO 64111
Date: June 16, 1989
Title: "Astronomy Versus Red Squirrel on Arizona Sierra"
Author: Tim McCarthy

SYNOPSIS: While few Americans know about this issue, protesters in Brussels, Belgium, drove a bulldozer to the basilica of Scherpenheuvel to dramatize the fierce battle between Native American Apaches and the University of Arizona (UofA).

The University of Arizona is the lead agency in an international project to build a $200 million observatory on Mount Graham, Arizona, a site considered by the Apaches to be sacred. Partners in the massive UofA project, which reportedly has connections with the Defense Department's Star Wars effort, include the Max Planck Institute in Germany, the Vatican and Italy's Arcetri Astrophysical Observatory.

Seven other original partners, such as Harvard University and the Smithsonian Institution, have withdrawn their financial support.

Fighting the project is a coalition of groups including the San Carlos Tribal Council, Friends of Mount Graham, the Apache Survival Coalition, Native Americans and their supporters.

Mount Graham is host to varied plants, insects and animals found only in this 615-acre national forest. The Apaches have used the site for hundreds of years for worship and burials and as a source for herbal medicines. In 1988, Congress approved a rider to the Arizona-Idaho Conservation Act exempting UofA from the National Environmental Act without public hearings or debate. An appeal to Congress resulted in exemption for the project from the Endangered Species Act and the National Forest Act.

Ignoring the history of the site and its extensive documentation, Father Coyne, S.J., director of the Vatican Observatory, cites the lack of title, written records and burial grounds as evidence the site is not sacred, and said that he "cannot find any authentic Apaches that consider the mountain holy." He adds, "This land is a gift from God to be used with reason and to be respected. We believe our responsible and legitimate use enhances its spiritual character." He denied the project's involvement with SDI research and funding.

One UofA anthropologist, Elizabeth Brandt, says "sacred sites are hard to record, but I have worked in this area for 20 years and I've never seen so much evidence detailing a sacred site."

Despite the massive effort against the project, investigative reporter Sal Salerno warns, "The powerful collusion of science, the military, the church and industry continues to trample on the rights of Native American people." Ironically, the centerpiece telescope for the observatory is named the "Columbus Project."

Though this story was first nominated in 1992, an earlier article on the issue (see the following "Comments" section) appeared in the June 16, 1989, issue of the *National Catholic Reporter*, written by Tim McCarthy, NCR foreign news editor.

Despite the numerous intriguing national and international aspects to this story and the fact that it is a cause célèbre in Europe, America's mainstream media have yet to put it on the national agenda. The media's spotlight on Mount Graham might help illuminate the conflict between an American university and Native Americans.

SSU Censored Researcher: Judy Bailey

COMMENTS: The failure of America's news media to cover this story defies logic. It has nearly all the ingredients the press could want in a "big story"—international intrigue, a major U.S. university versus

environmentalists, Native American religious rights versus the Pope, an interesting mountain-top setting and even the Defense Department's exotic Star Wars Program! Although these ingredients have attracted major international media attention, they have failed to interest much of the U.S. mainstream media.

Jennifer Rathaus and Sal Salerno, two of the investigative authors who have explored the issue, comment on this enigma and other issues involved in the Mount Graham Observatory story: "National news coverage of the Mount Graham Observatory has been insufficient in that it has consistently neglected the group most directly affected by the project, the San Carlos Apaches," says Jennifer Rathaus. "The *New York Times* and *Wall Street Journal* ran a few stories about opposition to the observatory because of the threat it posed to the endangered red squirrel and other potential environmental hazards.

"Only local Arizona and Native American newspapers have focused on the threat that the observatory poses to the San Carlos Apaches' sacred site and the implications it would have for them.

"In order to obtain permission to build the observatory, the University of Arizona, the Vatican and a few local politicians were able to circumvent, without public approval or knowledge, such laws as the Endangered Species Act, the National Historic Preservation Act and the American Indian Religious Freedom Act. Federal Agencies were pressured to accept hasty and flawed biological studies, and legislation was passed to exempt the project from environmental laws.

"The way in which the project has proceeded without appropriate legal regulation and with little public exposure sets a damaging precedent for future misuse of federal lands. Construction of the Mount Graham Observatory is a violation of Native American religious and cultural practices, and it also has serious ecological ramifications. Wider exposure of this subject can help give the general public an understanding, and perhaps an empathy, for Native peoples whose religious freedom is being obstructed. If the San Carlos Apaches' constitutional rights are being violated, all Americans are threatened.

"Among those benefiting from the lack of media attention to this subject are all of the companies involved in the project, along with the well-financed and politically influential developer, the University of Arizona. The university, which hired a powerful and expensive lobbying firm from Washington to obtain exemption from U.S. environmental laws, is blinded by the prestige and economic benefits it will receive."

Sal Salerno adds the following comments: "Coverage of the desecration of Native American sacred sites by extractive industries and commercial developers has not received coverage by national network news, news weeklies or major daily newspapers.

"The mainstream media blackout continues in spite of the fact that more than 60 different Native American and Native Hawaii sacred sites are currently under siege by developers. When the University of Arizona's project to build its colossal telescope monument to Columbus on a mountaintop sacred to the Apache people has received coverage in national newspapers, like the *Wall Street Journal* or *New York Times*, the articles have focused on the Mount Graham red squirrel, an endangered species threatened by the construction of the University's International Observatory. In Bush's so-called 'Year of the Indian,' the mainstream media have entirely avoided the issue of cultural genocide that is part and parcel of the wanton destruction of lands sacred to Native Americans and native Hawaiians.

"Most Americans are unaware that Native American religions are not protected by the Constitution, and assume that Native religions share the same protection afforded Christianity or Judaism. The Christian community would be horrified if plans were announced to build a radio tower on top of the Holy Sepulcher in Jerusalem. It is hard to imagine such plans not being on the front page of major newspapers, as well as the lead story on the nightly news. Since most important Judeo-Christian sacred sites are located outside the United States, American law has not addressed this aspect of religious freedom, a condition Walter Echo Hawk, an attorney for the Native American Rights Fund, has characterized as 'a crisis in human rights in Indian country.'

"The greed of developers not only denies basic First Amendment rights to Native people but ravages the earth's indigenous cultures and resources."

Author Salerno also notes that his articles, which appeared in *Huracan* and *Northern Sun News*, also appeared in the *Circle*, a monthly Native American newspaper edited by Ruth Denny, which has provided significant coverage of the Mount Graham issue.

Please note: For more information about The Circle, *which is scheduled to feature articles about Mount Graham by Sal Salerno, please write* The Circle, *1530 East Franklin Avenue, Minneapolis, MN 55404.*

CENSORED

Chapter 4

The Junk Food News Stories of 1992

P roject Censored has been the target of frequent criticism through the years, most of it ideological, coming from conservative groups such as Reed Irvine's organization Accuracy in Media or individuals like Jim Eason, San Francisco's KGO-Radio talk show host, who told tens of thousands of his listeners that Professor Carl Jensen is a "left-wing horse's ass."

However, some responsible observations from journalists and editors have warranted serious thought and response. For example, many news professionals have said that the issue isn't so much censorship (or self-censorship) per se as it is a difference of opinion about precisely what information is important to publish or broadcast. They also point out that there is a finite amount of time and space for news delivery—about 23 minutes for a half-hour network television evening news program—and that it's their responsibility to determine which stories are most critical for the public to know.

This struck me as a legitimate argument, so I decided to review the stories that editors and news directors considered to be most worthy of filling their valuable time and space. However, in the course of this research project, I did not find an abundance of hard-hitting investigative journalism. Quite the contrary. Indeed, what did become evident was a journalistic phenomenon I call Junk Food News (JFN), which, in essence, represents the flip side of the "Best Censored Stories."

The typical JFN diet consists of sensationalized, personalized and homogenized trivia, often generic to one of the following categories:

NAME-BRAND NEWS: Madonna's latest sexcapades. Fergie and Diana's Royal scandals. The Jay Leno/David Letterman/Arsenio Hall battle for insomniacs. The Oprah/Geraldo/Donahue battle for two-headed, cross-dressing, space aliens.

YO-YO NEWS: The stock market is up or down. The unemployment rate is up or down. The crime rate is up or down. The president's popularity is up or down. Gold, silver and pork bellies are up or down.

CRAZED NEWS: The newest diet craze, fashion craze, dance craze, sports craze, video game craze. And, inevitably, the always newsworthy, latest crazed killer.

PLAY-IT-AGAIN NEWS: The fire across town (dazzling, richly hued nighttime fires are particularly popular on television news). The routine freeway pile-up. A local drug bust. The earthquake of the day. The downtown bank robbery. Yet another Elvis sighting.

SEASONAL NEWS: Floods in the Northeast. Fires out West. Southeastern hurricanes. Midwestern tornadoes. But no natural phenomenon compares in bluster with the Political News Season and the torrents of rhetoric pouring from the mouths of earnest candidates, pledging to solve unemployment, reduce the deficit, lower prices, defy foreign invaders—and promising (sincerely) not to raise taxes. But trivial matters, these, compared with what inspires the biggest headlines as our esteemed politicos grapple publicly with charges of alleged infidelities and youthful indiscretions, proclaim or disclaim political leanings (Left or Right), champion their wives' cookie-baking prowess and exploit their pets' propensities for publicity.

The problem is not the lack of time and space for news, but the quality of the news selected to fill that time and space. We're suffering from news inflation—there seems to be more of it than ever before, but it isn't worth as much as it used to be.

News should be nutritious for society. We need more steak and less sizzle from the press. The news should warn us about those things that make our society ill, whether economically, politically or physically. And there *is* such news out there, as Project Censored has revealed time and again.

But the media continue to ignore many important issues while titillating the public with Junk Food News. At the end of each year, I survey the members of the national Organization of News Ombudsmen to solicit their selections for the most over-reported, least deserving news stories of the year.

You may recall some of the top-ranked JFN stories of the past:

 1984 Clara Peller's "Where's the beef?"

 1985 Coca Cola's new old classic, Cherry Coke

 1986 Clint Eastwood's campaign for mayor of Carmel

 1987 The tribulations of Jim and Tammy Faye

 1988 The trapped whales of Alaska

 1989 Zsa Zsa Gabor's cop-slapping trial

 1990 The marital woes of Donald and Ivana Trump

 1991 The William Kennedy Smith rape trial

The top ten Junk Food News stories of 1992, as cited by the news ombudsmen, are the following:

1. DAN QUAYLE MISSPELLS POTATO: the Vice President's final tutoring assignment
2. MADONNA'S BEST-SELLING *SEX*: from pop queen to porn queen
3. MURPHY BROWN/DAN QUAYLE: Dan's "family values" get low ratings
4. JOHNNY CARSON—THE FINAL DAYS: Wherrrrrrrrrrrrrrrre's Johnny?
5. ROYAL SCANDAL—FERGIE & DIANA: the naughty wives of Windsor
6. WOODY ALLEN vs. MIA FARROW: we liked him better when he was funny
7. GENNIFER FLOWERS: no shrinking violet
8. THE BARBARA/HILLARY COOKIE BAKE-OFF: let the chips fall where they may
9. THE ELVIS STAMP ELECTION: the youngest candidate won this election, too
10. U.S. OLYMPIC DREAM TEAM: the first single-sport Olympics in history

Rounding out the top 25 Junk Food News nominations of 1992 were Bush Tossing his Cookies in Japan, the Jay Leno/Arsenio Hall War, Clinton's Vietnam Record, Christopher Columbus: Hero or Heel?, Bill Clinton on Sax, Jerry Brown's 800 Number, Batman Returns/Superman Dies, Family Values, Polls-Polls-Polls, Sinead O'Connor Rips the Pope, Bouncing Checks in Congress, Sister Souljah, the Year of the Woman, the Elusive Michaelangelo Virus and Hillary's Projected Role in the White House.

Nominations not making the top 25 list were the following: the Rush to Buy Limbaugh's Book, Presidential Candidates' Sexcapades, Sexist Barbie Censored, Beer Belly Research Project, Jose Canseco's Off-Base Antics and the Pregnant Half-Man/Half-Woman.

As to why the media tend to sensationalize such stories, here are explanations suggested by some of the news ombudsmen who participated in selecting the top 1992 Junk Food News stories:

"Media types are gossips at heart who love scandal, controversy and bad news (all prime ingredients of news). Newspaper folk are driven to get it first—the scoop—generating the feeding frenzy." — Larry Fiquette, *St. Louis Post-Dispatch*.

"The belief that these are attention-grabbers, an easy 'hit,' and the reluctance of editors to stray from pack journalism." — Gordon Sanderson, *London Free Press*, London, Ontario, Canada.

"Too many wire editors feel pressured to duplicate in the next day's paper whatever was on last night's 'Entertainment Tonight' or any number of other pseudo-news programs. If there was a general understanding not to run this stuff in such a knee-jerk way, there'd be less reinforcement among our readers. Our stories legitimize junk news." — William Flynn, *Patriot Ledger*, Quincy, Massachusetts.

"This junk is easier to report, and it sells. It's harder to find out what your audience really wants and needs to know and to report it in an understandable way." — Jeff Langley, *Amarillo Globe-News*, Amarillo, Texas.

"[Junk Food News stories are] easier. Not one of these stories took much digging. The media helped Madonna sell her book and [Michael] Jackson sell more records. (But even the media couldn't rescue Batman.) How many reporters who wrote about Carson actually interviewed him? Newspapers contain misspellings every day. Media are holier than thou in making fun of Quayle." — Gina Lubrano, *San Diego Union-Tribune.*

"No single reason can be given to cover all cases. But I think a key factor in many of these is oversimplification of complex issues. There is also the tendency to focus on specific cases rather than on larger, more general issues. . . . The excuse for reporting every accusation, every denial, every charge and countercharge [in the Woody Allen affair] is that the issues are important: child abuse and foster families. Yet all too often, what's in the press and on the air is only about the specifics of the stars' lives—Woody and Mia, Soon-Yi and Dylan. And a serious look at societal problems becomes just another soap opera." — Henry McNulty, *Hartford Courant*, Hartford, Connecticut.

"Maybe [the media] enjoy the diversion these stories represent to a world that isn't otherwise much fun. Maybe in their quest for survival, they find it necessary to compete with media that know how to handle these sorts of stories better than anybody. Maybe they generally aren't deep thinkers about their craft. In any case, I've stopped being offended by it, as long as I can be sure the mainstream press is making a sincere effort to keep its collective eyes trained on its main mission: hard, serious news and analysis. We're getting better at it, I think. And if that's true, then

there ought to be room in our columns for some silliness. The question is one of balance, and that's the starting point for all sorts of nice arguments . . . and lists like this one, no?" — Art Nauman, *Sacramento Bee*.

"Many of the junk food stories this year centered on the presidential campaign. While it may be regrettable, I don't think the media have a good choice here: If the candidates talk about it—and they do—how can you ignore it?" — Frank Ritter, *Tennessean*, Nashville, Tennessee.

"Truly significant news is often oppressively dull or mentally taxing. The media welcome stories like these to leaven the loaf." — Kerry W. Sipe, *Virginian-Pilot*, Norfolk, Virginia.

"[Media tend to sensationalize stories for] ratings, circulation and general lip-smacking. Some of the stories are 'politically correct.' And, ironically, this year of all years, Christopher Columbus was politically incorrect, some said—so all said."
— Emerson Stone, *Communicator Magazine*.

"We live in a mass media, pop culture era. Everything is magnified by that fact, and often the trivial is elevated and the significant is subordinated or ignored. Editors and news directors are well aware of the numbers game. They know vastly more people are interested in Madonna or Fergie and Di than more substantive stories."
— Jim Stott, *Calgary Herald*, Calgary, Alberta, Canada.

"Most news organizations do not 'sensationalize' this stuff. It is not usually misrepresented, except in the sense that it is given too much space or time. Thus the significance, or at least the news value, is misrepresented. Editors play the stuff as they do because readers love it and read every word of it. Your question [Why do the media sensationalize certain stories?] is a little naive." — Robert Walker, *Gazette*, Montreal, Canada.

Henry McNulty, reader representative for the *Hartford Courant*, also had a news-diet tip for consumers: "I'm not bothered by a little JFN, just as I can tolerate some of the junk food it's named for. As long as there is showbiz there's going to be showbiz reporting, and there's nothing wrong with that. What's wrong is a way of eating that relies too heavily on empty calories and fat—and a diet of 'news' that consists mostly of trivia, gossip and mockery."

Surely there is, as McNulty points out, a need for news consumers to watch their diets. The person who gets all his or her news from the tabloid headlines at the checkout counter deserves little better. But, ignoring the chicken/egg argument, I maintain that the press has a responsibility to provide news the public needs, whether it wants it or not. As seen in the classic case discussed below, even the "nation's newspaper of record" can fail to fulfill that responsibility on occasion.

Pandering to the Bottom Line

To this day, an ongoing but little publicized controversy exists about the potential hazards of microwave radiation. It has now been more than 15 years since Paul Brodeur, in a series of *New Yorker* articles and a book, *The Zapping of America*, tried to sound a warning signal about the harmful effects of microwave radiation. But the major news media ignored the issue.

Then, in 1981, a significant event occurred. The New York State Worker's Compensation Board ruled that a telephone company supervisor had been killed by prolonged exposure to microwave radiation. It was the first official finding that long-term exposure to microwaves could cause death.

I believe that even the most diverse interpreters of "what news *is*" would agree that the first official death of an American citizen from microwave radiation had the makings of a significant news story. Experts have suggested that our nation is daily engulfed by microwave pollution that might endanger our health and lives. Confirmation that such pollution is indeed life threatening would seem to qualify as news we all should have. Despite the potential impact of that story, the *New York Times*, America's "newspaper of record," announced the finding in just three column-inches of space.

For comparative purposes, we should note that later that year, the *Times* devoted five column-inches to a story headlined "LONDON ZOO SAYS PANDA IS PREGNANT"—a story I believe fully qualifies as Junk Food News. Further, throughout 1981, the *Times* ran 20 separate items about pandas, which took up more than a hundred column-inches, while it referred back to the microwave death just once.

Personally, I have nothing against pandas. With the possible exception of Great Dane puppies, they may indeed qualify as the cutest animals on the planet. I am, however, intrigued by their awesome ability to attract the attention of our leading news media. I wonder if this might have been one of Richard Nixon's final jokes on the press.

For those who may have forgotten, pandas first burst onto our news scene in a major way when then President Richard Nixon gave two musk oxen to China. In response, Chou En-lai gave the U.S. two giant pandas—Hsing-Hsing and Ling-Ling. If you're curious, you'll find detailed, daily coverage of the pandas' fascinating trip from China to Washington, DC, reported in the *New York Times,* April 13 through April 18, 1972. (I've often wondered how much coverage our two musk oxen received in the Chinese media.)

The point, however, is that while the nation's most prestigious newspaper essentially ignored a story about death from microwave radiation that potentially affects millions of people, it found the space to report the most intimate details of a panda couple—a classic Junk Food News story that, without media coverage, would affect few of us.

It is time to question the news judgment of our media managers.

The irony of all this was compounded in late 1992 when Ling-Ling died, at the age of 23, in the National Zoo in Washington, DC. On December 31, 1992, the *New York Times* national edition devoted nine column-inches to her death—three times the coverage it gave the death of the telephone company supervisor in New York. The Santa Rosa *Press Democrat*, a northern California newspaper owned by the New York Times Company, featured Ling-Ling's demise with a blockbuster 33-column-inch photo caption on page A3, that read "Eulogy for a Panda." There was no comparable eulogy for the supervisor who died from microwave radiation.

Coincidentally, shortly before Ling-Ling's death, on December 7, 1992, Paul Brodeur published the latest of his ongoing "Annals of Radiation" exposés in the *New Yorker*. This one focused on the high incidence of cancer found in employees at a Fresno, California, elementary school located about a hundred feet from high-voltage transmission power lines.

Why Fight It?

Let's face it: the media will probably continue to satisfy the public's craving for Junk Food News. Why? Because:

- Junk Food News is easier and cheaper to produce.
- The pervasive influence of pseudo-news programs like "Entertainment Tonight" can't be ignored.
- Regular servings of JFN have undeniably boosted ratings and circulation across the board.
- In a fraught and complex world, JFN offers diversion from the gritty side of life.

But do we have to offer such gargantuan portions? Let's make some effort to trim them back. Takeshi Maezawa, columnist for the *Daily Yomiuri* in Tokyo, has written of one way the Japanese press has reduced the amount of Junk Food News published there. Noting the extraordinary amount of coverage given the wayward behavior of certain British royals, Maezawa says the Japanese news media mutually agreed not to cover the Japanese prince's search for a bride. This example of high-principled connivance may be impressive, but, in the United States, such a stand would be looked upon as a collective case of self-censorship.

There still may be time for us to get off the Junk Food News diet before we become hopelessly addicted to it. But to do this, we all have to participate. Corporate-level media owners should start to earn their unique First Amendment privileges. Editors should rethink their news judgment. Journalists should persevere in going after the hard stories. Professors of journalism should emphasize ethics and critical analysis, and turn out more muckrakers and fewer buckrakers. The judicial system should defend the freedom-of-the press provision of the First Amendment with far more vigor. And the public should show the media that it's more concerned with the high crimes and misdemeanors of its president than with the way the vice president spells "potato."

The effort will be worth it. America today is not the nation it once was—nor is it the nation it could be. We need a free and aggressive press more now than ever before, a press that will stand up to those who would control it and assume once again the independence it once celebrated. In November 1992, the nation voted for a change in the White House; now is the time to speak out for a change in news judgment.

CENSORED

CHAPTER 5

Censored Déjà Vu

Once cited as an early warning system for society's problems, Project Censored sounds the alarm on emerging social, environmental, economic and other issues—often while there's still time to respond to these problems before they get out of hand. However, too often these warnings go unheeded.

For example, had acid rain captured national media attention in 1977 when Project Censored first warned of its disastrous effects, this problem could have been resolved less expensively and before it took such a devastating toll on our environment and our health. The early warning system was ignored. Indeed, it was not until October 1992 that the Environmental Protection Agency (EPA) imposed long-delayed regulations on electric utilities that aimed at cutting sulfur dioxide emissions by half in a belated effort to control acid rain.

On the positive side, however, each year some of the issues first cited by the Project Censored "Early Warning System" attract media attention. Often, these stories take years to work their way onto the national news agenda. We call this phenomenon Censored Déjà Vu.

As George Santayana cautioned, if a society does not learn from the past, it is condemned to repeat it.

The Iran/Contra Issue

One of 1992's biggest déjà vu stories has to be the Iran/contra issue. As the year drew to a close, the Christmas Eve pardons and other revelations about the Iran/contra episode dominated the news.

However, this story was known as early as 1985 and surely should have been one of the key issues in the 1988 election of George Bush. Instead of focusing on Bush's deceit concerning Iran/contra, the media chose to ballyhoo the fact that Michael Dukakis was a card-carrying member of the American Civil Liberties Union. But Bush's role in Iran/contra wasn't a major issue in 1988.

In fact, it nearly wasn't a significant issue in the 1992 election. On October 30, just four days before the election, former Secretary of Defense Caspar Weinberger's "smoking gun" memo, implicating Bush in the arms for hostages intrigue, captured media attention—propelling this critical issue into election-year politics and news coverage for the first time.

In reality, the Iran/contra issue was available to the media for a number of years. The origins of the issue—the illegal aid to the contras—was a Censored story in 1985. The story pointed out that the aid to the contras was in direct violation of the U.S. Neutrality Act. It also revealed that the Reagan administration was well aware that the pro-contra groups in the United States were breaking the law by aiding the contra rebels in Nicaragua. Despite the alarming consequences of both issues, neither one was deemed worthy of major coverage in the mainstream media in 1985.

By 1986, while the Iran/contra story had taken on major proportions, some extraordinary aspects to the story still weren't being covered. Many Censored stories, including four of the top ten that year, addressed those issues:

▪ The #1 Censored story of 1986 revealed how the Reagan administration, in an effort to keep the lid on Central American issues, was violating the civil rights of American citizens. A three-part television report by San Francisco's KRON-TV "Target 4" anchor/reporter Sylvia Chase and producer Jonathan Dann, with help from Angus Mackenzie of the Center for Investigative Reporting, revealed that political opponents of the administration's Central American policies suddenly became targets of mysterious break-ins, IRS audits and FBI surveillance and interrogation. The report was ignored by the national media.

▪ Another story, which appeared in the Summer 1986 issue of the *CovertAction Information Bulletin* and was followed up with a story by Martha Honey in the March 1987 issue of the *Columbia Journalism Review*, revealed how the CIA paid Honduran and Costa Rican journalists and broadcasters for pro-contra media coverage.

▪ The fifth-ranked censored issue of 1986, based on stories by Eric Selbin in the August issue of the *UTNE Reader* and by George Martin Manz in the November issue of *Briarpatch*, exposed the influence right-wing and fascist groups had on President Reagan. It described how Reagan had supported the World Anti-Communist League, an international right-wing group so extreme that the John Birch Society shunned it.

▪ The fourth story of 1986, ranked #7, detailed the lawsuit filed by the Christic Institute that cited the "secret team," a group of paramilitary operatives, supporting the contra rebels. "Contragate", written by Michael Emery, an investigative journalist and journalism professor at California State University, Northridge, was published in the December 3 issue of the *San Francisco Bay Guardian*. It foretold many of the revelations publicized in late 1992, including the drug-trafficking ring operating out of contra bases on the Costa Rica property of John Hull, a shadowy U.S. rancher. It also discussed the attempted assassination of dissident contra leader Eden Pastora at La Penca.

The following year, Iran/contra continued to figure prominently in Project Censored's top ten.

In 1987, the #2 Censored story, based on a Christic Institute Special Report by Dan Sheehan, exposed a startling picture of large-scale drug trafficking under the auspices of the U.S. government/contra supply network. Additional articles that year in *Newsday*, *The Nation* and *In These Times* supported the Christic Institute's story.

By the time the 1988 election rolled around, substantial information was available about the Iran/contra issue and presidential candidate George Bush's involvement; but again the press failed to pursue the issue. This was just one of a series of issues cited in the #1 Censored story of 1988, titled "George Bush's Dirty Big Secrets."

One of the top ten stories of 1989 documented how five American officials, including a U.S. ambassador, were barred from ever setting foot in Costa Rica, a Central American country considered to be one of our friends. Oscar Arias, president of Costa Rica and winner of the 1987 Nobel Prize for Peace, permanently forbade the following Reagan officials from Costa Rica because of their involvement in drug smuggling activities: Oliver North, National Security aide;

John Poindexter, former National Security adviser; Major General Richard Secord; Joseph Fernandez, former CIA chief in Costa Rica; and Lewis Tambs, former U.S. ambassador to Costa Rica. Surely this story, charging leading U.S. officials with drug dealing, could have been considered as newsworthy as Zsa Zsa Gabor's cop-slapping trial, the well-publicized top "junk food news story" for 1989. Yet, the Ollie North, et al., story appeared in the October 1989 issue of *EXTRA!* and was never picked up by the mainstream media.

By 1990, the question "Where was George?" was being asked so often the media could hardly ignore it; yet, while material from Oliver North's diaries revealed that George Bush played a major role in the Iran/contra scandal from the start, the media continued to let him off the hook with his disingenuous "out of the loop" explanation.

Finally, by 1992, the press could no longer ignore the issue. The Iran/contra revelations were coming with such regularity that the thieves were stumbling over each other in their efforts to blame one another: Poindexter's cable revealed how Bush endorsed Reagan's plan to conceal specifics of the Iran initiative; General Secord charged that Bush "was not 'out of the loop'"; former National Security Council aide Howard Teicher claimed that Bush "knew from day one" about the details of the arms-for-hostages deal; a powerful *New Yorker* article (November 2, 1992) by Murray Waas and Craig Unger revealed Bush's emissary role during a Middle East trip in July and August of 1986; additional evidence was found in Caspar Weinberger's incriminating memo, which was supported by entries in Bush's own personal diary, reported in mid-January 1993 (all of which was fully confirmed by the memoirs of former Secretary of State George Schultz, as excerpted in *Time* Magazine in early February 1993).

And yet, as of this writing, George Bush has not been held accountable for his acts. The Iran/contra issue was an important story for the American people to have known back in 1985. At least two mainstream journalists, Robert Parry and Brian Barger, both with the Associated Press at the time, were onto the story that year. But according to an analysis by David Shaw, media critic for the *Los Angeles Times*, they encountered resistance to the story from their editors and finally got discouraged and left AP in mid-1986. Shaw's analysis of Iran/contra coverage, published December 20, 1992, also noted that, with the exception of the *Miami Herald*, most major news organizations failed to explore the story.

Ironically, while the story received good play in the alternative press in the U.S. at the time, the major media credited a Beirut magazine, *Al Shiraa*, with breaking the story about arms sales to Iran on October 31, 1986. It seems our mainstream media couldn't admit being scooped once again by our alternative press in the United States but apparently didn't mind if it came from a foreign publication.

The Nuclear Issue

Overlooked, undercovered and literally censored issues about the dangers of nuclear power dominated Project Censored's early years, starting in 1976. By 1992, a number of those Censored stories featured years ago were confirmed.

A classic example of Project Censored's role as an early warning signal is found in the #3 Censored story of 1978. This story appeared in the March 23, 1978, issue of *Rolling Stone*, titled "The Government's Quiet War on Scientists Who Know Too Much."

The story described what happened to Dr. Thomas Mancuso who, in 1964, had been commissioned by the Atomic Energy Commission (AEC)—predecessor to the Nuclear Regulatory Commission—to measure how safe nuclear plants are for the people who work in them. Dr. Mancuso and two associates had studied workers at the Hanford nuclear reservation in the state of Washington. As it turned out, they found evidence that low levels of radiation, previously thought to be safe, actually were quite deadly.

When Dr. Mancuso presented his findings, they were not what the AEC expected nor wanted. His contract with the government was promptly canceled, his research funds were cut off, his access to the workers' health records was denied. He was forced into premature retirement, and the government tried to take possession of his research material.

There was no major media follow-up to Mancuso's plight, the *Rolling Stone* article or to Project Censored's citation of it. No immediate action was taken to help the workers who may have suffered from exposure to the low-level radiation at Hanford, or was there any warning, based on Mancuso's findings, issued to workers at other nuclear production sites. Instead, the AEC turned to Battelle Pacific Northwest Laboratories, a research firm it often used, to review Mancuso's study. Battelle attributed the unnatural cancer rate to statistical bias rather than radiation. The AEC found this conclusion to be satisfactory.

This was the situation until December 8, 1992, when journalist Matthew L. Wald reported in the *New York Times* that the first independent study of the health records of thousands of workers at the Hanford site confirmed Mancuso's original warnings. The study was conducted by Dr. Alice Stewart, one of Mancuso's original research colleagues. *Times* reporter Wald also revealed that, for decades, the federal government had limited access to the Hanford health data to scientists of its choosing. These scientists have generally concluded that the radiation exposure had done little harm.

This story suggests that while important, well-documented news and information may be reported in the alternative press, the mainstream media sometimes fail to investigate it on their own. Further, it confirms that the federal government has, on at least one provable occasion, attempted to censor critical information by soliciting research that would appear to discredit that information.

Ironically, on December 2, about a week before the *New York Times* revelation, *USA Today*, in a major feature commemorating the 50th anniversary of the nuclear age, cited the Hanford nuclear reservation as an example of how failure (the discovery of a massive radioactive environmental tragedy) can bring success (an economic boom as workers and business rush in to clean up the mess). There was no mention, however, of Dr. Mancuso's early study revealing how low-level radiation could cause cancer.

Other nuclear issues cited previously by Project Censored received mainstream coverage in 1992: Portland General Electric Co. votes to close Oregon's only nuclear power plant 15 years before its license expires—dangers of nuclear power plants have been recurring Censored stories since 1976; deregulating radioactive waste to "Below Regulatory Concern" so it can be dumped at local landfills remains a threat—Censored story #6 in 1989; a sunken Russian nuclear submarine off the Norwegian coast leaks radioactive cesium from its damaged reactor—dangers of nuclear accidents on the high seas was the #8 Censored story of 1983; profitable illicit smuggling and sale of radioactive materials are discovered—inadequate nuclear reactor safeguards and flawed accountability of nuclear materials was the #6 Censored story of 1976; scientists protest the launch of a nuclear reactor into space as part of the Strategic Defense Initiative, warning that leaking radiation could block most of the space-based scientific studies of the universe for more than a year—the dangers of nuclear reactors in space was the #10 Censored story of 1986.

In each of these cases, and in other instances, an early warning about a potential danger was issued ... but ignored at the time by the mainstream media.

Other Déjà Vu Stories of 1992

• **GULF WAR MEDIA COVERAGE GAVE U.S. FALSE PICTURE**—In a candid, though belated, case of mea culpa, the press and its pundits finally acknowledged in 1992 that the media too often went along with the Gulf War

cheerleading efforts by the White House and the Pentagon. Stanley W. Cloud, *Time* Magazine's Washington bureau chief, acknowledged, "Desert Storm was certainly the worst-covered major U.S. conflict in this century." The inadequate coverage of the events leading up to the Gulf War was the top Censored story of 1990, while the filtered and biased war coverage in 1991 was the top Censored story of that year. The news media censorship was so bad that Walter Cronkite, America's longtime top-ranked television news anchor and most trusted man, charged that the Pentagon's censorship was "the real horror of the Persian Gulf war."

• **THE POISONED U.S./MEXICAN BORDER**—In February 1992, an agreement by President Bush and Mexican President Carlos Salinas de Gortari to clean up the poisoned border was widely publicized; not publicized, however, was a 1988 story that revealed a similar U.S./Mexican presidential agreement in 1987 was routinely being violated by U.S.-owned plants along the border. What does this portend for the latest presidential agreement?

• **AMERICA'S POLITICAL PRISONER**—Leonard Peltier, accused of murdering two federal agents in a shoot-out near Wounded Knee, South Dakota, in 1975, was the subject of Censored nominations in 1985 and 1986. While Peltier, described variously as America's Andre Sakharov or an American "political prisoner," has been widely publicized in the international media, he has never been put on the American news agenda by our mainstream media. And while he was the subject of a critically acclaimed documentary, "Incident at Oglala," produced by Robert Redford in 1992, Peltier remains in a federal penitentiary at this writing.

• **TEACHING KIDS TO SMOKE**—In July 1985, an extraordinary single-subject issue of the *New York State Journal of Medicine*, edited by Alan Blum, M.D., warned about the tobacco industry's appeals to children; but the special issue was ignored by the news media. In 1992, the U.S. Surgeon General, the American Medical Association and others, including the media, finally attacked

tobacco companies for promoting smoking with "Joe Camel" and other morally questionable appeals to young people. Now it remains to be seen whether their efforts will continue in the face of a well-funded counter-attack by the tobacco industry.

• **OVER-THE-COUNTER DRUGS MAY BE DANGEROUS TO YOUR HEALTH** — A new congressional report by the General Accounting Office in 1992 challenged the safety and effectiveness of over-the-counter drugs and the Food and Drug Administration's (FDA) failure to supervise them properly. The FDA subsequently acknowledged that hundreds of ingredients in over-the-counter medications don't do what they say they are supposed to do. The #9 Censored story of 1976 was based on an FDA report warning that people who purchase such drugs are "victims of a gigantic medical hoax." And the FDA should know.

• **THE WORST U.S. CIVIL DISORDER IN THE 20th CENTURY**—The media's role in the events leading up to, during and after the tragic Los Angeles riots in 1992 were predicted in the "1968 Report of the National Advisory Commission on Civil Disorders," also known as the "Kerner Commission Report." The Censored story of the King rebellion and the riots did not address what happened nor why nor how the media covered it; the real story was that we had not learned from the past. The #1 Censored story of 1977, "The Myth of Black Progress," issued a warning signal that was ignored.

• **THE COSTLY MYTH OF THE BIG RED SCARE**—The top Censored story of 1984 was "The Myth of the Soviet Military Build-up." It charged that CIA estimates of Soviet military spending were highly inflated. On May 20, 1992, CIA Director Robert Gates admitted that CIA intelligence data had been cooked to portray the Soviet economy as stronger than it was. Critics say the false statistics led to the budget-busting defense build-up that peaked in 1985 under President Ronald Reagan.

• **CHEATING AT SEARS WAS AN OLD STORY**—In June 1992, the California Department of Consumer Affairs charged Sears, Roebuck and Co. with systematically bilking customers in its automobile repair shops. Ed Brennan, Sears chair and CEO, denied the charges, stating Sears "would never intentionally violate the trust customers have shown in our company for 105 years." Brennan apparently forgot a 1976 Censored story that reported how Sears went to court for engaging in illegal bait-and-switch selling tactics. In early September 1992, Sears settled auto-repair fraud cases in California, Michigan, Pennsylvania and other states for $46.6 million, the largest settlement ever for such fraud.

- **DDT MAKES A COMEBACK**—In 1992, 20 years after being banned in the U.S. and Canada, the pesticide DDT was found to be increasing in fish and wildlife throughout the Great Lakes. Speculation was that the DDT was being blown into the region from Mexico, Central America and South America. Sales of pesticides banned in the U.S. to Third World countries—a Censored story in 1976, 1980 and 1989—continue to this day.

- **AMERICA HELD HOSTAGE BY THE NRA**—In the aftermath of John Lennon's murder and Ronald Reagan's assassination attempt, the skyrocketing murder rate finally emerged as a national news story. Yet the proliferation of handguns was cited as a Censored story in 1980. In 1992, the American Medical Association acknowledged that murder was "a national epidemic" as the nation's murder rate reached its highest point since Prohibition. On November 13, 1992, the Associated Press reported the results of a major new study by the National Research Council that concluded the United States is the most violent nation in the industrial world. And on December 11, 1992, ABC-TV's "20/20" broadcast an investigative piece that revealed it was more difficult for a person to get a driver's license than a license to sell guns because of lax control by the Bureau of Alcohol, Tobacco, and Firearms. This can be traced back to congressional representatives' willingness to kowtow to pressure from pro-gun groups.

- **BABY FORMULA SALES FRAUD**—In 1992, the Federal Trade Commission charged Abbott Laboratories, the largest U.S. infant formula-maker, with fixing prices in a government program for poor women and children, and settled related charges with Mead Johnson and American Home Products. Abbott Labs and American Home were both prominent players in the #5 Censored story of 1979, which revealed how infant formula manufacturers employed exploitative and deceptive tactics to sell their infant formula products in Third World countries.

- **THE CENSORED SAGA OF EAST TIMOR**—It took the brutal beatings of two journalists, Allan Nairn of the *New Yorker* and Amy Goodman of Pacifica Radio, before the press finally asked itself, "Why Did Press Ignore East Timor Massacre?" in the July/August 1992 issue of the *Washington Journalism Review*. The tragedy in East Timor was the #7 Censored story in 1979 and the #3 Censored story in 1985. However, the message finally appears to be getting through; in October 1992, for the first time in 17 years, Congress reduced aid to Indonesia because of the genocidal attacks on the East Timorese.

- **OCCUPATIONAL SAFETY FAILURE IS AT LEAST 16 YEARS OLD**—An "Eye on America" segment on the CBS-TV "Evening News" in June 1992 featured the failure of the Occupational Safety and Health Administration to protect American workers. The same issue was cited as the #7 Censored story in 1976 and #5 in 1979.

- **HISTORY'S BIGGEST BANKING SCANDAL**—U.S. federal agencies received more than 700 tips and leads about illegal activities at BCCI (Bank of Credit and Commerce International) between 1979 and 1991; yet it was still a Censored story in 1990. In 1992, the Associated Press finally acknowledged that BCCI represents the "biggest banking scandal" in history; but even now the scandal remains far from being resolved or fully explained to the American people.

- **SLAPP SUITS: A THREAT TO FREE SPEECH**—In August 1992, the *Washington Post* published an informative article, titled "Suing to Squelch: A New Way to Keep Activists Quiet," about the dangers of SLAPP suits—Strategic Lawsuits Against Public Participation. The SLAPP suit threat to First Amendment rights was the subject of the #17 Censored story of 1989.

- **THE SPECTER OF STERILITY**—The #7 Censored story of 1978 revealed how industrial and agricultural chemical pollution caused the average sperm count among American men to drop substantially since a landmark study done less than 30 years earlier. A new study, in 1992, has now confirmed changes in sexuality, ranging from fertility to sexual orientation, as a result of pollution from Dioxin, PCBs and other chemicals, as cited in the 1978 story.

- **AFRICA: PLAGUED BY FAMINE AND NOW TOXIC DUMPING**— The #2 Censored story of 1989 revealed how Africa was in danger of being transformed into the world's garbage can for toxic dumping. In September 1992, it was reported that a Somalian warlord signed a contract with a Swiss-based firm to allow thousands of tons of Europe's toxic waste to be dumped in Somalia, a tragic land already suffering from famine and anarchy.

- **TRUE HORROR OF EL SALVADOR REVEALED**—The censored horror of what was happening in El Salvador in the early 1980s finally found its way into mainstream media in 1992, when forensic experts unearthed skeletons of children and babies in El Mozote, El Salvador. Their findings confirmed that hundreds of civilians were killed in the largest massacre of that country's civil war. "Distorted Reports of El Salvador Crisis," #1 Censored story in 1980, and "The Real Story of Central America," #5 Censored in 1982, were just two of a number of stories about atrocities being committed in El Salvador and Central America cited by Project Censored at the time.

- **AMERICA'S SUPER-SECRET SPY COURT HAS A PERFECT RECORD**—The #2 Censored story of 1982 exposed the little-known U.S. Foreign Intelligence Court, which reviews intelligence agency requests to spy on Americans in this country. At that time, the Washington-based court had heard 962 requests for electronic surveillance since it was launched in May 1979 and had approved all 962 requests. Stephen Aftergood, editor of *Secrecy & Government*

Bulletin, updated the secret spy court record in the *Bulletin*'s November 1992 issue. Through the end of 1991, the court had received a total of 6,546 requests since it started and had approved all 6,546 of them. Not one of the thousands of surveillance requests has been rejected. Obviously, this must be the most efficient court in world history! Another question, not asked by the mass media, is, who are these 6,546 Americans that our intelligence agencies are spying on?

• **WATER, WATER (DISAPPEARING) EVERYWHERE**—In late 1992, an authoritative new book, titled *Last Oasis: Facing Water Scarcity*, by Sandra Postel (vice-president of the Worldwatch Institute), warned of a water crisis in the 1990s similar to the oil crunch of the 1970s. The #5 Censored story of 1981, "Our Water Is Running Out and What's Left Is Being Poisoned," provided an earlier warning that went unheeded.

• **HIGH-TENSION POWER LINES INCREASE THE RISK OF CAN-CER**—Hundreds of thousands, if not millions, of Americans living near high-voltage power lines have never heard about one of the top 25 Censored stories of 1978, titled "High Voltage: Hazards Over Our Heads." Fifteen years ago, it warned people that the electromagnetic fields (EMFs) surrounding high-voltage power lines have adverse effects on humans, plants and animals. Nonetheless, utility company executives at the time said the lines were safe and, in fact, encouraged people to use surrounding rights of way for farming and recreation. On November 13, 1992, the news media reported on two authoritative Swedish studies that confirmed EMFs produced by power lines may cause cancer and that increased exposure to EMFs increased the risk of cancer. If the news media had covered this issue, as it should have 15 years ago, hundreds of thousands of people might not have had to endure this risk.

Revisiting old problems that could have been resolved years ago if the media had sounded that warning is just like Yogi said: "It's déjà vu all over again." Only it ain't funny.

CENSORED Reprints

W e've tried to include reprints of as many of the source articles for the top ten "Censored" stories of 1992 as possible. In some cases we weren't able to do this because of time constraints, costs, copyright restrictions, etc. Nonetheless, we were able to locate and obtain reprint rights to most of them. We believe you will find the original stories to be interesting, important and relevant. And, once again, we hope you will wonder why they weren't published in your mainstream media. Following is a guide to the reprinted stories.

Story #1 The Great Media Sell-out To Reaganism
Article: *Mother Jones* • May/June 1992 • "Journalism of Joy"

Story #2 Corporate Violators Dwarf Street Crime and Violence
Article: *Multinational Monitor* • December 1991 • "Corporate Crime & Violence in Review: The 10 Worst Corporations of 1991"

Story #3 Censored Election Year Issue
Article: *Common Cause* Magazine • April/May/June 1992 • "Bush's Ruling Class"

Story #4 United States: The World's Leading Merchant of Death
Article: *World Press Review* • September 1992 • "The World's Top Arms Merchant: The U.S. Grabs More of a Shrinking Market"

Story #5 Iraqgate and the Silent Death of the Watergate Law
Article: *The Paper* • October 22, 1992 • "Iraqgate: Is Bush a Felon?"

Story #6 "We Are Winning the War on Drugs" Was a Lie
Article: *EXTRA!* • September 1992 • "Don't Forget the Hype: Media, Drugs and Public Opinion"

Story #7 Trashing Federal Regulations for Profit
Article: *The Nation* • March 23, 1992 • "Bush's Regulatory Chill: Immoral, Illegal and Deadly"

Story #8 Government Secrecy Makes a Mockery of Democracy
Article: *Issues in Science and Technology* • Summer 1992 • "The Perils of Government Secrecy"

Story #9 How Advertising Pressure Can Corrupt a Free Press
Article: Center for the Study of Commercialism • 1992 • Excerpt from "Dictating Content: How Advertising Pressure Can Corrupt a Free Press"

Story #10 The Pentagon's Post Cold War Black Budget
Article: *Mother Jones* • March/April 1992 • "The Pentagon's Secret Stash"

Journalism of Joy by Ben H. Bagdikian;
Mother Jones • May/June 1992

In a roundup of the 1991 recession, an intriguing article in the *New York Times* contained this paragraph: "There is little mystery about what caused the economic problems. The country is suffering a hangover from the mergers, rampant speculation, overbuilding, heavy borrowing and irresponsible government fiscal policy in the 1980s."

It's true. There is little mystery about how the 1980s caused our economic (and social) problems. But if you watched television and read the daily papers during that era, you did not receive a picture of the accumulating wreckage produced by Reaganism. You were fed a steady diet of positive news about the "miracle" of the 1980s, the brilliant achievements of the "Reagan Revolution."

If it's all so unmysterious now, where was our news establishment at the time? Did it sell out?

In a word, yes. And it's clear why it did. The great majority of big media owners have always been happier with conservative Republicans, but in the 1980s they had reason to be ecstatic; as they were dispensing their relentlessly positive news about Reaganism, they were being allowed by the government to create giant, monopolistic media empires.

During the 1980s, for example, the three big news networks were taken over by corporations that might have been deemed unqualified under earlier standards set by the Federal Communications Commission. ABC went to Capital Cities, a large newspaper chain whose acquisition increased cross-media domination. NBC was taken over by General Electric, which not only has a major stake in the news as a leading defense contractor and maker of nuclear reactors but has a remarkable history of convictions for fraud and antitrust violations. And a big real-estate operator, Laurence Tisch, took over CBS and decimated what used to be the best news and documentary operation in the United States.

The FCC also relieved broadcasters of traditional requirements for public service, made it almost impossible for citizen groups to challenge renewal of station licenses, and lifted limits on the number of stations that a single corporation can acquire.

The owners of the daily print press got their share of special government treatment too. The daily-news business was already controlled by monopolies in 98 percent of U.S. cities, but in the 1980s the administration further sedated the antitrust laws to permit the biggest newspaper chains to sweep up these local monopolies. In addition, the National Labor Relations Board became stacked with pro-management members, and the media giants went on a ten-year spree of union busting.

Like all of big business, the broadcasters and print publishers benefited from Reagan's shift of corporate taxes onto the middle class and poor, but Americans did not see much coverage of that on television or in the printed news. Ditto with unemployment. To this day, joblessness continues to be reported as though it were a mysterious plague falling unbidden from heaven rather than a natural result of the speculative corporate debt, financial manipulations that rewarded big investors but weakened the products, and fabulous rake-offs by the merger artists of the 1980s.

When, for example, Time, Inc., and Warner Communications were permitted to merge into the world's largest media firm, the descriptions in the news were like those of all big mergers. It was an exciting battle between empire builders; it would produce more efficiency and creative "synergy." As in other cases, when citing "winners" and "losers" in the takeover battles, the news mentioned only the Wall Street adventurers, not the workers and consumers. Only in 1990 did we learn that one of the merger operators who manipulated the Time-Warner deal, Steven Ross, received an annual compensation of seventy-eight million dollars. The next year he laid off six hundred Time, Inc., employees.

It is clear why owners were happy to delude themselves and the public about Reaganism. But what about the 100,000 print and broadcast journalists who did the actual reporting and editing? Did they, too, sell out the American public?

Unlike their bosses, the majority of working journalists certainly did not acquire more money or power during the 1980s. Like the rest of the middle class, they experienced a decline in real purchasing power.

Journalists as a class are hardly exempt from the sins of vanity, sloth, or greed, but this does not explain the misrepresentation of reality that they helped create. For one thing, during the 1980s, local print and broadcast news outlets periodically produced serious stories about the growing economic and social problems in their own communities. The same was true from time to time at the national level. Though major network documentaries practically disappeared, an occasional mini-documentary produced powerful evidence of the social dislocations caused by Washington policies; daily newspapers occasionally reported the underside of the 1980s, as well.

But for every story of that kind there were dozens of the cheerleading variety, which quickly wiped out the impact of the critical stories. Isolated reports seldom frame the citizen's view of the world; rather, news items that are treated briefly and not pursued soon become forgotten bits of flotsam and jetsam in the great tides of information that hourly and daily inundate the public. It is the *pattern* of coverage that creates the dominant impression.

Nevertheless, even the occasional bits of realistic news were enough to bring White House complaints to media owners and executives. Any negative story was in danger of official condemnation. Meanwhile, the president's spin doctors were orchestrating daily photo ops and sound bites, which were meant to brush aside any notion that all was not well at 1600 Pennsylvania Avenue or in the country.

Media owners and managers openly spread the idea in U.S. newsrooms that the news needed to be upbeat. Allen Neuharth, then chief of Gannett, the country's largest newspaper chain, announced that it was time for reporters to practice what he called the "journalism of hope."

Soon, the normal restraint exercised by most media owners over inserting corporate propaganda into the news crumbled. For twenty years, neoconservative intellectuals had been hammering U.S. journalists as liberal ideologues who tilted the news against business and conservatives, often against the reporters' own bosses. It was an absurd claim, given the similarity of voting patterns between journalists and all professionals with college educations in the liberal arts. Even so, the campaign bore spectacular fruit. There has always been pressure in newsrooms to "prove you are not being unfair to conservatives." In the 1980s, it simply reached new levels of mandated blindness.

Systematically, David Gergen and other White House "communications" operatives complained to news executives that stories exposing gross consequences of Reagan policies—growing hunger, unemployment, poverty—were "unfair" and "unbalanced," invoking the magic words of the twenty-year campaign against independent journalism. These complaints found sympathetic ears among owners and top editors.

If, in the field, a correspondent showed the White House to be lying, as did the *New York Times*' Ray Bonner in El Salvador, that reporter was pulled back in favor of more congenial correspondents. Eventually, this process led to reporters such as Shirley Christian covering the area. Her stories, it would be fair to say, seemed closer to those that people like Elliott Abrams and Oliver North would favor. It is no surprise that the Iran-contra operation was disclosed by an obscure magazine in Beirut and not by any of the three thousand U.S. correspondents in Washington.

When reporters tried to penetrate the propaganda barricade at the White House, their own managements blocked their efforts. One example involved coverage of the president himself. The White House wanted to project an image of the titular leader of the "Reagan Revolution" as a shrewdly insightful, compelling visionary of policy, a natural genius in command of his administration.

The truth was that, left on his own with reporters, Reagan would have revealed himself to be one of the most ignorant men ever elected president, beating out even Calvin Coolidge, whose picture Reagan proudly remounted in the White House. He was subject to alarming fantasies about himself, slept through crucial meetings, and, even when awake, was easily confused by his own three-by-five cue cards.

What Reagan was really good at was B-movie acting—the cocky toss of the head, the gee-whiz smile of the guy next door, and the John Wayne posture on horseback. So the White House media staff came up with the ideal strategy: no words, just pictures, pictures, pictures. As reported by journalist Mark Hertsgaard, the president's media managers ordered Washington news bureaus to stop sending reporters to cover daily events like visits by foreign leaders. Only TV cameras and still photographers would be permitted. The reporters rebelled, but their home offices ordered them to obey. The result was the constant countrywide repetition on TV and front pages of the image of a masterful policy chief.

The owners' abandonment of their reporters gave White House propaganda a free ticket into the nation's news. During his administration, the media regularly referred to Reagan as the most popular president in the history of U.S. public-opinion polling, even though basic Gallup survey data showed he was not. Franklin Roosevelt, Eisenhower, Kennedy, and Johnson had higher peaks; all except Johnson had higher averages. But the White Houses's spin doctors got away with their own version.

The eagerness of media owners to accept the propaganda is what did the trick. And the false image of the most popular president in history intimidated his opponents. After Reagan left office, Michael Deaver, coordinator of White House image making, admitted that "Reagan enjoyed the most generous treatment by the press of any president in the postwar era."

The mechanism by which owners control the news succeeds because it is invisible to the public. All owners carefully select their top editor or producer with their corporate needs in mind. In turn, this news executive assigns reporters and camerapeople and decides whether the stories and footage that come back will be used or thrown out, whether they will lead the news report emphatically or be relegated to brevity and obscurity, whether they will be pursued as a theme in future stories or dropped at once. No owner hires a top news executive who is expected to spoil the owner's breakfast too often, nor keeps one who does.

Top editors have always been meticulously screened to make sure that they will not be inclined to offend corporate desires. But during the 1980s, a new twist was added: top editors were made part of the business-management team, responsible for keeping up ad linage and often sent to business schools for special training to make them think more like corporate executives.

To intensify corporate control over top editors, most newspapers now grant annual bonuses and stock options for those who remain in the good graces of the business side. One example, though more grandiose than for most newspapers, involves the managing editors of Time, Inc.'s, publications. They receive about $250,000 in annual salary, plus bonuses of from 50 to 75 percent of this figure—all at the discretion of corporate bosses. In addition, many *Times* editors have options letting them buy stock that in the past has sold for as high as $182. They, like many newspaper editors, can, if they continue to please the corporation, retire as millionaires. It is not surprising that these editors start thinking more like stock-brokers and less like journalists.

Owners and media companies vary in the latitude they permit editors and news staffs. But even firms with the best journalistic reputations will eject esteemed editors and producers if they do not sufficiently conform to corporate wishes. Gene Roberts is probably the most respected news editor of this generation. More than anyone else, he personally fashioned and operated the strategy that converted the old *Philadelphia Inquirer* from a national joke to one of the most respected (and prosperous) newspapers in the country. The result was a daily that swept the field in its city and region. Then, last year, Roberts unexpectedly "resigned." As with most such disappearances, the victim said little in public to condemn his old paper and bosses, but his closes associates made it plain that the reason for his departure was his refusal to accept new conditions laid down by the parent firm, Knight-Ridder. The same thing happened to Bill Kovach, the editor who reversed the downward slide of the *Atlanta Journal & Constitution* and re-established it as a respectable force in its area. He had reported important news that too often embarrassed powerful friends of the owners.

Editors learn from these emblematic events. The result is deep and widespread self-censorship from the top down in U.S. journalism. The internalized censorship can continue for years or decades after a single, dramatic demonstration by an owner shows that serious punishment will follow if independent news judgments offend that owner's politics or friends.

The same conditioning and self-censorship occur even more readily among reporters. Like their editors, reporters do not need constant reminders of the penalty for defying censorship imposed from the top. In 1982, a time when such stories, if reported nationally, might have prevented the current banking disasters, Earl Golz, a reporter with thirteen years of experience at the *Dallas Morning News*, wrote that federal bank examiners were alarmed about a local bank with unannounced bad loans. After the bank chairman told the paper's owners that Golz's report was a lie, Golz was fired, as was the editor who had approved the story. The bank failed two weeks later, and the examiners forced the dismissal of the chairman who had indignantly denied everything. But neither the reporter nor his editor was rehired. For a long time thereafter, no reporter or editor needed to be told that stories that anger influential bankers may end your career.

Even the most courageous reporter stops wasting time on stories that won't get on the air or into the paper. Self-censorship becomes epidemic. But it is an invisible epidemic, and all the harder to counter because the public never finds out about it.

Most censorship remains invisible for an ironic reason. Journalistic ethics among working reporters have risen enough to make it embarrassing if the censoring hand of the corporation leaves telltale fingerprints on the news. A frank statement by an editor to a reporter that a story was killed for corporate reasons could end up in one of the country's journalism reviews, or even at another news outlet. For example, when Golz and his editor were fired because of the Dallas bank affair, the *Wall Street Journal* carried the whole embarrassing story.

Owners, like their journalists, have egos. And they prefer to avoid negative publicity that could also affect favorability of the medium for advertising. So most owners have learned not to post embarrassing memoranda. Except for a few crude operations, editors no longer tell reporters, "The boss wants no more stories like this." Instead, reporters are given professionally acceptable reasons. These include decisions that could be legitimate editing judgments, like "No one's interested in that" or "We did that once." When the real reason involves orders from above or corporate anger at the truth, it is never stated.

Lawrence Grossman, former head of NBC News, revealed recently that, following the stock-market crash in 1987, Jack Welch, CEO of NBC's owner, General Electric, called to say that he did not want the network's newscasts to use language that might depress GE stock. Grossman says he did not tell his staff about the call. He has not disclosed whether the private pressure from the top affected his decisions over what to allow on the news.

There is another management practice that may deeply diminish good journalism for a long time. More than ever before, major news corporations are conducting systematic screenings of new reporters to keep out journalists who might not readily comply with corporate wishes or who might join newsroom unions. Some major news companies, including the nation's second-largest newspaper chain, Knight-Ridder, do the screening through mandatory, lengthy psychological questionnaires of all potential new reporters. Others, including some papers in the largest newspaper chain, Gannett, order editors to be deliberately blunt in interviews so that the applicants know the company wants only "team players" who will not rock the boat and are not in favor of unions. Hiring reporters who are not inclined to question authority is one way to guarantee bad journalism.

While there is widespread cynicism about such procedures, they seem to have had real consequences. Ben Bradlee, former editor of the *Washington Post*, says that, today, "reporters are more conservative than the previous generation." Older correspondents in the gulf war, for instance, were appalled by the number of younger war correspondents who reported transparent military propaganda as if it were fact.

It is not simple to change trends like these. Strictly for profit reasons, the news monopolies tend to hew closely to overwhelming public sentiment. Consequently, it will take a real alteration of the country's political and social atmosphere to force the media to work harder to serve the public more and its owners' favorite political and economic causes less.

But viewers and readers are not powerless. Protests to the media can produce some change. Clear and individually composed letters and phone calls seldom fail to make an internal impact, even if news organizations pretend they do not. Without such audience response, complaints from the organized right-wing and the powerful will dominate pressure on the news. In the end, the media needs the audience to stay in business.

Within journalism, professional news staffs in corporate media should be permitted to elect their own top editor and have a substantial voice in long-range journalistic policies, as is done at some of the most prestigious newspapers in Europe. This would decrease the invisible corporate influence over the news. But such a reform will not come until media owners recognize that the public is losing confidence in increasingly monopolistic and arrogant industry.

During the degradations of the 1980s, government lying was too willingly supported by the media; high crimes and misdemeanors by the president of the United States became an accepted public boast; looting the public treasury and cheating the citizens were treated by most editors as necessary for liberation of the marketplace. For almost ten years, the media remained silent on the obvious—that Reaganite politics were taking a frightful toll in human suffering and crippling the economy.

The mass media gave the country a dismal demonstration of what George Orwell saw forty years ago: "...political chaos is connected with the decay of language....Political language is designed to make lies sound truthful and murder respectable, and to give an appearance of solidity to pure wind."

From that kind of public morality neither the country nor journalism will soon recover.

Ben H. Bagdikian is the author of The Media Monopoly *and a former assistant managing editor of the* Washington Post.

Corporate Crime & Violence In Review: The 10 Worst Corporations of 1991 by Russell Mokhiber; *Multinational Monitor* • December 1991

The past year has seen corporate crime and violence on the move at an accelerating pace—public corruption, environmental degradation, financial fraud, procurement fraud and occupational homicide are all on the increase.

Criminal corporate collectivist action has inflicted injuries on the planet and its people that even the most evil of individuals acting alone could not dream of inflicting—the growing hole in the ozone layer, global warming, and increasing cancer rates, to name a few.

Yet, many people in positions of authority continue to deny this reality and defy common sense.

The vast majority of crime shows on television today, for example, focus on street crime, not corporate crime.

Earlier this year, *Washington Post* columnist Richard Cohen wrote that "Young black males commit most of the crime in Washington, D.C." This statement is demonstrably false. In making it, Cohen ignored the research of corporate criminology, which has found that all corporate crime and violence combined inflicts far greater damage on society than all street crime combined.

Apparently, Cohen did not take into account Exxon, International Paper, United Technologies, Weyerhauser, Pillsbury, Ashland Oil, Texaco, Nabisco, and Ralston-Purina, all convicted of environmental crimes in recent years. All of these convicted corporations operate in Washington, D.C. None of them are young black males.

All of the 46 individuals convicted in the Operation Ill-Wind prosecution of defense procurement fraud were white males. The six corporations convicted in that operation—Cubic, Hazeltine, Loral, Sperry/Unisys, Teledyne, and Whittaker—are controlled by white males. And of the people convicted in the recent Wall Street insider trading scandals, the vast majority were white males. Cohen apparently redlines these white-collar criminals and their Washington associates from his definition of crime.

Jeffrey Parker, an associate professor of law at George Mason University School of Law, put forth the idea earlier this year that "there is no corporate crime—only individuals can commit crime."

"Crime can only be committed by an individual human being who can be held morally responsible through punishment," Parker wrote. "The idea of 'corporate crime' is a corruption of the core meaning of crime and a dilution of the underlying ethic of individual moral responsible and autonomy."

Parker's theoretical idea that a "corporation has no mind, and therefore cannot commit crime" defies reality. Sure, a corporation doesn't have a mind in the human sense, but as Thomas Donaldson points out in his book, *Corporations and Morality*, corporations have "practical and theoretical knowledge that dwarfs that of individuals."

And their crimes dwarf those of individuals, too. In support of a different view of criminology, specifically, that a corporation can commit a crime, that white people commit more crime than black people and that television is still a vast wasteland, we present the Ten Worst Corporations of 1991.

ALYESKA: Invasion of Privacy

Charles Hamel is a former oil industry executive in Alaska. He left the business when he discovered that oil he was sending to foreign customers was significantly diluted with water. Hamel investigated the problem and found that the oil companies were aware of the water problem but failed to take action to correct it. "Instead, they denied the truth, and apparently hoped that I would forget about my business, the damage to my credibility and reputation and my lost income," Hamel says.

In 1985, Hamel decided to expose the "dishonesty of the oil industry." In addition to the water-in-the-oil problem, Hamel concluded that "the oil industry was turning Alaska into an environmental disaster."

Hamel focused his attention on Alyeska Pipeline Service Co., the consortium which represents the major oil companies operating in Alaska.

"The more I heard, the angrier I got about what was going on," Hamel told a congressional committee earlier this year. "Alyeska was polluting the water by introducing toxic sludge, including cancer-causing benzene, into the pristine waters of Port Valdez and Prince William Sound. Alyeska was poisoning the Valdez fjord's air by venting extremely hazardous hydrocarbon vapor directly into the atmosphere."

Alyeska insiders began turning information over to Hamel about environmental and other violation committed by Alyeska. Hamel passed the information to federal enforcement agencies, to the media and to Congress.

Hamel's advocacy led to enforcement actions, news stories, congressional investigations and growing public awareness of the problems of oil in Alaska. He became a major thorn in the side of the industry.

Then, Alyeska sought to silence Hamel. The company hired Wackenhut Corp., a major security firm, to investigate Hamel. Alyeska claims that it hired Wackenhut to recover "stolen documents." But Representative George Miller, D-California, who investigated the Alyeska/Wackenhut operation, said that the surveillance operation "involved the much more sinister and disturbing motives of silencing environmental critics and intimidating whistleblowers."

Wackenhut created a fake environmental group to try to trick Hamel. "One day in April 1990, a Dr. Wayne Jenkins came to me," Hamel told Representative Miller's Committee on Interior and Insular Affairs earlier this year. "He described his company, Ecolit Groups, as a well-funded group of attorneys who wanted to help me. They would provide me the tools to protect these workers who had turned to me for help. Ecolit could help protect their jobs, and supply me support staff and assistance to manage what had become a full-time, financially costly job of protecting whistleblowers and coordinating government investigations. I thought it was too good to be true." And it was. Dr. Wayne Jenkins was in fact a Wackenhut investigator. Wackenhut surreptitiously videotaped the meetings with Hamel. And that was only the beginning.

"Alyeska authorized stealing our trash, monitoring and taping our telephone calls, concealing video cameras in a hotel room, stealing our mail and illegally obtaining our personal and financial information," Hamel testified.

Based on the information gathered through this surreptitious operation, Alyeska fired a number of employees who fed Hamel information.

Virginia state police are investigating allegations that Alyeska and Wackenhut might have violated state laws by secretly intercepting Hamel's telephone calls.

Miller's committee believes that the Wackenhut/Alyeska operation may have violated federal mail and wire fraud statutes, and laws governing theft, eavesdropping, tape recording and obtaining telephone toll records. Both companies deny engaging in any illegal activities.

"I refuse to believe that any citizen of this country has to tolerate the invasion of privacy that I have been subjected to simply because I have exercised my Constitutional rights and responsibilities as a citizen to petition Congress," Hamel says.

AMERICAN HOME PRODUCTS:
Puerto Rican Racket

What do Chef Boyardee pasta, Jiffy Pop popcorn, Wheatena, Advil, Anacin, Robitussin, Dristan have in common? They are all made by American Home Products Corp., a company that cares little about its worker.

In November 1990, AHP announced that it would close down its Whitehall plant in Elkhart, Indiana, throw its 775 employee out of work and move the facility to Guyama, Puerto Rico.

Unfortunately for American Home Products (AHP), its Indiana workers refused to go quietly into the night. Last year, the Oil, Chemical and Atomic Workers Union (OCAW) launched a grassroots campaign called "Keep Whitehall Open: Hometowns Against Shutdowns" to prevent the plant from closing [See "American Home Products Moves Abroad," *Multinational Monitor*, April 1991]. The campaign has seen a number of street actions and numerous lawsuits against AHP, including a $100 million racketeering lawsuit. The National Labor Relations Board has charged the company with numerous labor law violations.

"The closure of Whitehall looms like a death sentence over our members," says Connie Malloy, president of OCAW local 7-515. "American Home Products has displayed a total lack of respect for the law and a total lack of respect for [its] long-term employees."

In Puerto Rico, U.S. District Court Judge Jaime Pieras agreed with Malloy, at least in part. In August 1991, Pieras cited AHP for an "outrageous violation" of a discovery order in connection with the racketeering lawsuit. Pieras held that AHP had improperly withheld thousands of documents which the labor union had requested.

OCAW's racketeering lawsuit, filed in January 1991, alleges that American Home Products fraudulently obtained federal tax benefits by falsely certifying that the plant would not harm existing employment in company facilities on the U.S. mainland. Under federal tax law, corporations cannot utilize a number of tax breaks available in Puerto Rico if mainland jobs will be lost as a consequence.

CLOROX: Mud Ball

Everybody's Business: A Field Guide to the 400 Leading Companies in America, by Milton Moskowitz, Robert Levering and Michael Katz, calls Clorox "a good corporate citizen in their hometown of Oakland."

But the giant bleach manufacturer has its dirty side, too, and that side reared its ugly head earlier this year when a public relations firm prepared a "Crisis Management Plan" for Clorox, advising the company on how to deal with the environmental movement.

The plan, prepared for Clorox by the public relations division of Ketchum Communications, recommends labeling environmental critics as "terrorists," threatening to sue "unalterably green" journalists, dispatching "independent scientists" on media tours as a means to counteract bad news for the chlorine industry and recruiting "scientific ambassadors" to tout the Clorox cause and call for further study. The Clorox plan makes reference to studies linking chlorine use to cancer, and suggests key ways to discredit the findings if they ever become public.

The plan was apparently prompted by fears that the environmental group Greenpeace would target household use of chlorine bleach and call for its elimination.

And those fears proved correct later in the year when Greenpeace issued a scathing report, "The Product Is Poison: The Case for a Chlorine Phase-Out." According to the report, chlorine is one of the world's most severe toxic pollutants and should be phased out. The report also called for plans to protect the 10,000 to 20,000 workers employed in the chlorine industry and the communities where such industries are located. The report found that in U.S. and Canadian populations, 177 organochlorines have been identified in human fat, breast milk, blood, semen and breath.

Greenpeace has instituted an international program aimed at ending the use of chlorine in the pulp and paper industry. Greenpeace's slogan, "Chlorine-Free in 1993" is cited in the Clorox crisis management plan, which outlines numerous "worst case scenarios" in which Greenpeace and "unalterably green" journalists figure prominently.

Water pollution from the use of chlorine in the paper industry has contaminated rivers, streams and lakes throughout the world. Chlorine is the base chemical in DDT, PCBs, Agent Orange, CFCs and many other persistent toxic pollutants, according to Greenpeace's Shelly Stewart.

Fred Reichler, Clorox's director of corporate communications, backed away from the plan when stories about it hit the press in May of this year, saying that the plan was "rejected by Clorox." But, he added, "all responsible corporations must be aware of issues that may affect their products and services."

Du PONT: Worst Polluter

Earlier this year, E.l. Du Pont de Nemours & Company began running a television advertisement featuring sea lions, otters, dolphins and penguins playing in their natural environments while Beethoven's "Ode to Joy" plays in the background. The 30-second commercial shows a shoreline and pans the horizon, as the narrator remarks, "Recently, Du Pont announced that its energy unit would pioneer the use of new double-hulled oil bankers in order to safeguard the environment."

Friends of the Earth's Jack Doyle points out, however, that Du Pont's oil subsidiary, Conoco, does not have any double-hulled ships in service and that its fleet will not be doubled hulled until the year 2000. And the company has no plans to put double hulls in two of its supertankers, according to Doyle.

The advertisement "is doubly effective, because it doesn't just make us feel good about Du Pont—it makes us feel good about Du Pont the environmental company," Doyle says.

In fact, Du Pont is the nation's number one corporate polluter. According to an exhaustive report issued by Friends of the Earth earlier this year, Du Pont has paid out nearly $1 million in fines, penalties or lawsuit settlements for alleged environmental and public health problems between March 1989 and June 1991. Du Pont reported that it emitted 348 million pounds

of pollution in 1989—14 times more than Dow Chemical, 20 times more than Chrysler, and 30 times more than Mobil. The Friends of the Earth report, "Hold the Applause," found that, among the largest 10 companies in 1989, Du Pont had the highest ratio of pollution to profit and the lowest value of sales generated per pound of U.S. pollution.

According to the study, Du Pont has dumped pollutants into the world oceans, invented chemicals which are now destroying the earth's protective ozone layer, injected millions of pounds of hazardous wastes underground with unknown consequences, produced pesticides that have infiltrated the world's foodstuffs and drinking water, sold lead additives for gasoline in developing countries and lobbied Congress, state legislatures and foreign governments to oppose or weaken environmental measures.

An incident reported earlier this year sheds light on the company's callousness and disregard for human life. The *News Journal* of Wilmington, Delaware reported that, in its quest to develop a method of dry-cleaning women's clothing, Du Pont exposed volunteers to Freon 113 during early experiments, leading to the death of a company secretary. Du Pont continued the experiments even after the death of 44-year-old Beverly B. Manning, according to company documents obtained by the *Journal*.

But if large megacorporations go the way of the dinosaurs, Du Pont will probably be most remembered for producing chlorofluorocarbons (CFCs), the chemicals which destroy the earth's protective ozone layer. The Environmental Protection Agency estimates that increased exposure to ultraviolet rays brought on by ozone destruction will result in 200,000 additional U.S. skin cancer-related deaths over the next 50 years.

"Du Pont is perhaps most culpable for stringing out the CFC era for its own business reasons and for delaying a shift to safe alternatives," asserts Doyle [See "Du Pont's Disgraceful Deeds: The Environmental Record of E.l. Du Pont de Nemours," *Multinational Monitor*, October 1991].

ETHYL CORPORATION:
Poisoning Third World Children

The hazards of lead to children are well known: low birth weight, decreased intelligence, behavioral abnormalities and other life-long, irreversible damage. A public education campaign in a number of Western countries forced governments to ban lead additives in gasoline.

However, a U.S. corporation still produces tetraethyl lead (TEL), a toxic gasoline additive—for export to Third World countries.

"Ethyl is exporting a developmental toxin to developing countries," says Kenny Bruno, coordinator of Greenpeace's Hazardous Exports Prevention Campaign. "Lead was taken out of gasoline in North America after it poisoned countless children, but Ethyl continues to export lead additives abroad. Ethyl's decision to fuel profits by exporting this deadly [chemical] demonstrates contempt for children around the world" [See "Poison Petrol: Leaded Gas Exports to the Third World," *Multinational Monitor*, July/August 1991].

While most industrialized countries have banned or reduced the use of leaded fuel, Ethyl, which manufactures TEL at a plant in Canada near Sarnia, Ontario, applied for permission to double its production capacity of the additive. Later, under pressure from environmentalists, the company abandoned its expansion plans, announcing that it would instead buy TEL from other suppliers.

Ethyl is one of only three companies in the world that produce TEL. The others are Du Pont and the United Kingdom-based Octel. Ethyl, the second-largest producer of the additive, insists that TEL is not linked to lead poisoning.

But, according to Dr. Sergio Piomelli, a hematologist at Columbia University who has published a number of studies on lead poisoning, there is very strong evidence that lead exposure even at low levels interferes with the intellectual function of the developing brain.

"The removal of lead from gasoline in this country has had a fantastic effect on children's health," Dr. Piomelli says. "It is unfair and immoral to inflict more exposure to lead on children in developing countries."

Many Third World countries still rely exclusively on highly leaded fuel. According to David Schwartzmann, professor of geology at Howard University, lead poisoning of children in the Third World cities "can be expected to be truly epidemic."

Bruno concludes that "there is no technological impediment to preventing almost all of the lead contamination stemming from the use of leaded gasoline."

It's the political impediment—Ethyl Corp and the other lead additive producers—that's blocking change and creating health problems worldwide.

GENERAL ELECTRIC:
Bringing Nasty Things to Life

After a two-year absence, General Electric (GE) is back on the Ten Worst List. General Electric is still a criminal recidivist company, it is still heavily engaged in building weapons of mass destruction, and it still trying to whitewash its image by flooding the national media with its catchy jingle, " GE Brings Good Things to Life."

But the people at INFACT, the Boston-based public interest group that is calling for a consumer boycott of all GE products, want you to know that GE has brought some very bad things to the environment, too—namely extensive pollution and contamination.

In a report released last year, "Bringing GE to Light: General Electric's Trail of Radioactive and Toxic Contamination from the Company's Nuclear Weapons Work," INFACT found that GE's nuclear weapons work has created environment health and safety nightmares across the United States.

INFACT charges that GE knowingly contaminated residents of Washington, Oregon and Idaho with radioactive contamination from its Hanford nuclear weapons facility. Workers and communities faced similar dangerous contamination problems at GE facilities throughout the country.

In addition, the report found that:

▪ GE ranks number 1 in Superfund sites, being a "potentially responsible party" at 51 sites as of August 1990.

▪ GE released more cancer-causing chemicals into the environment than any other U.S. company during 1988.

▪ While conducting a nationwide repair program for over one million of its refrigerators, GE intentionally released more than 300,000 pounds of CFCs into the atmosphere where they destroy the Earth's protective layer.

▪ For over 30 years, GE dumped hundreds of thousands of pounds of PCBs, which cause birth defects and may cause cancer, into New York's Hudson River. Over 250,000 pounds remain in the river bottom. All fishing is banned in sections of the river and commercial fisheries for striped bass had to be shut down as far as Long Island.

▪ In 1977, an epidemiologist noticed high levels of cancer and leukemia among workers at GE's plant in Pittsfield, Massachusetts. He began a study that initially showed an excessive number of deaths. Then GE took over the funding and the provision of employee records for the study. In 1990, GE announced that the study failed to find a link between toxics used at the plant and cancer deaths, and that there would be no further studies. A closer look at the present study shows a number of "associations" between toxics and specific cancers found among workers at the plant.

And in a report released earlier this year, "Workers At Risk: A Survey of OSHA's Enforcement Record Against the 50 Largest U.S. Corporations," Essential Information's James Donahue found that of the 50 largest industrial corporations surveyed, General Electric was by far the most frequent violator of federal workplace and safety health laws. From 1977 through 1990, GE received 2,017 citations and paid a penalty for 27.3 percent of those citations. GE received 550 penalties during the period, more than any other corporation in the survey.

GE was also heavily involved in killing in the Persian Gulf. INFACT reported that GE received nearly $2 billion in U.S. military contracts for systems employed in the Gulf War effort.

GE owns NBC, the television network. During the Gulf War, as the media watchdog group FAIR has pointed out, "Conflicts of interest at NBC were an ongoing problem, as when the network aired a laudatory segment on the Patriot missile (1.18.91), for which GE produces parts. [NBC anchor Tom Brokaw] called the Patriot 'the missile that put the Iraqi scud in its place.'"

FAIR also reported that "the government of Kuwait is believed to be a major GE shareholder having owned 2.1 percent of GE stock in 1982, the last year for which figures are available."

Conflicts of interest at NBC have not been confined to the war. When NBC's "Today" show did a segment on consumer boycotts around the country, many consumer products from Spam to Marlboros were mentioned. GE's light bulbs were left out. Todd Butnam, editor of the National Boycott News, says a "Today" show staffer told him "We can't do that one [GE]. Well, we could do that one, but we won't."

Another "Today" producer joked that he would be looking for a job if he publicized the GE boycott on NBC.

G. HEILEMAN BREWING CO.:
Racist Marketing

In June of this year, G. Heileman Brewing Co., the Milwaukee brewer of Old Style, Schmidt, Tuborg, Carling Black Label, Iron City and a number of other college favorites, decided to focus its energies on the African-American community. Heileman unveiled PowerMaster, a malt liquor that contained 31 percent more alcohol than other malt liquors, including Colt45, also manufactured by G. Heileman, and 60 percent more alcohol than regular beer. PowerMaster had an alcohol content of 7.5 percent and was marketed primarily in minority neighborhoods already plagued by high rates of alcohol-related diseases.

But unlike other sexist and racist advertising campaigns launched by the alcohol industry in recent years, the PowerMaster campaign died a quick death after a flood of public interest criticism. Within a week of press reports that PowerMaster was hitting the street, a coalition of 21 community, consumer and health groups called on G. Heileman to halt the marketing of PowerMaster and asked the Bureau of Alcohol, Tobacco and Firearms (BATF) to require malt liquor products to have no more alcohol than regular beer. In a letter to Heileman, the groups called on the company to remove PowerMaster from the market and charged that "given the growing public concern and outcry about the extent of alcohol-related disease and crime problems facing urban America, we believe that the targeting of the product to inner-city communities is particularly irresponsible." Boycotts of other G. Heileman products were planned in 25 cities.

U.S. Surgeon General Antonia Novello said she wanted G. Heileman to change the name of PowerMaster and scrap a marketing campaign aimed at minority consumers who were already at risk for alcoholism. *Food and Drink Daily* reported that the BATF was examining all malt liquor ads and labeling. Fathers Michael Pfelger and George Clement were arrested while trying to meet with Heileman officials. In Chicago, liquor stores posted signs saying "We will not sell PowerMaster in this store!! Save our Children!!"

Reverend Calvin Butts of the Abyssinian Baptist Church in Harlem condemned Heileman and the "insidious and diabolical marketing methods" of this new malt liquor.

"PowerMaster is marketed to primarily low-income, powerless people so you get a feeling of euphoria and [a sense] that you are powerful and masterful when in fact things that make you powerful and masterful you are not doing— you're drinking malt liquor," said Reverend Butts.

"Nightline" even did a show on Power-Master. The already bankrupt Heileman couldn't take the public pressure and buckled. In July, it announced that it was scrapping its plans to market PowerMaster, and by October, the potent brew was reportedly off the market.

"The withdrawal of PowerMaster puts out the message to all the other malt makers and to tobacco and alcohol companies in general that we aren't sitting back and watching you stomp and kill and destroy and then just saying 'that's too bad,'" Reverend Pfleger of the St. Sabina Church in Chicago told the *Wall Street Journal*. "That era is over."

KELLOGG'S: Harassing the Police

"Kellogg's constantly lies about its products. I don't believe anything Kellogg's tells me."

Who said this? A person giving an on-the-street interview? An agitated consumer? No, it's Stephen Gardner, a tough cop with a rough edge.

Gardner is an assistant attorney general in Texas, and chief of the attorney general's consumer protection division.

Gardner led Texas and five other states into legal battle with Kellogg's, charging the giant cereal maker with making false nutritional claims about a number of its cereal products.

"I do believe that Kellogg's lies about its products to the public," Gardner says. "And I do believe that Kellogg's has lied to me and to the court on any number of occasions to gain an advantage in the litigation. I don't trust them."

In May 1991, Kellogg's sued Gardner for slander accusing him of launching a "media assault" against the company.

In fact, what probably disturbed Kellogg's the most was Gardner's idea of protecting the public trust. During the late 1980s, Gardner led Texas, Iowa, Minnesota, California, Florida and Wisconsin in an investigation of Kellogg's claims about a number of its cereals, including Special K and Sugar Frosted Flakes and Heartwise. The states alleged that Kellogg's deceptively promoted Special K as a high protein cereal which dieters could use to "keep the muscle but lose the fat." The states charged Kellogg's with using "scare tactics" by telling dieters they would lose their muscle tone without eating enough protein. "That's simply not true," Gardner said.

The states also investigated Kellogg's Heartwise cereal. In 1990 Gardner's office determined that in marketing Heartwise, Kellogg's was actually promoting a laxative as a breakfast cereal. There is a fundamental issue about whether it's safe to put a laxative in a breakfast cereal, Gardner said. This is compounded by the fact that Kellogg's admittedly has received over five dozen complaints of allergic reactions from people who ate Heartwise.

Kellogg's has since stopped making the disputed claims for each of the three products but has refused to settle with the states.

Kellogg's slander complaint alleges that on a WFAA-TV news telecast in Dallas, Gardner made the "false statement" that the intended use of this stuff [referring to Heartwise] is going to give you diarrhea. And the state of Texas wants to know if Kellogg's ought to be selling mommies and daddies laxatives to feed their kids at breakfast time.

"These statements constitute a slanderous attack on the good name and reputation of Kellogg's Company," a company spokesperson said.

Texas Attorney General Dan Morales calls the slander suit against his associate Gardner "a harassment suit."

Gardner isn't backing down. "I believe that if we have to, we can establish that Kellogg's is a liar," Gardner says. When—as I anticipate—

Kellogg's does violate the law in some new and novel way in the future, we'll be in touch with them."

HOFFMAN LA ROCHE:
80 Dead and Counting

The giant Swiss drug manufacturer F. Hoffman La Roche discounted early warnings by its U.S. counterpart that a drug used as a sedative and an anesthesiac could cause deadly side effects if sold in a highly concentrated form, according to internal company documents released earlier this year.

The documents indicate that the company's marketing division felt that the problem was "less significant" than the "commercial exploitation" of the drug. Roche went forward and sold the drug, Versed, in the more concentrated form. Versed has been linked to about 80 deaths and many more near fatalities.

In July 1991, Public Citizen's Health Research Group called on the Bush administration to launch a criminal investigation of the company for failing to report key findings about the hazards of Versed to the government. The Bush administration has yet to act.

"It is clear from FDA's own chronology of the events between initial U.S. approval of the concentrated (5mg/ml) dosage form in December 1985 and the eventual introduction of [the safe, less concentrated] (1mg/ml) dosage form in July 1987, that FDA had not been informed of Roche's internal evidence that the concentrated dosage form was so dangerous for many patients, especially those getting the drug for diagnostic procedures so-called conscious sedation where an anesthesiologist is not present," says Public Citizen's Dr. Sidney Wolfe.

The company has denied that the more concentrated form of Versed is unsafe and that it discounted safety concerns for marketing considerations.

The incriminating documents include correspondence between Roche's U.S. affiliate in Nutley, New Jersey and its Swiss headquarters in Basel, Switzerland. The documents also include a summary and analysis of the correspondence between the Basel headquarters and the Nutley division prepared by the Washington D.C. law firm of Arnold & Porter prior to a Food and Drug Administration investigation into the marketing of the drug.

The Arnold & Porter memorandum, marked confidential, concluded, "One interpretation possible from these documents is that Roche/Nutley disregarded its own concerns for safety of the drug in favor of the marketing and political pressure from Roche/Basel."

"When the drug came out, I was very surprised at the concentration and I ran some of the dosage numbers and found it was a dreadful mistake—that the drug was too concentrated for physicians to use responsibly," says Dr. Robert M. Julien, an anesthesiologist based in Portland, Oregon.

"My feeling was that the company was desperately trying to protect its Valium market with a very expensive brand-named drug," Dr. Julien says. "When it was marketed in early 1987, it was purported to be a Valium replacement and Valium look alike. It is clear that Versed is about four to six times as potent as Valium—although it was purported to be equal to Valium."

Dr. Julien calls Roche "irresponsible" and says that he thinks the company should remove the highly concentrated form from the market.

Public Citizen's Dr. Wolfe is calling on the FDA to punish Hoffman La Roche. "Roche was well aware of this problem and that it was essential to also provide a more dilute dosage form in order to prevent deaths and serious injuries," Wolfe wrote to FDA chief David Kessler. "This important information appears to have been withheld from FDA for a significant amount of time, resulting in dozens of preventable deaths in this country. According to FDA officials, the belated introduction of the more dilute dosage form has been accompanied by a significant reduction in these tragic

preventable deaths. The full force of the law must be applied to the Roche officials responsible for these lost lives. Even a fine of hundreds of thousands of dollars would be far too lenient. We hope that your investigation will also lead to imprisonment for the Roche officials."

PROCTER & GAMBLE:
Of Dirty Rivers, Disposable Diapers and Coffee from El Salvador

You would think that a company that makes products with such names as Ivory Snow, Mr. Clean, Sure and Sunny Delight would keep its operations clean, sure and sunny. Think again.

Every day, Procter & Gamble's cellulose plant in Florida dumps 50 million gallons of wastewater into the Fenholloway River, which was once known for its healing mineral springs.

Health officials have told residents not to eat fish from the river because of dioxin contamination. Chemicals have seeped from the river into drinking water wells. Procter & Gamble (P&G) now supplies bottled drinking water for area residents and for workers at its plant.

Environmental Protection Agency (EPA) officials say that, in parts of the river, fish are no longer found. In other parts female fish have been found with male characteristics.

The pollution of the river has been going on for years. Earlier this year, Julie Hauserman, a reporter with the *Tallahassee Democrat*, pushed the plight of the Fenholloway into the public spotlight with a series of articles titled "Florida's Forgotten River."

According to the *Democrat*, since March 1991, environmentalists have petitioned the EPA to overstep Florida environmental officials and upgrade the river from its industrial classification to a recreational river where fish can survive and people can swim. State officials are now undertaking the most extensive review of P&G's permit since the plant was opened to determine whether it should retain its permit.

"It's the worst river I've ever seen," says David Ludder, an attorney with the Tallahassee-based Legal Environmental Assistance Foundation. Ludder says the contaminants released into the river include a wide range of chemicals such as ammonia, bromide, organic nitrogen, oil and grease, dioxin, lead, mercury, phosphorus, magnesium and phenols. "The color in the discharge has effectively prevented sunlight from reaching the bottom of the river as well as from reaching the bottom of the Gulf of Mexico where the Fenholloway flows," he says. "The result is that plant life and the aquatic organisms that depend on sunlight can't survive. Chemicals have consumed the available oxygen in the water."

Ludder says that P&G has polluted the river without violating state and federal environmental laws, but that enforcement action may be possible for the contamination of the groundwater.

P&G, the maker of Luvs and Pampers disposable diapers is the nation's largest disposable diaper manufacturer. Earlier this year, attorneys general from 10 states forced P&G to agree to refrain from claiming on labels and in advertising that its diapers are readily degradable.

New York Attorney General Robert Abrams said that the company's advertisements create the overall impression that the diapers are completely biodegradable and make it appear to consumers that they need not worry about the solid waste problems posed by disposable diapers because they will somehow turn into environmentally benign dirt in a matter of months.

"To make an environmentally informed choice, consumers need truthful and accurate information not slogans aimed at making them feel good," Abrams said. "By promoting their disposable diapers as compostable, when facilities that accept diapers for composting are virtually unavailable, Procter & Gamble is deceiving consumers who are concerned about the trade-offs between using disposable diapers and limiting solid waste."

One last thing—Neighbor to Neighbor is into the third year of its boycott of P&G's Folgers coffee because the company buys its coffee beans from El Salvador, where a small group of elite families controls coffee production (and the rest of the economy) and where death squads and the military have murdered tens of thousands of civilians over the last decade. Earlier this year, P&G announced that it is developing a new blend of coffee that does not contain coffee beans from El Salvador. But for now P&G is still using El Salvador beans in Folgers, so the boycott is still on.

#3

Bush's Ruling Class by Jeffrey Denny, Vicki Kemper, Viveca Novak, Peter Overby and Amy E. Young. Interns Katherine Leo, D.E. Spealman and Alison Widmer contributed research; *Common Cause* Magazine • April/May/June 1992

A *Common Cause* Magazine investigation reveals a pattern of special favors for the president's inner circle of $100,000 donors.

At a California campaign fundraiser in February, President Bush asked Howard Leach, a wealthy Salinas farm investor, what worried the local citizenry. Water, Leach said. Because of the lengthy drought, the Interior Department had cut off agribusiness's subsidized federal water from the Central Valley Project, a massive system of dams and reservoirs.

Bush "was obviously sensitive to this," Leach says. "He clearly was interested and sympathetic."

Ten days later, the president unveiled a 326 billion-gallon emergency allocation of Central Valley water for local growers—enough to serve five million urban customers for 18 months. With one quick move, Bush reversed the Interior Department's plan to release no water this spring.

Naturally, regional growers were pleased. But none could have been happier than the single largest user of Central Valley Project water, the controversial land trust operated by longtime Leach acquaintance J.G. Boswell and his son James W. To a much smaller extent it also helped Leach's old friend Howard Marguleas and his produce marketing firm Sun World International, which grows fruit on a 960-acre Central Valley spread.

Leach, James Boswell and Marguleas have something else in common: All three are members of President Bush's Team 100, the 249 wealthy individuals who poined up at least $100,000 each in "soft money"—a total of $25 million—to help elect Bush in 1988. Soft money is used to evade federal campaign laws, which, among other things, limit contributions to a presidential candidate to $1,000 per election.

Administration officials claim that heavy February rains, not political favoritism, made the water available. But taxpayers can be forgiven for wondering.

Boswell officials did not return telephone calls. Leach says he's not sure whether he benefits.

President Bush's policy reversal raises an important question: Given the political potency of Bush's Team 100, to what extent have donors been able to pull strings in the executive branch at the expense of the public?

A six-month investigation reveals that by financing the president's election with six-figure contributions, Team 100 has ensured access and influence in the executive branch while seeking, obtaining and protecting:

- executive-branch pork barrel handouts;
- vigorous import-export assistance;
- high-level intervention on regulatory and other matters;
- appointments to ambassadorships and federal advisory commissions;
- broad national policies for wealthy Wall Street, oil, real estate and cable television interests.

Bush's clean air proposal to Congress, for example, included special provisions promoting alternative automobile fuels important to three Team 100 members: ethanol to benefit Dwayne Andreas's company Archer Daniels Midland (ADM); natural gas to benefit T. Boone Pickens's Mesa company; and reformulated gasoline to benefit Lodwrick Cook's Atlantic Richfield (Arco).

While direct quid quo pros are inherently difficult to prove, a clear pattern of questionable actions and policy reversals favorable to Team 100 members emerges from government records, corporate reports, interviews, and industry and press reports.

The White House did not respond to a written request for comment.

INNER CIRCLE

Who would give $100,000—the average American's four-year earnings and 100 times the legal limit—to help elect the president?

"Most who give in that range are giving with some political self-interest," says Thomas McBride, associate special Watergate prosecutor whose campaign finance task force won conviction of several corporate Nixon donors. "They're hoping for an ambassadorial or government appointment, hoping they'll be fondly remembered for White House social events, hoping for access to high decision-making counsels. Or it's even more directly related to some pending matter in the government."

Bush's $100,000 donors are among the nation's wealthiest individuals and represent a number of influential special interests who've also thrown political money around Congress for years. Along with Manhattan real estate mogul Donald Trump, Wall Street takeover artist Henry Kravis, and convicted S&L kingpin Charles Keating, Bush's team includes top executives of major investment firms, oil companies, government contractors and multinational corporations enriched by federal subsidies and protected by import barriers.

Two of Bush's $100,000 donors were invited to join the president on his controversial trip to Japan in January, which directly helped one of them close a business deal. At least four Team 100 donors—Kenneth Good, Louis Marx, Jackson Stephens and Bill Daniels—have done business with or given jobs to the president's sons.

Since 1988, a number of Team 100 donors and the companies they represent have continued to make large soft money contributions to the Republican National Committee (RNC) and the so-called "President's Dinner," a GOP fundraising drive hosted by Bush.

Team 100 members retain expensive, well-connected lobbyists and top-flight regulatory lawyers—including a number of former Bush administration and current campaign officials. Charles Black, a Bush campaign senior adviser, is retained by the Trump Organization and A. James Clark, the nation's third-largest general contractor. James Lake, the Bush campaign's deputy chair, represents Central Valley water users like Boswell and Marguleas.

These $100,000 donors not only give money, but also help raise it for Bush. Texas oilman Bobby Holt is finance chair of Bush-Quayle '92, and Kravis and Florida sugar baron Jose "Pepe" Fanjul are chair and vice chair, respectively, of the campaign's finance committee.

Robert Mosbacher, a longtime Bush intimate and chief political money man, masterminded the Team 100 fundraising drive in 1988; he recently quit his job as secretary of commerce to chair Bush's reelection campaign.

WATERGATE REDUX

The Bush administration's actions on behalf of $100,000 donors raise striking parallels to the Watergate scandal, which broke 20 years ago this summer.

Among other things, fundraisers for CREEP, Nixon's Committee to Reelect the President, dunned corporate executives whose firms had extensive matters pending before the administration, offering to include them in a "select class" of $100,000 donors.

As the Watergate scandal unfolded, the Nixon administration's decision to raise milk price supports was linked to the milk producers' pledge of funds to Nixon's 1972 campaign. And an internal memo written by International Telephone & Telegraph (ITT) lobbyist Dita Beard suggested that the Nixon Justice Department had dropped three antitrust suits against the firm in return for its $400,000 pledge to help finance the GOP convention in 1972. Several CREEP donors were rewarded with ambassadorships.

George Bush (whom Nixon chose as national party chair in the midst of the Watergate scandal), has invited $100,000 donors back into the business of financing presidential elections and influencing the White House. Several Team 100 members in fact were CREEP donors, including insurance executive W. Clement Stone; ADM Chair Dwayne Andreas; Florida developer Alec Courtelis, who took over Team 100 from Robert Mosbacher in 1989; and Mosbacher.

According to Sam Dash, chief counsel of the Senate Watergate Committee and now a Georgetown University law professor, the reappearance of these names indicates "a lack of respect for what it was that angered the American people in Watergate. And they're back because they're hardball players."

Stone's campaign contributions helped finance Bush's failed Senate campaign in 1970, according to the *Washington Post*. Bush and Mosbacher, his finance chair even then, received $106,000 from "Operation Townhouse," a secret operation run by two Nixon aid-es who later pleaded guilty to running an illegal campaign fundraising operation. Four checks of $10,000 each came from Stone.

"It has come to my attention that you sent down a fantastically generous contribution to my campaign," Bush wrote Stone in 1970.

"Thanks ever so much.... I really believe we will win and I'm most grateful to you for your help."

Just this spring, Nixon addressed a gathering of Bush's $100,000 donors at a California hotel. Team 100 gave Nixon a two-minute standing ovation.

SHORT-CIRCUIT

Does Team 100 operate with a different set of rules, or does it just seem that way?

After more than a decade of political and legal wrangling, Denver area officials were relieved when workers broke ground on the area's new $2.7 billion international airport in 1989.

But last year, George Doughty, Denver International director of aviation, began hearing ominous rumors. A small, general aviation airfield just five miles away, Front Range, suddenly was courting big cargo carriers like Federal Express and United Parcel Service (UPS).

Doughty didn't believe it; big jets couldn't land on Front Range's short, light-duty runways.

"They were planning, and didn't tell us, to amend their airport layout plan to extend and strengthen those runways" with a $35 million federal grant, says Doughty—violating a regional council of governments agreement and luring away some of the paying traffic Denver International had counted on.

Denver officials soon learned that Front Range's plans are inextricably tied to those of a group of private developers—including William Lloyd Davis, a California real estate investor who gave $100,000 in soft money to help Bush's 1988 campaign and another $76,540 since then to Bush's national party. The group wants the small airport upgraded to be the hub of an industrial park project called Centerport they plan to build next door.

Davis's involvement seemed to explain a lot. Doughty says he and other city officials were told by Federal Aviation Administration (FAA) authorities that Front Range was likely to get the federal grant and they should not stand in the way. Still hoping for additional federal money for their own Denver International, city officials relented, signing an agreement with Front Range officials saying the two airfields would compete for cargo traffic. They also dropped objections to the project's environmental assessment.

"The political influence of the Centerport folks certainly was a factor" in what he believes was an end run by Front Range, Doughty says. "They at least had entree into the [transportation] secretary's office and into the White House." Then-Secretary of Transportation (now White House Chief of Staff) Samuel Skinner told him he had met with Centerport representatives, Doughty says.

"There was a much higher level of interest in this by the FAA than the project ever should have gotten," Doughty continues. "The [FAA] associate administrator for airports [Leonard Griggs] was trying to broker an agreement with us."

Griggs did not respond to requests for an interview, but an FAA spokesperson says Griggs did meet with Centerport representatives, as did other FAA personnel.

"The Centerport people have been very involved," says Randy Broderson, administrator of Adams County, which runs Front Range. "I know that they have been meeting with FAA people in Washington and locally and regionally."

An FAA spokesperson denies that Davis's contributions influenced the agency's actions.

Doughty isn't so sure. "Mr. Davis is a major contributor to the Republican Party," he says. "Our point is this is a federal subsidy of a private corporation."

The Environmental Protection Agency (EPA) also raised questions in objecting to the project's environmental assessment. The FAA is supposed to evaluate the need for major airport projects before it can proceed. The only need for this one, said EPA, is to "meet a 'strategic business plan' promoting a privately envisioned market mission"—meaning Centerport.

Nonetheless, in mid-March the FAA approved the environmental assessment. It was a major victory for the Front Range-Centerport backers: Had the FAA nixed the document, they would have had to go through the much more time-consuming and costly process of preparing a full-blown environmental impact statement.

The approval came two weeks after Davis vice-chaired a $1,000-a-plate fundraiser for Bush-Quayle, which brought in more than $1.25 million.

Though Denver tried to win back the major cargo carriers, Federal Express and UPS committed to the smaller airport in early April.

Many who have fought for Denver International remain angry. "I can't believe the FAA would allow another airport with major jet traffic to operate so close" to Denver International, says one city council aide. "With the right kind of influence, I guess you can get a lot of things done."

POWER PLAY

It's still not clear why the Justice Department killed a federal criminal investigation involving one of the nation's largest public utility companies.

In February 1988 Georgia Power accountant Gary Gilman paid a secret visit to the IRS. Gilman claimed that Georgia Power and its parent, Southern Company Services, had written off some $50 million in spare parts that were still on the shelf, and may have done so improperly. To keep track of the spare parts, Gilman said, officials devised an "off the books" accounting system and instructed personnel to destroy or take documents home, according to an affidavit filed in U.S. District Court in Atlanta by IRS Special Agent Arthur McGovern.

Gilman went back to work outfitted by the IRS with a hidden recording device. He taped

hours of damning conversations with higher-ups and provided IRS agents with company documents and diagrams of offices. "I mean if the IRS comes in... you're dead," one company officer said on tape.

The ensuing investigation turned into one of the largest white-collar criminal cases in Georgia history. But in early 1990, just when things looked bleakest for the utility company, the head of the U.S. Justice Department's tax division, Shirley Peterson, killed the case.

In doing so, Peterson, a Bush political appointee, took the unusual step of overriding her top career lawyers, say sources close to the case who spoke on condition of anonymity. "It was total shock when the answer came down. Disbelief. From a lot of people," says one observer. "Some of the potential defendant's lawyers were surprised.

In the absence of any other explanation, one lingering theory is that Southern Co. President Edward Addison's Team 100 membership played some role in the case being killed.

In the two-year investigation, federal agents had raided company offices, seizing records and computer disks. McGovern's affidavit charged that officers of the Southern Co., its subsidiaries and its auditor "schemed and conspired to willfully attempt to evade federal income taxes [and] aided and assisted in the filing of tax returns" known to be false. The Justice Department had authorized the U.S. attorney's office in Atlanta to bring evidence before a grand jury; reportedly more than 500 subpoenas were issued and some 200 witnesses called.

In late 1989 Assistant U.S. Attorney James Fagan told company lawyers he would recommend criminal indictments against six utility employees, as well as Southern Co. and Georgia Power. If tried and convicted, the companies would face up to $200 million in back taxes, penalties and interest.

As Justice Department rules require, Fagan requested permission from the tax division to seek grand jury indictments. Stanley Krysa, chief of the division's criminal enforcement section and a 35-year Justice Department veteran, expressed doubts that the government could prove the highly complex tax allegations, sources say. But Krysa agreed there was evidence of a conspiracy to mislead the IRS and recommended giving Fagan the go-ahead on that part of the case.

Nevertheless, not long after Southern's lawyers pleaded their case at a special meeting with tax division staff lawyers in Washington, criminal allegations were dropped.

In an interview at the Justice Department with Krysa and James Bruton, acting head of the tax division, Krysa noted that only 6 to 10 percent of the criminal cases the division reviews are rejected. However, Bruton, Krysa and Fagan all declined to talk about the Southern case. The Justice Department rejected formal requests for documents pertaining to its review, indicating that their release could interfere with ongoing enforcement proceedings. An attorney representing Southern indicated that a civil case is continuing, but a company official says the firm faces only routine IRS audits.

It's not unusual for executives of the Southern Co., the nation's largest investor-owned electric utility, to communicate with top Bush administration officials. Addison heads a task force of the Business Roundtable, a group of prominent CEOs from 200 of the nation's largest corporations. Last year President Bush joined Addison in a ceremony to present a Roundtable environmental award.

Southern officials "act like people who think they have a lot of power in Washington," says a House of Representatives aide who works on public utility issues.

A lawyer for the company rejects speculation that contributions and politics played a part, arguing, "It's incredible that someone would think [Addison] influenced the case. Shirley Peterson is a fine public servant we should be proud to have in the government."

Southern spokesperson David Mould says the company was innocent all along. Peterson refused to comment on the Southern case, but said in a letter to *Common Cause* Magazine, "I will, however, state categorically that neither the White House nor any party's political affiliation affected any decision made by me during my time with the Department [of Justice]."

Early this year, Peterson was appointed by Bush and confirmed by the Senate as commissioner of the IRS.

HOTWIRED

Addison also spends time in Washington as a vice chair of the Edison Electric Institute, a leading trade group, funded in large part by Southern, that has lobbied the administration to reduce regulation.

Addressing Edison's annual convention in San Diego last year via satellite, Bush vowed to help out. "Work with us," Deputy Energy Secretary Henson Moore—now White House deputy chief of staff—added. "Our common purpose is great."

The administration has proved it. In an April 25, 1991, letter to Energy Secretary James Watkins and EPA Administrator William Reilly, Edison complained about EPA plans to enforce a provision of the recently adopted Clean Air Act. EPA's draft rules governed which power plant modifications would require installation of new smokestack "scrubbers" to fight sulfur dioxide emissions, which contribute to acid rain. Edison wanted fewer plants covered by the new rule.

A few days later, acting Assistant Energy Secretary Linda Stuntz wrote to EPA making the same complaint, saying the draft rules weren't "responsive to the needs of the electric utility industry." Stuntz offered changes requested by Edison. EPA officials balked. "This is mostly garbage," an EPA attorney scribbled in the margin of Stuntz's proposal.

In stepped White House economic adviser Richard Schmalensee, demanding that EPA accept Stuntz's proposal. EPA capitulated and is currently expected to offer rules reducing the number of power plants that will have to install scrubbers. Stuntz told the *Washington Post* that Edison's complaint had had a "significant impact" on her action.

"What's left," charged Rep. Henry Waxman (D-Calif.), chair of the House health and environment subcommittee, "in essence is a rule written by polluters to benefit polluters."

TRUST FUSS

Not long after his promotion to U.S. attorney general in 1991, William Barr announced a Justice Department plan to prosecute, under U.S. antitrust laws, companies in Japan's "keiretsu" system of interlocking firms, buyers and suppliers. The action was aimed at forcing the so-called cartels to let American firms in.

Barr's plan, denounced as "loopy and dangerous" by the *Washington Post*, seemed to come from nowhere. But insiders knew it came from T. Boone Pickens, corporate raider, oilman and $100,000 Bush donor. "Before Boone came along nobody knew a keiretsu from a kimono," says a Pickens spokesperson.

Since Pickens's $100,000 contribution to help Bush in 1988, he and his Mesa companies have given another $202,660 in soft money to the RNC and the President's Dinner fund. In late 1991 Bush showed up at Pickens's home for a Texas GOP fundraiser that netted more than $600,000.

In mid-1990 Pickens met privately with high-level Justice Department officials. He was angry because, despite being the largest single stockholder of the Japanese auto parts firm Koito Manufacturing, he was denied a seat on its board of directors. Toyota, the second largest shareholder, had three seats.

"If the Japanese want to operate in this country, they should do so only in complete compliance with all of our laws," Pickens said at the time. "If they refuse, then they should face the same civil and criminal penalties as other antitrust violators."

Barr's action came too late for Pickens—last year he pulled out of Koito. Still, he praised Barr, calling his initiative "a breath of fresh air."

CHARGE IT

Paul Hebner, an executive vice president (since retired) of Occidental Petroleum, gave $100,000 to Team 100 in 1988—the same year the Department of Energy's (DOE) Office of Hearings and Appeals announced it would hold Occidental liable for a whopping $710 million in fines and interest for alleged violations of federal oil price controls.

But four years have passed, and one of the largest, longest-running and most controversial oil overcharge cases in DOE history remains unresolved. The company has so far avoided paying penalties to the U.S. Treasury, 14 state governments and millions of oil customers—although Oxy and Hebner have managed to pump another $234,780 in soft money into the RNC and the President's Dinner fund.

In late 1988 Occidental appealed the $710 million charge—and lost. But in February 1989 DOE's Economic Regulatory Administration (ERA) announced a proposed settlement with Oxy of just $150 million, or 21 cents on the dollar, to be paid over an eight-year period. Even with interest, its payments would total only $205 million.

The affected states vigorously protested the reduced fine. And a 1990 General Accounting Office (GAO) investigation identified several irregularities in ERA's handling of the case. Among other things, ERA's lead attorney on the case was excluded from key negotiating sessions with the company.

In May 1991, responding in part to "the public's widespread perception that the settlement terms are unreasonable," ERA formally withdrew the settlement offer. Occidental and the Energy Department could not agree on a new principal amount for the fine, so the matter was back in litigation. The company could appeal the matter all the way to the Supreme Court. Final resolution of the case "could be very far in the future," says an official familiar with the case.

Occidental officials did not return phone calls.

FARMED OUT
Farmworkers' rights advocates blame sugar baron Jose "Pepe" Fanjul's personal ties to the Bush administration for the Labor Department's failure to crack down on his company's abuse of Caribbean workers. The plight of the workers, brought to the United States for the back-breaking work of cutting cane, was the subject of a congressional report.

The Fanjuls' Flo-Sun company dominates the Florida sugar industry, with 160,000 acres and three processing mills, plus another 240,000 acres in the Dominican Republic. Jose Fanjul splits his time between a 26-room mansion in Palm Beach and a 7,000-acre estate in the Dominican Republic.

The Fanjul family is enriched by a complicated arrangement of quotas and government price supports that restricts sugar imports and props up domestic sugar prices. U.S. sugar programs cost U.S. consumers about $3 billion a year, while reportedly providing the Fanjuls some $50 million.

Team 100 member Fanjul and his company have given $200,000 in soft money to help elect Bush and to the RNC since then. Fanjul was a Bush fundraiser in 1988 and is a finance committee vice chair for the '92 Bush-Quayle campaign. He also is close to Robert and Georgette Mosbacher; in 1989 they spent their first Bush administration Christmas at the Fanjuls' resort in the Dominican Republic. Upon taking the helm at the Commerce Department, Mosbacher hired Wayne Berman, a Fanjul lobbyist, as his chief legal adviser.

Van Boyette, Fanjul's current lobbyist, sees nothing wrong with the family's political generosity. "It's not a quid pro quo," he says. "[The campaign money] comes from the bottom of their hearts."

According to congressional investigators, the Labor Department determined that the Fanjuls' Okeelanta sugar mill had violated minimum wage and work rules in 1988 and 1989 and levied a $267,000 fine. But more than a year passed without the Labor Department collecting the fine. Meanwhile, it allowed Okeelanta to import workers for the 1990 season "without requiring any proof of discontinuation of the unlawful employment practices found in the prior year," a congressional report notes—and even though the fine hadn't been paid.

Company lawyers are negotiating with the Labor Department to reduce the fine. A reduction seems likely; after fining Okeelanta $2.5 million for 1987 and 1988 violations, the department settled for 12 cents on the dollar.

Labor Department officials deny the Fanjuls influenced their handling of the Okeelanta cases. Okeelanta denies charges that the company mistreated its workers or violated labor rules, and company spokesperson Joseph Klock says Fanjul's political contributions actually make Labor officials more willing to scrutinize his client.

But the way Mike Hancock, executive director of the Farmworkers Justice League in Washington, sees it, the Fanjuls' political contributions and connections have helped to make the Bush administration "solicitous" toward Okeelanta in the labor case.

"There's no smoking gun, but there's clearly indications" of inordinate influence, Hancock says.

WELFARE FOR FAT CATS
How Team 100 members get and protect government giveaways.

One of President Bush's key reelection campaign strategies is to attack Congress for bringing home the bacon. "Those who reject these pork barrel projects will stand with me and the American taxpayer," Bush said in March.

"Those who support them will have to explain in November why the public interest has been denied."

Bush's hit list of pork barrel projects did not include one of USDA's most controversial handouts: the Market Promotion Program, which gives U.S. companies money to buy billboard space and television advertising touting their brand-name products overseas.

The program distributes some $200 million a year—$1 billion since 1986—to U.S. food, tobacco and liquor producers, including Team 100 members' firms.

A major share of USDA's $8.9 million grant to promote Kentucky bourbon overseas since 1990 went to Brown-Forman distilleries, headed by Team 100 member W.L. Lyons Brown. The money pays for advertisements for Jack Daniel's whiskey and Early Times bourbon. "Brown-Forman's overseas business enjoyed another year of record volume," Brown wrote company shareholders in 1991. He and his firm have given a total of $305,000 in soft money to elect Bush, to the RNC and to the President's Dinner fund.

The Dole Food Co., the worldwide fruit concern chaired by Team 100 member David Murdock, was among the highest recipients of USDA export promotion money in 1991, reportedly receiving more than $4 million. Murdock and his firm have given a total of $335,000 to elect Bush and to the RNC and the President's dinner.

"It's a huge sieve in the agriculture budget that provides no useful service except as a form of corporate welfare for companies that don't need [it]," says Bob McCarson, a spokesperson for Rep. Charles Schumer (D-N.Y.).

"WATER IS LIKE DEMOCRACY"

When Bush announced the emergency federal water allocation for California farmers in March, it wasn't the first time he had taken care of James Boswell's business interests.

Three years ago, in the face of a 960-acre cap on the size of farms eligible for federal low-cost water, the J.G. Boswell company split its 23,000-acre farm into parcels smaller than 960 acres and sold them at bargain prices to the Westhaven Trust, which was set up in the name of 326 employees.

Boswell's ploy worked: The Interior Department ruled that Westhaven Trust would be eligible for subsidized federal water. Interior Secretary Manuel Lujan later conceded Boswell's arrangement was counter to the spirit of the water program but has let it stand.

As a result, Boswell's Westhaven Trust receives federal water at $13 per acre-foot, less than one-third the price charged to large farms, at a cost to the government of about $2 million a year, according to the GAO. And while Boswell's firm technically doesn't own the farm, it does continue to live off the land: The Westhaven Trust reportedly pays the firm more than $1 million a year to manage the farms and, according to a congressional aide, Boswell still owns the ranch's railroad line, cotton mill, business offices and subsurface mineral rights.

Helped by the low-cost federal water, Boswell's California operation—not some muddy southern plantation—is the nation's top cotton producer. "Water rights are like democracy," J.G. Boswell once said. "Once you have them you spend a lifetime defending them."

The Bush administration has rejected calls from environmental groups and members of Congress to overhaul the water program. While city dwellers and wildlife suffer water shortages, some 80 percent of the federal supply goes to growers, many of whom have 40-year leases and raise federally subsidized produce. A reform measure sponsored by Sen. Bill Bradley (D-N.J.) recently was blocked in committee thanks to an effort led by yet another Bush $100,000 donor—California Republican Sen. John Seymour.

WHITE LIGHTNING

Early in his tenure Bush invited officers of a corn growers' group to the White House to talk about ethanol, a corn-distilled alcohol that's mixed with gasoline to make gasohol. Bush later drove an ethanol-powered car around a Nebraska test track. "President Bush has repeatedly made clear his support for the development of ethanol," says Edith Munro, spokesperson for the Corn Refiners Association.

The chief beneficiary of Bush's enthusiasm for ethanol? ADM, which has cornered some 70 percent of the nation's ethanol market. In fact, about 10 percent of its profits come from making ethanol out of corn. At the helm is globetrotting $100,000 Bush donor Dwayne Andreas.

Ethanol continues to fuel controversy—critics say it wouldn't be a gasoline alternative if not for Andreas's clout with the White House and Congress. Without a federal tax exemption of about 54 cents a gallon—almost $5 billion during the 1980s—gasohol would be a lot more expensive than regular gasoline; it takes as much energy to produce as it gives off and some question whether it really curbs air pollution.

Nevertheless, Bush recently signed legislation extending the ethanol subsidy to the year 2000 at an estimated cost to taxpayers of $3.43 billion. The Treasury Department has ruled that the subsidy could also fund the ethanol derivative ETBE at a projected additional cost of $192 million. Ethanol also benefits from federal price supports for corn and sugar.

With Bush's support, the Clean Air Act of 1990 will require smoggy cities to offer ethanol-blend gasoline. The bill is expected to boost the ethanol market by 50 percent; one farm analyst estimates it could add 22 cents to ADM's per-share earnings.

Republican oil-state senators, usually Bush allies, are less enthusiastic about ethanol subsidies. "I do not have anything against ADM, but that is where most of the benefits are going to go," Oklahoma Sen. Don Nickles said.

EPA recently raised ADM hackles with a new regulation that excludes certain ethanol-blend gasolines from the Clean Air Act's reformulated gasoline program, saying that they emit too many smog-producing volatile compounds. But under pressure from the ADM-dominated Renewable Fuels Association, EPA agreed to a new round of industry comments.

ADM did not respond to requests for comment. But Andreas's history of political generosity, Capitol Hill connections and clout is a common theme in press accounts.

Andreas became a focal point in the Watergate scandal when his $25,000 check to the 1972 Nixon campaign was discovered in the bank account of Watergate burglar Bernard Barker, helping to link the break-in to the White House. Andreas was indicted but later acquitted in connection with his $150,000 contribution to Democrat Hubert Humphrey's 1972 presidential campaign. Andreas and ADM have given a total of $652,000 in soft money to elect Bush and to GOP committees since.

Andreas told the *New York Times Magazine* that he never lobbies Bush on ethanol during his periodic White House visits. But as White House counsel C. Boyden Gray told the TIMES, Andreas suggested at a 1988 dinner that one way for candidate Bush to win votes was to tout the environmental benefits of ethanol.

GAS ATTACK

In December 1990, as U.S. military forces massed on the Iraqi border, T. Boone Pickens, the Texas oilman and Team 100 donor, called on the administration to reduce imported oil's "stranglehold" on the U.S. economy by increasing the country's reliance on natural gas. Pickens, chair and CEO of Mesa Inc., a natural gas producer, even had a plan: The government should convert 500,000 of its vehicles to compressed natural gas, and it should stop buying gasoline-powered vehicles after 1991.

Bush's 1989 clean air proposal called for natural gas-powered cars, but his national energy strategy, released three months after Pickens's speech, was more specific. It called for a substantial phase-in—90 percent of new purchases by the year 2000—of natural-gas and other alternative-fuel vehicles in business-owned fleets.

On March 6, one month after Mesa made a $100,000 contribution to the RNC, Bush announced new regulations designed to promote the use of natural gas-powered vehicles.

TRADING FAVORS
Blocking imports, pushing exports, whatever works for Team 100.

President Bush and the GOP have preached the free-trade gospel for years. "It is the politicians and special interests who use protectionism to cover up their failures and enrich themselves at the expense of the country as a whole," the 1988 Republican platform proclaimed.

But free trade and protectionism are flexible concepts. The Bush administration has shown that it can bend over backward to protect a certain industry—or Team 100 contributor—from free market realities.

Take the domestic cement industry, which since 1960 has repeatedly attempted to block imports from Mexico, Japan, Venezuela and other nations. Since 1975, five straight petitions had been rejected, including two during the Reagan administration.

All that abruptly changed when George Bush came to office. His administration has ruled favorably on all three anti-dumping petitions filed by the domestics. Leading the charge was the nation's third-biggest cement maker, Southdown Inc. of Houston, whose corporate counsel is Bush $100,000 donor Edgar Marston III.

"We were pleasantly surprised" by the Bush administration's help, says John Bloom, Southdown's director of corporate planning.

On September 26, 1989, eight months into the Bush administration, a Southdown-led group of U.S. cement manufacturers asked for protection from Mexican imports.

Three days later, Southdown gave the Republican National Committee $25,000.

Within two months, Robert Mosbacher's Commerce Department decided that imports were hurting the domestic manufacturers. The following April, the International Trade Commission (ITC) ruled that Mexican cement was being "dumped"—sold at less than fair value—even though it often cost more than domestic cement.

One success led to another, and another. By early 1992, responding to petitions spearheaded by Southdown, the Bush administration had virtually driven out cement imports from Mexico, Japan and Venezuela, clearing the way for domestic producers to raise prices.

Thus Southdown could tell stockholders last year that it was possible "to achieve a price increase despite the precipitous drop in cement consumption."

Marston denies there is any connection between the contribution and his company's plea for help. "That money was given because Dukakis was running for president," Marston says.

Ironically, Southdown had made millions of dollars importing Mexican cement in a joint venture with Cemex, the largest Mexican producer. Southdown sold out in 1989. Less than three weeks later CEO Clarence Comer signed the document asking the administration to investigate Cemex and other Mexican producers.

As one cement industry economist points out, "This is a very concentrated industry. If you can kill off your major competitor, you can keep prices up."

Higher prices were critical to Southdown, which had increased its corporate debt five-fold buying up competitors in the 1980s. Now the construction industry was collapsing.

Two separate bureaucracies, the Commerce Department and ITC, handle anti-dumping cases. The Commerce Department found that Mexican cement was being dumped. At the ITC, the case took three odd turns.

First, anti-dumping petitions must be supported by manufacturers of "all or almost all" of the product in a region. But Southdown and its allies produced just 62 percent of cement in the southern states.

Second, Southdown presented unsubstantiated statistics on Japanese cement prices, and the ITC used them to bolster the case against Mexico.

Third, the commissioners split over how to calculate domestic production, a key element in assessing any economic damage. One commissioner concluded that the domestic industry had already bottomed out and Mexican cement was not suppressing prices. But two other commissioners found material injury. Southdown won.

Mexican imports dropped about 60 percent and disappeared from some markets. Domestic prices went up.

The Mexican government called for bilateral negotiations, which failed. It has appealed to the U.S. Court of International Trade and the General Agreement on Tariffs and Trade (GATT) in Geneva, arguing that no government has ever before mixed proven and unsubstantiated data in a multinational dumping case.

Despite all the help, Southdown still had problems in Florida, which depends on both imported and domestic cement. Venezuelan cement had replaced the Mexican imports, although imports overall weren't gaining market share. In May 1991 Southdown and other domestics filed an anti-dumping petition charging that the Venezuelan government subsidized the imports; importers said the subsidies had stopped months earlier.

The petition also brought cries from independent U.S. cement companies that used imported cement.

"I would ask of you to please consider what the real motives are behind this suit," Roger Charles of Charles Redi-Mix Inc. wrote to Mosbacher. "Might there be an underlying motive of total control of the cement market? Should these producers gain this control, they could conceivably... force the independents to be at their mercy, and mercy does not appear to be one of their strong characteristics."

The ITC and the Commerce Department discovered that Venezuelan cement usually cost more than the domestic product, but ruled that it was being dumped anyway. Practically speaking, the Venezuelans lost.

TOBACCO DIPLOMACY

Tobacco's links to cancer spur many nations to restrict cigarette sales and advertising. But the Bush administration has pulled out the stops to spread U.S. tobacco products abroad, to the benefit of Team 100. American tobacco firms "play our free trade laws and export policies like a Stradivarius violin," said James Mason, a top official of the Department of Health and Human Services (HHS) in a 1990 speech.

Tobacco interests represented on Team 100 have contributed a total of nearly $1.8 million in soft money to help elect Bush, to the RNC and to the President's Dinner fund.

KKR and RJR Nabisco, which it controls, lead the pack. Former RJR Nabisco CEO F. Ross Johnson, company attorney W.G. Champion Mitchell III, and KKR principals Henry Kravis and George Roberts each gave $100,000 to help elect Bush in 1988. Since then, RJR Nabisco has given $438,930 in soft money, Roberts $50,000, and Kravis $25,000 to the RNC. KKR executives Robert MacDonnell and Paul Raether also gave $125,000 and $130,000.

Louis Bantle, chair of the Greenwich, Conn.-based U.S. Tobacco Co., contributed $100,000 to help Bush in 1988. Since then, his firm has given another $204,760 to the RNC.

While not a member of Team 100, Philip Morris has given more than $224,000 in soft money to the RNC since 1988; the industry-funded Tobacco Institute has contributed $77,500.

Despite shrinking sales in the U.S., the tobacco companies are healthy—thanks in large part to exports, which reached $1.5 billion in 1991. The Commerce Department helped Philip Morris and RJR negotiate a deal to export 34 billion cigarettes to the Soviet Union in 1991, a transaction reportedly worth some $50 million to Philip Morris and $40 million to RJR Nabisco.

In 1989 U.S. Trade Representative (USTR) Carla Hills joined R.J. Reynolds, Philip Morris and Brown & Williamson in a fight to overturn import and advertising restrictions in Thailand. They won most of their case before GATT in October 1990. Now the administration is pressuring Taiwan to drop its proposed sterner warning labels and bans on cigarette advertising and smokeless tobacco.

HHS finds itself caught in the conflict between health and tobacco. Secretary Louis Sullivan and Surgeon General Antonia Novello criticize the industry for targeting children and minorities, but HHS has been powerless to affect export policies.

"When push comes to shove," an industry critic says of HHS, "they're going to back off."

In most cases the entire industry has benefited. But according to State Department cables, diplomatic correspondence and interviews, the Bush administration has taken extraordinary action to help a single Team 100 member's firm, U.S. Tobacco.

U.S. Tobacco makes Skoal and Copenhagen oral snuff, shredded tobacco that health experts say causes an excruciating form of mouth cancer. The company is pushing to build its overseas sales.

In 1989, shortly after his country banned oral snuff, Australian Attorney General Michael Duffy tried to schedule a meeting at the State Department in Washington. To Duffy's surprise, his appointment with Assistant Secretary of State Richard McCormack was put off several times. When the meeting finally began, Duffy found out why: U.S. Tobacco executives wanted to attend.

Duffy felt ambushed, an Australian attache says, adding, "The process was somewhat quaint, to say the least."

Nicholas Buoniconti, the former football star and then president of U.S. Tobacco, placed tins of tobacco on the table and complained about Australia's oral snuff ban for 10 minutes. Duffy politely disagreed; the executives said thanks and departed.

"Clearly the money contributed by U.S. Tobacco resulted in the administration giving undue attention to a product that causes cancer and has no real market overseas," in the view of Greg Connolly, chair of a World Health Organization study group that helped five nations ban products made by U.S. Tobacco. The company did not respond to requests for comment.

Meanwhile the Commerce Department and the USTR's office were attacking a British proposal to ban oral snuff. Britain cited a 1986 U.S. surgeon general's report on its dangers. A U.S. diplomat shot back, "If the U.K. adopts this ban, it could become a contentious bilateral issue."

The ban was adopted. A month later Secretary of State James Baker raised the issue with the British foreign minister. Mosbacher mentioned it in London. McCormack and Deputy USTR Linn Williams spoke to British attaches. Officials of the Commerce and Agriculture departments also pushed the issue, as did North Carolina's senators, Republican Jesse Helms and Democrat Terry Sanford.

The British government stood fast. U.S. Tobacco went to British court twice and got the ban rejected on procedural grounds. After each ruling, U.S. Ambassador Henry Catto (a Bush fundraiser) urged the British not to appeal. U.S.

Tobacco offered concessions, including a vow not to market Copenhagen to children, Catto noted in a 1991 letter to the British government. He added: "We think [this] offer ... would allow us to put this issue, which has caused considerable consternation and high-level political concern, behind us."

U.S. Tobacco ultimately lost that battle to a European Community continent-wide ban on smokeless tobacco. Still, Bantle's generosity continues. Last June, U.S. Tobacco supplied $83,174 worth of chardonnay and cabernet sauvignon in glasses inscribed with the company logo to the 1991 President's Dinner.

When the master of ceremonies announced that Bantle had pledged a $100,000 soft money contribution, according to UPI reporter Tom Ferraro, the tobacco magnate proudly stood as the crowd cheered.

LANDED GENTRY

A quarter of Team 100 hails from the real estate industry. When they talk, Bush listens.

In 1986 Ronald Reagan and Congress abolished the "passive loss" tax shelter for real estate investments as part of the tax reform package that lowered income tax rates for the wealthy.

But in his January State of the Union address, President Bush called on Congress to bring it back—at least for big real estate developers. Treasury Secretary Nicholas Brady and Federal Reserve Chair Alan Greenspan had cautioned against reviving the break in congressional testimony a month earlier, but apparently they were no match for Team 100.

Some 60 individuals involved in real estate are on Team 100. All told, they have given $7.9 million to the Bush bid in '88 and to the RNC since.

Before it was abolished, the passive loss break helped spur the speculative commercial overbuilding of the 1980s, which in turn helped sink the nation's S&Ls. The shelter provided a classic write-off: New properties actually could make money by losing money.

The real estate industry never got used to tax reform. The elimination of the write-off "was just an absolute catastrophe for the country, for the real estate industry," Team 100 member Donald Trump told Congress last fall. "It has to be brought back.... It has to be taken care of."

Last December representatives of a dozen real estate trade groups got a crucial meeting with Bush, where they pleaded for its restoration. Among those present was Robert Larson, chair of the National Realty Committee.

The Realty Committee speaks for major developers and investors. Several of Bush's $100,000 donors or officers of their companies are on its board of directors. Larson is a top executive of the Taubman Companies of Bloomfield Hills, Mich., a shopping mall developer headed by Team 100 donor Alfred Taubman. Other Team 100 members represented on the committee's board include:

• Donald Bren, chair of the Irvine Co. of Newport Beach, Calif., who is on *Forbes* magazine's list of the 400 richest people in America;

• Trammell Crow, chair of the Trammell Crow Co. of Dallas, Texas, the nation's No. 1 developer;

• Peter Bedford, president of Bedford Properties of Lafayette, Calif.; and

• A. James Clark, chair of Clark Construction of Bethesda, Md., another *Forbes 400* luminary and one of the largest builders in the D.C. area.

Since the 1988 election, Bren's Irvine Co., whose holdings include a chunk of coastal California four times the size of Manhattan, has given another $205,100 in soft money to the RNC. In February Bren co-chaired a $1,000-a-plate dinner in Los Angeles that raised more than $1.25 million for Bush-Quayle '92. Bren and Irvine Co. officials declined to comment.

Bush heeded the industry's call. His passive loss tax break for developers would cost taxpayers nearly $2.5 billion over five years, the Treasury Department estimates.

A proposal in Congress supported by the National Association of Realtors, which operates the nation's largest PAC, would have provided the tax break to realtors as well. In contrast, "Bush's plan would restore passive loss write-offs for big real estate developers only," notes Citizens for Tax Justice, a Washington-based policy group.

While Bush vetoed (for other reasons) a tax bill with a modified version of his proposal, his stance has set the stage for further action.

REGULATOR END-RUN

Team 100 members have dozens of ways of making their interests known to the White House, but one of the most direct may be through Vice President Dan Quayle's Council on Competitiveness. The panel has weighed in on issues ranging from product liability to air pollution and repeatedly gutted regulations that resulted from months or years of work by federal agencies.

Quayle's council "has usurped power, holds secret meetings with industry groups and violates administrative procedures on public hearings and public access to information on decision-making," Rep. Henry Waxman (D-Calif.) charged in an interview with the *Washington Post*.

The council claims exemption from the Freedom of Information Act and it stonewalls the press, watchdog groups and Congress. Quayle meanwhile solicits industry comments on regulatory matters and holds closed-door meetings around the country with business executives who are big GOP donors.

For some Team 100 donors from the real estate and oil and gas industries, one of the hottest issues is the definition of wetlands, which Quayle's panel has taken great interest in.

Wetlands are ecologically delicate areas that filter out groundwater contaminants, help control floods, and harbor birds and other

wildlife. Wetlands use, on private as well as public land, is federally regulated.

The attack on wetlands dates back to wetlands definitions issued by the government in 1989. Industry charged that they would needlessly restrict development and other uses in many areas.

Last summer, over the objections of EPA Administrator William Reilly, an administration working group heavily guided by the council proposed weaker definitions. This time it was environmentalists—and environmental scientists, engineers and others who work in the field—who hit the roof.

The administration, which has received 70,000 letters on the proposed redefinitions, must now decide whether to finalize them, start over or kick the whole matter over to the National Academy of Sciences, as some have suggested. "It's very political stuff," says one EPA staffer.

In the meantime, the Quayle Council has solicited the advice of at least one pro-industry group with close Team 100 ties: the National Wetlands Coalition.

A creation of the lobbying firm Van Ness, Feldman & Curtis, the coalition includes Phillips Petroleum, whose chair C.J. Silas gave $100,000 in 1988 and which has given $115,000 in corporate funds to the RNC and the President's Dinner fund since then; the International Council of Shopping Centers, which includes Team 100 donors Al Taubman and Edward DeBartolo; and the Koll Co., headed by California developer Donald Koll, another Team 100 donor. All told, Team 100 members in the coalition and their companies have given more than $1.9 million in soft money to Bush and the GOP.

A Van Ness partner, Robert Szabo, has met with the head of the White House Domestic Policy Council's wetlands task force, and in January he met with two Competitiveness Council staffers to discuss the wetlands issue.

New definitions could make an enormous difference to the coalition's members and others in real estate. In Orange County, the Koll Co. has agreed to preserve about 1,000 acres in a coastal area the company is developing called the Bolsa Chica. The administration's proposals could mean a dramatic turnaround: "If the redefinition takes hold, up to 70 percent [of the 1,000 acres] will fall out of federal protection," says Adrianne Morrison, executive director of the Amigos de Bolsa Chica, a wetlands preservation group.

Lucy Dunn, a senior vice president with Koll, says the company will honor the agreement but adds that other Koll projects could be affected by the redefinitions. "I'm very supportive of the redefinitions," she says. "Eco-terrorists across the nation will say that everything's a wetland, so don't touch it."

In fact, according to EPA, at least 75 percent of California's seasonal wetlands—most of the wetlands in the state—will no longer be protected if the Bush proposal stands.

Also imperiled is a tiny songbird, the California gnatcatcher, which lives in the same Orange County habitat as some of Bush's richest donors.

The U.S. Fish and Wildlife Service (FWS) has proposed listing the gnatcatcher as an endangered species, which could block numerous development plans. Leading the opposition: the Building Industry Association of Southern California (BIA), whose Orange County chapter includes companies headed by Team 100 donors Lyon, Bren, Kathryn Thompson and James Baldwin. In a recent flyer, the BIA proclaimed itself "an awesome force."

Some BIA members, including Bren and Baldwin, have formed the Coalition for Habitat Conservation to block gnatcatcher listing; they are pushing an alternative program that environmentalists say wouldn't do the job.

But the Bush administration seems receptive. In a September 1991 press release announcing the proposed listing of the gnatcatcher, FWS praised the alternative program and even Bren's Irvine Co. by name.

In December FWS Director John Turner "dropped by" a California fundraiser for the alternative program, according to Laer Pearce, a public relations consultant who both heads the coalition and speaks for BIA.

And in early March, Turner's deputy Richard Smith met with four real estate industry lobbyists on the gnatcatcher question, including Hank Hankla, whose clients include both the BIA and the coalition, and William Ferguson Jr., who represents the Irvine Co.

Pearce makes no apologies for taking his clients' fight to the highest levels. "We feel that if we leave it to [FWS] staff, none of our questions will be satisfactorily addressed," he says. "We have to cover those [political] bases."

The gnatcatcher's fate is expected to be decided by September.

LET'S BE FRIENDS

From Wall Street to the oilfields, Bush wants what his donors want.

Just before his '89 inauguration, George Bush made reference to the political good fortune of his friends in the oil business. "They got a president of the United States that came out of the oil and gas industry, that knows it and knows it well."

Not surprisingly, 20 oil interests are represented on Team 100, including some of the biggest in the business. Altogether they have given more than $3.8 million to Bush's '88 election bid and to GOP national committees since then.

But one company stands head and shoulders above the rest. Atlantic Richfield (Arco) tops its competitors in the amount of soft money it has contributed to the team and in its impact on key policy proposals. While some in the industry—particularly smaller, independent companies—might complain about specific administration proposals, Arco has repeatedly benefited.

Thanks to Lodwrick Cook, chair of Arco, the company's relationship with the White House is strong and well-financed. In 1988

Cook and company president and CEO Robert Wycoff each contributed $100,000 to Team 100; since then the company has donated $462,360 in soft money to the RNC—plus $200,000 to the President's Dinner fund. All in all, Arco has contributed $862,360 in soft money to the '88 Bush effort and GOP national committees. For years Cook has been a GOP stalwart: He chairs the Ronald Reagan Presidential Library Foundation; he's a Bush and Reagan golfing partner; and in August, he will host the "GOP Gala Luncheon" at the party's national convention.

Arco spokesperson Al Greenstein acknowledges that Cook's "access is related to the fact that he is a supporter of President Bush."

FILL 'ER UP

Whatever the explanation, the company's impact on the policy process seems extraordinary. Take the issue of clean air.

A funny thing happened on Bush's way to announcing his clean air plan in 1989. According to spokesperson Greenstein, Cook "talked to the president [and] told him how excited he was" that Arco had successfully tested a new gasoline formula.

Thus began a sequence of events that left government fuel experts stunned and disillusioned and found other oil companies playing catch-up. What was to have been a major, environmentally sensitive push from the White House for truly alternative—that is, non-oil based—fuels, was changed in a matter of days to protect Arco's interests.

Government and industry officials say it happened like this: Days before Bush unveiled his clean air plan, executives from Arco and other major oil concerns met with the president. "The White House was pretty receptive to the oil industry coming forward [and] said 'We'll politically support you,' " a government official close to the talks recalls.

Bush's guests were concerned that his clean air plan would threaten the $100 billion-a-year gasoline business and exerted "a lot of pressure" on Bush, the official says.

White House advisers were promoting methanol, a natural gas derivative and personal favorite of White House Counsel C. Boyden Gray. After years of research, EPA scientists had concluded that methanol was the auto fuel of the future.

"The oil industry thought it was facing a very large methanol mandate," says Doris Dewton, director of government relations at the National Petroleum Refiners Association. "That's when it invented reformulated gasoline."

Unlike methanol, which is made from natural gas, or ethanol, produced from corn or sugar cane, reformulated gasoline is nothing more than the traditional oil-based fuel modified to reduce polluting emissions. In fact, it uses even more oil than regular gasoline. And it's still in the experimental stage.

"Reformulated gasoline was not even a concept when the [clean air] debate started," recalls Jeff Alson, an official at EPA's vehicle emissions lab in Ann Arbor and co-author of Bush's original, methanol-based alternative fuels proposal.

Nevertheless, at a Camp David session with top advisers the weekend before Bush announced his clean air proposal, reformulated gasoline made its way into the president's plan.

The oil company that would benefit most? Arco. Pushed by tough anti-pollution standards in its native California, Arco had already begun modifying its refineries and was producing a cleaner-burning gas for older cars. "Arco gets most of the credit" for reformulated gasoline being in the Clean Air Act, Dewton says.

The rest of the industry, well behind in reformulating gas, didn't appreciate Arco's role. The American Petroleum Institute waged a $1 million ad campaign pointing out that "no testing has been done to show 'Government Gas' is less polluting, more efficient or affordable."

The General Accounting Office (GAO) concluded in June 1990 that mass production was years away and would require substantial investment in new refinery equipment. "It could adversely affect small refiners, increase the cost of gasoline to consumers and require additional imports of crude oil."

Still, a reformulated gas provision was adopted by Congress as part of the Clean Air Act. Now, almost two years later, "We don't really know yet what reformulated gasoline is.... It's a big guess at this point," Dewton says.

"Reformulated gasolines are not the answer," EPA's Alson says. "Other fuels would be 80 to 90 percent cleaner."

NORTH TO ALASKA

President Bush also took special care of Arco in his national energy strategy. The cornerstone of his proposal—and one of Bush's favorite causes—was the opening of Alaska's Arctic National Wildlife Refuge (ANWR, or "Anwar"). Administration and industry officials argued that ANWR's coastal plain represented the nation's last great hope for a large domestic oil find.

Before George Bush took up residence in the White House the Department of the Interior's Bureau of Land Management (BLM) estimated the probability of recovering significant quantities of oil from ANWR at only 19 percent. But shortly after the administration released its energy proposal, Bush's BLM released new figures: a 46 percent chance of large recoveries.

When the Natural Resources Defense Council, a leading environmental group, charged that the new figures were politically motivated, Interior Department officials countered that they were based on "proprietary" oil industry data, which it refused to release.

Among those who would benefit most from the opening of ANWR: Arco, the second-largest oil producer in Alaska (after British Petroleum). In 1990 Arco netted $700 million from its Alaskan holdings. Arco's Greenstein says Cook "never remembers discussing ANWR with the president," adding that he had "no need to, because his position is so public."

As the Senate prepared to vote on ANWR, Bush held sessions in the Oval Office to lobby individual senators. But in the wake of the Exxon Valdez oil spill and with strong opposition from environmentalists, the Senate defeated the measure.

Energy bills currently pending in the House and Senate lack an ANWR provision, but the Bush administration apparently has other plans. According to Becky Gay, ANWR coordinator for Alaska Gov. Walter Hickel, "The president and some congressmen have told us they'd be willing to look at ANWR in the context of a jobs bill." Gay described the state's $800,000 print advertising campaign, which in March urged Congress to open ANWR to drilling because of the jobs it would provide, as "just bolstering the president's efforts."

SEEING EYE TO EYE

One way the industry makes its views known to Bush is through its official role in the administration: the National Petroleum Council (NPC), a federal advisory committee comprised of some 150 oil and gas executives appointed by the secretary of energy. This panel includes the top brass of several companies represented on Team 100: Amerada Hess, Arco, Fina, Michel T. Halbouty Energy, Hamilton Oil, Mesa, Occidental Petroleum, Phillips and Pruet Drilling.

In 1990, when Congress was debating the Clean Air Act, Department of Energy Secretary James Watkins requested NPC studies on natural gas production and oil-refining methods. "I anticipate that the results of your work will be able to contribute significantly to the development of the Department's policies and programs," Watkins wrote to then-NPC chair Lod Cook.

In January 1991 Cook submitted to Watkins an NPC report calling for the creation of a "petroleum-related National Defense Executive Reserve," a group of oil-industry executives that would advise the government during emergencies. In fact, the Department of Energy had consulted key industry officials during the Persian Gulf crisis.

But standard conflict-of-interest laws restrict the government's capacity to employ or consult individuals who have a financial stake in the policy actions on which they are making decisions or offering advice. The NPC report complained that "existing laws make it difficult for companies within the petroleum industry to make a contribution to government."

Within months the Bush administration proposed legislation to give the president exclusive authority to waive such conflict-of-interest rules in times of national emergency. The proposal awaits further action.

SEND A CABLE

The name Bill Daniels may not be a household word, but it should be. As "the father of cable television," he sent the first TV signal from Colorado to Wyoming in 1953.

With an estimated worth of $325 million, Daniels has been an active Bush supporter. He hosted a 1987 fundraiser for Bush's election at his Denver home, a 20,000-square-foot abode called Cableland, that hauled in more than $300,000. Daniels was a Team 100 donor in 1988 and has given another $124,000 in soft money since then. The biggest chunk— $99,000—was given in March, when legislation to regulate the cable industry was chugging through Congress.

All told, cable interests gave $700,000 in soft money to help elect Bush in 1988 and more than $200,000 to the RNC since.

Daniels is known for his philanthropy: His $10 million donation to the University of Denver enabled it to incorporate ethics classes in its MBA program. Not long ago, he provided a job for President Bush's embattled son Neil. Embroiled in conflicts of interest while a director of Denver's now-defunct Silverado Banking

Savings & Loan, Neil Bush recently became director of new business development for a consulting firm that is part of Daniels's cable empire.

A personal friend of the Bush family, Daniels has not hesitated to communicate his views to the president on the sticky question of whether cable TV should be "reregulated"—industry lingo for bringing back some of the consumer rate protections lost when cable was deregulated during the Reagan years. Asked at the time of Neil Bush's hiring if he planned to speak to the president, Daniels emphatically said yes. But, he added, "I don't want anything from the White House. I have never asked a politician for a favor in my life."

Well, yes and no. In May 1990, when Congress was poised to pass legislation giving consumers some relief from skyrocketing cable TV rates, Daniels wrote to Bush, "It is my hope that your administration would take a strong stand now against reregulation. If not, momentum [for enactment] will build."

When momentum brought the bill to the Senate floor that September, the White House "played a real aggressive role in killing" it, says one Commerce Committee aide.

Also lobbying the Senate was Robert Mosbacher, then in charge of the Commerce Department, which advises the White House on telecommunications policy. In a letter to Sen. Fritz Hollings (D-S.C.), chair of the Commerce Committee, he declared, "Competition rather than regulation creates the most substantial benefits for consumers and the greatest opportunities for American industry."

In fact, notes Gene Kimmelman of the Consumer Federation of America, "There is nothing in this theory of competition for the consumer in the near or mid-term."

More than 99 percent of the nation's cable systems operate without direct competition; once one company has invested the millions of dollars it takes to lay copper wire, another company is not likely to do the same. Thus whoever holds the local franchise can charge whatever the market will bear. Not surprisingly, cable TV rates have soared in recent years—last year at three times the rate of inflation.

State and local governments could regulate rates except for one thing. In more than 75 percent of all cases they are barred from doing so by the cable deregulation legislation enacted under President Reagan.

The Bush administration argues that competing technologies will control costs. But futuristic fiber optic telephone wiring, satellites and other delivery systems carry their own costs and face stiff barriers in a market dominated by a few giant cable operators.

Anyone lucky enough to be on the inside is guaranteed a profit. According to industry analysts, cable companies pay so little in overhead that nearly half of every dollar they take in is profit. Much of the rest typically goes toward interest payments on the massive loans cable operators take out to acquire the franchise and lay wire.

With all that money flowing around, cable companies are in an ideal position to buy time in Washington. Since 1989, when Congress began making noises about cable reregulation, the industry has poured more than $1 million into congressional campaign coffers.

Legislation to reregulate the industry has passed the Senate and is moving forward in the House. Bush has said he will veto it.

THE KRAVIS CONNECTION

Few things gladden the hearts of those in the financial community more than President Bush's constant call to cut capital gains taxes—undoing the work of his former boss, Ronald Reagan, who had virtually eliminated the tax break for capital gains in exchange for lower overall income tax rates in the 1986 Tax Reform Act.

A reduction would be a boon to financial interests across the board—old-line investment bankers and securities brokers, S&L and bank operators, buyout artists and corporate raiders. This is a group that has invested heavily in

Bush: All told, Team 100 members and their companies who are in the money business have donated nearly $9 million in soft money to help Bush and to his party in 1988 and since.

Financial engineer Henry Kravis, who knows Bush personally because their fathers were friends, is the ringleader. At the same time he was turning Wall Street upside-down with a form of corporate takeover dubbed the LBO (leveraged buyout), he dug into his own pocket and urged others to do so in support of the Bush regime. Kravis and his partners at Kohlberg Kravis Roberts & Co. (KKR) have contributed $505,000 to the Bush bid in 1988 and to the RNC since. KKR's influence is magnified by the nearly $809,000 given by RJR Nabisco (which KKR controls) and RJR's executives to the 1988 Bush effort and GOP national committees.

Indeed, Kravis's ability to raise money for Bush is legendary. In 1987 he organized a Wall Street fundraiser that took in more than $500,000, and he served as New York finance co-chair of the '88 campaign. This election he's co-chairing the Bush-Quayle national finance committee.

Kravis told Sarah Bartlett, author of "The Money Machine," a book on KKR, that Bush sends him handwritten notes all the time, adding, "He calls me and stuff, and we talk," often about financial issues.

Kravis's financial industry colleagues on Team 100 include:

▪Goldman Sachs partners, three of whom gave $100,000 each in 1988, with one giving another $57,450 in soft money to the RNC since then.

▪Team 100 members Theodore and Nicholas Forstmann and Brian Little of the leveraged buyout firm Forstmann Little & Co., who together have given $505,000 in soft money to help Bush in '88 and Republican national committees since.

▪$100,000 donor Stephen Schwarzman of the Blackstone Group.

■Morgan Stanley & Co. executives Joseph Fogg and Dudley Schoales and his wife, who have given $410,000 in soft money to the Bush bid and the RNC since.

■Cincinnati corporate raider Carl Lindner Jr., who is in a class by himself. He and his American Financial Corp., a holding company with insurance, banking and other subsidiaries, have given a whopping $845,460 to the Bush election bid in 1988 and Republican national party committees.

One top priority for these financiers is a cut in taxes on capital gains, or income earned on investments. And Bush has been most cooperative, having called on Congress repeatedly to bring back the tax break for capital gains that ended in 1986. He sent Congress a proposal earlier this year that would cut the capital gains tax rate from 28 percent to as low as 15 percent for those in the highest tax brackets. "We were happy with it," says Edward O'Brien, president of the Securities Industry Association, whose members include a number of firms represented on Team 100.

Studies indicate the measure would help neither the economy nor the little guy. It would provide an average tax reduction of $8,500 a year for those with incomes over $200,000—America's richest 1 percent—while costing the government $15 billion in lost tax revenue over the next five years, according to Congress's Joint Committee on Taxation.

MONEY GAMBITS

Kravis and KKR are the undisputed masters of the LBO, a form of takeover financed by large amounts of debt in loans and junk bonds, and they have raked in billions of dollars by engineering these deals. Bought-out firms must work doggedly to reduce their debt, typically by selling assets, slashing jobs and cutting funds for research and development and capital improvements.

Buyouts grew at a feverish pace through the '80s, but the biggest of all came in 1988 when KKR grabbed RJR Nabisco for $26 billion.

Critics said these unproductive deals did little to help U.S. manufacturers compete in the world marketplace, and political pressure began mounting to crack down on them. At a pre-inaugural press conference, Bush indicated he might be willing to cut back corporate tax deductions that were fueling the buyout market. Treasury Secretary Nicholas Brady sounded a warning at congressional hearings a few weeks later. "I have a gnawing feeling that we are headed in the wrong direction," said Brady, "when so much of our young talent and the nation's financial resources are aimed at financial engineering while the rest of the world is laying the foundation for the future."

Encouraged, the House Ways and Means Committee developed some options to help curb the buyout mania. But—to the certain pleasure of Wall Street—the administration backed off. A Brady emissary, testifying nearly four months after Brady's telling comments, not only failed to offer specific suggestions on how to deal with the problem but rejected those of the committee as well. "Treasury's taken a vacation on this issue," said Rep. Byron Dorgan (D-N.D.). Members of Congress had their own reasons to back down—including the fact that many of their campaigns are also funded by financial interests—so little was done.

"No special treatment was ever asked for or received by any of the contributors" from KKR, said a spokesperson for the donors.

Still, critics believe a different administration might have scrutinized KKR's doings more closely. One case in point: In February the Federal Trade Commission (FTC) surprised even antitrust experts by reversing an administrative judge's decision that would have undone a KKR takeover.

The chain of events began in 1987, when KKR took over the nation's largest glass container company, Owens-Illinois. Later that year, the bought-out Owens-Illinois went after Brockway, one of its main competitors. The FTC tried to block the merger with a court injunction but failed. Owens thus obtained control of about 40 percent of the glass container market.

An internal memo from an Owens official to its president establishes that the company went after Brockway to exert greater control over market prices, court documents show. In September 1989, an FTC administrative law judge found that the merger was likely to hurt consumers by making price fixing easier. Noting the glass container industry's history of antitrust violations, he ordered Owens to sell Brockway's glass container business within a year.

Owens appealed the order, meanwhile conducting business as it pleased, including shutting down some of Brockway's plants and putting thousands of people out of work. Two-and-a-half years went by.

Then this February a panel of FTC commissioners overturned the administrative judge's order and dismissed the complaint against Owens.

"To me it's a distressing decision," says Lawrence Sullivan, a professor at Southwestern University School of Law and author of a widely used textbook on antitrust. "If you have any merger policy that takes the problems of [market] concentration at all seriously, this just doesn't pass muster.... The real motivation of the [corporate] decisionmakers is ignored [by the FTC] and it is assumed that their motivation is innocent, although it isn't."

A footnote: Late last year a federal jury found Owens-Illinois, Brockway and one other glass container manufacturer guilty of price fixing from 1970-1987. The defendants won a new trial but settled the case in February.

BANKING ON DISASTER

A number of Bush's $100,000 donors have cashed in on the $500 billion savings and loan disaster by snapping up government-seized thrift assets at fire-sale prices, a process likened to raiding a piggybank.

Team 100 donors Robert Bass, Amway co-founder Jay Van Andel, cosmetics magnate Ronald Perelman, and mega-builders A. James Clark and Trammell Crow were among the major shareholders and officers of companies that cut "sweetheart deals" for thrift assets in late 1988, according to a Center for Responsive Law study. Every $1 the investors paid was worth $78 in assets and government benefits, according to congressional estimates.

Other high-flying Team 100 donors contributed to the S&L crisis and took a tumble when the disaster unfolded. In April, Team 100 member Charles Keating, former head of Lincoln Savings and Loan Association and its parent American Continental Corp., was sentenced to 10 years in prison on California securities fraud charges. The central figure in Capitol Hill's "Keating Five" scandal awaits trial on federal charges. Meanwhile the federal bailout of Lincoln will cost taxpayers about $2 billion.

Team 100 member Thomas Spiegel also has fared poorly. The U.S. Supreme Court recently refused to hear an appeal by the former Columbia Savings & Loan CEO of a regulatory order that requires him to post $21 million before facing a hearing on charges that he looted the thrift. Regulators say he used the thrift's funds to pay for a luxurious lifestyle and loans to his friends. The bailout of Columbia is expected to cost taxpayers some $1.5 billion.

Columbia's downfall also involved the tangled dealings of Team 100 member Michael Parker, who contributed $100,000 in 1988. Parker founded two firms that both recently went bankrupt. Parker was sued by Columbia and arrested by the FBI on charges that he defrauded the thrift of as much as $11 million between 1983 and 1987. A bankruptcy examiner said Parker gambled away some of Columbia's money at Lake Tahoe. Parker is now free on $1 million bail, but a vice president of one of his companies last year pleaded guilty to conspiracy and tax evasion in the case.

ISN'T THIS ILLEGAL?

Corporations were barred from making campaign contributions in the wake of a 1904 presidential campaign scandal involving contributions from oil companies, railroads and insurance companies. Labor unions have been similarly barred since the 1940s. In Watergate's aftermath, Congress prohibited individuals from giving federal candidates more than $1,000 per election, and enacted a system of spending limits and public financing for presidential elections.

The Supreme Court has upheld campaign contribution limits not only on grounds that they prevent corruption. "[O]f equal concern ... is the impact of the appearance of corruption stemming from public awareness of the opportunities for abuse inherent in a regime of large individual financial contributions," the court noted in the 1976 *Buckley v. Valeo* decision.

With all this, how did 249 people manage to give $100,000 apiece to support Bush's election? They gave through a convoluted system that critics say is nothing short of political money laundering.

Just after Bush's nomination in 1988, his campaign's finance chair, Robert Mosbacher, set up shop at the RNC, where he tapped a nationwide network of wealthy executives. They joined the elite Team 100 by giving at least $100,000. Team 100's money was channeled to key state GOP committees and spent on Bush campaign "ground war" activities such as get-out-the-vote drives.

The Dukakis campaign's finance chair, Robert Farmer, set up a similar $100,000 club—in fact, several Team 100 donors gave equally to the Dukakis effort. If Michael Dukakis had been elected president, actions his administration took on behalf of his $100,000 donors in 1988 would raise similar questions to those Bush now faces.

GOP officials claim that Team 100's contributions were raised to help the party, not elect Bush. But comments of some Team 100 donors make it clear they gave with Bush in mind.

California developer Kathryn Thompson described herself as "a Team 100 member, one of a group of individuals who have contributed $100,000 to the [RNC] in support of President Bush." Denver oil and gas magnate Bruce Benson—who raised $1 million for Team 100, including $100,000 of his own—describes Team 100 as "the best thing we ever did."

"I can ask somebody for $100,000 and tell them they can go see George Bush and have dinner at the White House, or I can ask for $5,000 and they can come see me," Benson says. "I think they'd rather give $100,000 and go to the White House." Benson has given another $120,000 to the GOP soft money fund since 1988.

Both the Republicans and Democrats plan huge soft money fundraising drives for the 1992 presidential race. The Democrats have upped the ante by seeking $200,000 donations.

As Republican party chair, Rich Bond will help oversee the new six-figure contribution drive. He will be a different man from the Rich Bond who was Bush's deputy campaign manager in 1988. Before Mosbacher set up Team 100, Bond attacked the Democrats for raising $100,000 contributions to help elect Dukakis.

"It's illegal on its face," Bond said then.

Who They Are	What They Gave*	What Happened
William Lloyd Davis Developer Santa Monica, Calif.	$176,540	FAA clears way for $35 million federal grant for Denver air terminal adjacent to industrial park sponsored by Davis's group.
J.W. Boswell Agribusinessman Los Angeles, Calif.	$125,000	Bush releases federally subsidized water which supports Boswell's agribusiness concern in California's Central Valley.
Edward Addison President, Southern Company Services Atlanta, Ga.	$105,000	Justice Department kills two-year, $50 million criminal tax probe of Southern, a major electric utility.
Heinz Prechter President, American Sunroof Corp. Southgate, Mich.	$183,100	Joins Bush's trip to Japan; lands lucrative deal for his company.
Edgar Marston III General Counsel, Southdown Inc. Houston, Texas	$125,000	At Southdown's behest, administration imposes first cement tariffs in 26 years.
60 Real Estate Executives	$7.9 million	Administration backs real estate tax shelter, weakened wetlands protections.
Lodwrick Cook Atlantic Richfield	$862,360	Reformulated gas provision in Bush clean air proposal; White House push for Alaska oil drilling.
T. Boone Pickens Oilman, corporate raider Amarillo, Texas	$302,660	Pressed by Pickens, administration inserts natural gas proposal into national energy plan.

* Includes individual and corporate contributions to Team 100 and GOP committees.

These totals include corporate and individual soft money contributions to help Bush and to GOP committees.

Lodwrick Cook
Atlantic Richfield (Arco)
$862,360

Dwayne Andreas
Archer Daniels Midland
$652,000

Carl Lindner
American Financial
$845,460

Henry Kravis
Kohlberg Kravis Roberts (KKR) Partners*
$505,000

RJR Nabisco And Executives
$808,930

* KKR also controls RJR Nabisco.

The World's Top Arms Merchant: The U.S. Grabs More of a Shrinking Market by Frederick Clairmonte; *World Press Review* • September 1992

In the 1980s, global arms-spending rocketed to nearly $1 trillion yearly—or about $2 million a minute. The magnitudes have tapered off slightly since 1991, and what augurs a qualitative reduction has been the exit of the former Soviet Union, one of the paramount international death merchants. But its place will be taken by others, with the U.S. being the grand trafficker leading the pack. Of the almost $1 trillion spent on arms annually in the 1980s, around $860 billion was spent by the advanced capitalist countries and the command economies and $140 billion by the Third World. Hitherto dominated by the two superpowers, which grabbed two thirds of arms exports to the Third World between 1983 and 1990, the arms bazaar is a concentrated market. Sales to the Third World during that time were worth more than $301 billion, with the Middle East accounting for more than 50 percent of the traffic.

Saudi Arabia, which spent $57.3 billion, and Iraq, which spent $30.4 billion, were recipients of almost one third of Third World purchases. U.S. policy has contributed massively (and not only in Israel, where there are 300 nuclear warheads) to the militarization of the Middle East.

Ten countries have accounted for 85-90 percent of worldwide exports: the U.S.S.R., the U.S., France, Britain, Germany, China, Czechoslovakia, Poland, Italy, and Switzerland. Conversely, seven countries in the Middle East and three in the Indian subcontinent (India, Afghanistan, and Pakistan) have absorbed the bulk of arms imports. In the arms traffic, the two leading arms merchants were running neck and neck in 1983, when the U.S.S.R. spurted ahead, a trend that has been drastically reversed. The enhancement of U.S. market share in the Third World and the Middle

East was discernible prior to the collapse of the Soviet Union. There was nothing fortuitous in this. It had become an explicit marketing objective of the Pentagon.

It appears highly improbable that President Boris Yeltsin's Russia will ever be able to recoup anything near the lost market share of the former U.S.S.R.—and its implications for international arms traffic—transpired precisely when the world business cycle was dropping and the resources to buy arms in the Third World and elsewhere had diminished. This deceleration of global capitalism is matched by yet other factors: the drive to Third World self-sufficiency, of which Iran, India, and Pakistan are prime examples, and the shift of many leading Third World countries from conventional to non-conventional arms: biological, nuclear, and chemical.

Undoubtedly, the U.S. and other arms sellers will continue to push arms sales. But one perceives, nonetheless, an upper limit. For most Third World countries, debt-servicing and military outlays take up 50-70 percent of central government revenues. Moreover, there is the escalating cost of arms. Since World War II, prices of U.S. high-tech weapons have climbed 200-fold. Given the cumulative impact of these factors, the prospects for the Third World's being a sustained dumping ground for the arms are not so sanguine.

The international arms trade is a mere 2.6 percent of global trade. There is an upper limit to the number of laser-guided and television-guided bombs, computerized radar systems, Patriot missiles, and so forth that the Third World and the Middle East can absorb. There is, of course, another palpable element at work, and that is the mounting hostility of world opinion against militarization.

U.S. President George Bush's foreign-policy obsession distracted public opinion from the abysmal failings of the U.S. economy, but public mood has drastically shifted. The continued pathology of U.S. arms-spending can only further intensify the problems in America.

Not only did U.S. productivity decelerate in the 1970s and 1980s, but real hourly wages declined, as well. The crescendo of poverty in the U.S. has attained deafening proportions.

This is the entrenched affliction that President Dwight Eisenhower bravely sought to correct—unsuccessfully. "Every gun that is made, every warship launched, every rocket fired signifies in the final sense a theft from those who are cold and are not fed. This world in arms is not spending money alone. It is spending the sweat of its workers, the genius of its scientists, the hopes of its children." This was his warning against the menace of frantic proliferation that he branded "the military-industrial complex," a Frankenstein monstrosity whose growth in the decades to come Eisenhower could only dimly have conceived. In every year from 1951 to 1991, military outlays exceeded the combined net profits of all U.S. corporations.

There is ample reason to celebrate the exit of the Evil Empire from the first circle of death merchants. But, distressingly, the lessons to be drawn from the tragedy of the U.S. military-industrial complex and its connections with the Third World have yet to be understood by the U.S. political caste. But even in Bush's America, populist, anti-militarist, and other pressures are inexorably climbing. This is a movement that will gather momentum in the years ahead.

#5

Iraqgate: Is Bush a Felon? by Stephen P. Pizzo; *The Paper: Sonoma County's Independent Voice* • October 22, 1992

I hope, as president, that I have earned your trust. I've admitted it when I made a mistake but then I go on and try to help solve the problems. I hope I've earned your trust because a lot of being president is about trust and character. And I ask for your support for four more years to finish this job.

> —George Bush's concluding remarks in the first presidential debate

Amidst the din of election year rhetoric a new "gate" has been added to the political lexicon: "Iraqgate." What hasn't yet been understood is how serious a matter this new scandal is. The gravity of the Iraqgate affair was brought home to me one day when I went to the mailbox. There I found a reporter's most blessed sight—a fat manila envelope with no return address. Even better, it bore a Washington, D.C., postmark.

When I opened the package, I found a stack of government documents still arrogantly sporting their official "Classified" and "Secret" stamps. The documents had been organized in chronological order beginning with a June 12, 1984, Department of State document memo addressed to Donald Gregg at the White House. Gregg was then Vice President George Bush's national security adviser. The memo was a cover letter for "talking points for the Vice President in calling Eximbank Chairman William Draper concerning Exim financing" for Iraq.

As I peeled back page after page, a remarkable drama unfolded before my eyes. Even before I reached the final page, I had concluded that President George Bush had participated in at least two felonies and could be impeached. Here is what the documents showed.

A short history. The Reagan/Bush administration had spent a good portion of its first term in office secretly selling arms to Iran in an abortive attempt to get our hostages in Lebanon released and a more successful program to fund a rogue Contra supply network. The nation would not learn much about that until well into their second term.

Meanwhile war had broken out between Iran and Iraq and by 1984 Iran was licking Iraq. The administration had to figure out how to balance the fight so that neither side could actually win. But they could hardly go to Congress for funding to aid Iraq since then they might have to explain why Iran was so well equipped.

So the administration again chose the now familiar covert route. They had already gotten Congress to remove Iraq from the list of countries harboring terrorists, clearing the way for non-military trade. All Iraq needed now was funding. The administration decided to supply the funding via two federal loan-guarantee programs administered by two executive branch departments, Agriculture and Commerce, and overseen by the State Department.

The two loan programs—the Export/Import Bank (Exim) and Commodity Credit Corporation—could funnel billions of dollars secretly to Iraq by simply authorizing that the bank loans made to Iraq carry a 100 percent U.S. payback guarantee. Of course, the law limited the loan proceeds to specific, non-military uses, such as buying grain from American farmers. But never mind. That little problem could be easily overcome if they used the right bank.

The little bank that could. The bank they chose for this specialized operation was the Banco Nazionale del Lavaro (BNL), an Italian-owned bank that just happened to have a branch in Atlanta, Georgia. This was no ordinary bank. BNL also just happened to have former Secretary of State Henry Kissinger on its board of advisers, and his consulting firm, Kissinger Associates, represented BNL. At the time the loan program began in 1985 the vice chairman of Kissinger Associates was Larry Eagleburger (now acting Secretary of State) and the KA's president was Brent Scowcroft (now White House National Security Adviser.)

(On the international scene BNL had even more interesting connections. Its wholly owned subsidiary in Zurich, Lavaro Bank, AG, was headed by Dr. Alfred Hartmann, a mysterious Swiss banker who was also a director of the Bank of Credit and Commerce International (BCCI). Hartmann also was president of the Swiss Chemical Manufacturer's Society. Stories in the Swiss press quote Hartmann in 1986 complaining that sales of Swiss chemical producers was way down and that new markets had to be developed. In 1989 the U.S. Federal Reserve would report that tens of millions of dollars were funneled from BCCI through Lavaro Bank to BNL/Atlanta and then to Iraq at the very time Saddam Hussein was building his chemical warfare capabilities.)

With the CCC/Exim loan program in place at BNL/Atlanta, the administration approved $1 billion a year for five years in CCC and Exim bank loans to Iraq—$5 billion in all. At least $2.6 billion of the money was directly spent on military equipment, particularly on Iraq's chemical, nuclear, and ballistic missile programs. What American grain and rice Iraq did buy with the money was more often than not shipped to third countries and bartered for additional military equipment.

When George Bush became president in 1988 the loan program was perking right along. Not only had a rearmed Iraq fought Iran to a stalemate, but Bush had the added bonus of being able to brag to U.S. farmers that he was helping them sell grain through the CCC loans to Iraq. After the 1988 election, Larry Eagleburger and Brent Scowcroft left Kissinger Associates and joined the new Bush administration. Henry Kissinger remained on BNL's board and his firm continued providing advice to BNL.

But by early 1989 the Iraq loans began making some administration officials nervous. The classified documents show that Treasury Secretary Nicholas Brady, Commerce Secretary Robert Mosbacher, and Agriculture Secretary Clayton Yeutter were getting squeamish. One 1989 memo from Exim Bank officials warned the White House, Commerce, and Treasury that Iraq was a very bad credit risk and probably would not repay the money, leaving the taxpayer to pick up the tab. Also CIA memos to the White House warned that Saddam Hussein was using his money to buy gear for his budding nuclear bomb program. Still the White House pushed for continued approval for Iraq's CCC loans.

Then in August 1989 a monkey wrench was thrown into the machinery that threatened not only to end the loan program, but to expose the White House's role in the scheme. The Iraqi loan program's real purpose had been considered so sensitive by the administration that no one had briefed the FBI or Customs. So when those two agencies got a tip that something was rotten at BNL, they raided the bank and hauled off its records.

The raid caused panic in both Washington and Rome. If the U.S. Congress got wind of the loan scam, it could strip the CCC loans of their U.S. guarantee, leaving Italy holding the bag for Baghdad's $5 billion in loans. A still classified cable to the State Department from the U.S. ambassador to Italy expressed the Italians' alarm. Also Italy had seen how Israel had been embarrassed when its involvement with the Reagan administration in the Iran/Contra affair was aired during congressional hearings. The Italian ambassador told the U.S. ambassador to let the White House know that his government wanted the BNL affair "raised to a political level...to achieve some kind of damage control."

But damage control was already on the White House agenda. An uncontrolled investigation into BNL would certainly compromise the White House. To further complicate George

Bush's life, all this happened just when Iraq was due for its 1990 fiscal-year CCC loan. And Iraq sent its foreign minister, Tariq Aziz, to Washington to personally collect. No one ever accused Iraq of being either shy or subtle and Aziz was not interested in George Bush's little problem down in Atlanta. He said Iraq wanted its $1 billion, all of it, and right now—BNL scandal or not.

It was around this time that House Banking Chairman Henry Gonzalez (D-Texas) began asking the White House just how this crooked little Italian bank had gotten approval to make so many U.S. guaranteed loans to Iraq. Attorney General Thornburgh tried to silence Gonzalez by inviting him to a private briefing. Gonzalez told Thornburgh if he had anything to reveal about BNL, he could do so under oath when he testified before his committee. Fearing they'd be dragged deeper into the BNL affair, the secretaries of Treasury, Commerce, and Agriculture began hedging their support of the Iraqi loan demand.

But none of this reduced President Bush's enthusiasm for the Iraqi loan program and he insisted that the full $1 billion loan be approved. In order to give his three nervous agency secretaries the political and legal cover they needed, Bush signed National Security Directive 26 on Oct. 4, 1989, less than two months after BNL was raided. NSD-26 ordered all executive branch agencies to do everything possible to facilitate and expand cooperation and trade with Iraq. Under cover of NSD-26 the agencies fell into line, and under intense lobbying from Eagleburger at State, they each approved the release of the first $400 million of Iraq's $1 billion in 1990 CCC loans.

But Saddam decided not to wait for the rest of the money. In August 1990 he used his U.S.-financed arms to attack and occupy Kuwait. Now the White House had a real problem. Bush had to rally the nation and a shaky coalition of Arab states into a unified force to fight a righteous battle. How could he pull off such a feat if it was revealed that he had been Saddam Hussein's personal banker?

The cover-up begins. So phase 1 of the BNL scandal ended as phase 2, the cover-up, began. The White House General Counsel's Office phoned Gale McKenzie, the assistant U.S. attorney in Atlanta. Department of Justice officials in Washington phoned her, too—just to inquire about the case, they later said, nothing improper. But notes of that conversation scribbled by a department official indicate that the Atlanta prosecutor "was sensitive to the embarrassment potential" of the case. Sensitive enough, it turned out, to hold off bringing indictments in the case until one day after the shooting stopped in the Gulf.

But even when the war in the Gulf was over, the danger the case posed to the administration was as great as ever, and now the administration turned its attention to solving the problem once and for all. First the U.S. attorney in Atlanta was replaced. But the new appointee, Joe Whitley, was forced to recuse himself from the BNL case when the *Atlanta Journal* disclosed that his law firm had represented an Ohio company, Matrix-Churchill, which had been one of the key U.S.-Iraqi front companies funneling the CCC loan money into illegal military purchases. Just a coincidence, Whitney said. Small world.

The case was then turned completely over to Assistant U.S. Attorney Gale McKenzie, who in early 1992 announced she had finally cracked the case. Indicted and blamed for the entire $5 billion scheme was Christopher Drogoul, BNL's Atlanta branch manager. Drogoul, 45, was charged with over 300 counts of bank fraud and agreed to plead guilty to 65 counts. No U.S., Iraqi, or Italian officials were charged—or even questioned.

But U.S. District Judge Marvin Shoob was uneasy about accepting Drogoul's plea. He complained from the bench that he believed that federal prosecutors were not revealing everything they knew about BNL. Ms. McKenzie

assured the judge that it was a simple case and that Drogoul was the culprit—the only culprit. Unconvinced, Judge Shoob put off Drogoul's sentencing until September 1992.

But as his sentencing approached, Drogoul began to realize that neither the Italian government nor anyone in U.S. intelligence was going to come to his rescue. Drogoul began to openly complain to the media that he was being made the fall guy for what he claimed was an approved covert operation. His complaints reached famed Atlanta trial lawyer Bobby Lee Cook, who agreed to represent Drogoul without charge.

In court, Cook savaged the prosecutor's case, peppering the court with classified government documents he claimed had been "shoved under his hotel room door during the night." However Cook got the documents, they were the final straw for Judge Shoob, whose angry glare finally convinced Ms. McKenzie to agree to allow Drogoul to withdraw his guilty plea and go to trial.

Two weeks later another shoe dropped. The court now knew that someone within the U.S. government had deliberately withheld evidence from the court. With a full-blown trial coming up, Cook was certain to produce even more government documents that the prosecutor had earlier claimed didn't exist. That's obstruction of justice—a felony. Someone had to cook up an explanation for the missing documents, and pretty quick.

On Oct. 5, CIA Director Robert Gates suddenly admitted that the CIA had withheld documents relating to the BNL affair. The Department of Justice breathed a sigh of relief and was quick to claim that, had the CIA told it of this evidence, it would have certainly shared it with the court.

But wait. Why would the CIA, which rarely admits or denies anything it does, voluntarily step forward and admit this? The same question occurred to Senate Intelligence Committee Chairman David Boren, who summoned the CIA behind closed doors and demanded some straight answers. Gates owed his confirmation as director of the CIA to Boren, who vouched for him when others on the committee wanted to deny confirmation because of his role in the Iran/Contra affair. On Oct. 8, under Boren's angry questioning, Gates admitted that the CIA had not withheld the documents on its own. He said the agency had been instructed to withhold the documents by senior officials at the Justice Department. Attorney General Barr, who now headed the department, had come there from the CIA several years earlier.

(It was not the first time an administration had tried to have the CIA take the fall in order to stop a growing scandal. Richard Nixon's first try at containing Watergate was to pin it on the CIA and attempt to throw the cloak of national security over the whole matter.)

The Justice Department angrily denied the CIA's charge, and a remarkable public fight broke out between the two federal agencies. FBI Director William Sessions had been watching all this from the sidelines. When federal Judge Shoob first began complaining that he believed someone in government was hiding information from the court, Sessions had suggested to his Justice Department superiors that the FBI investigate the charge. But Sessions was denied permission to investigate. On Oct. 10, after the CIA admission, Sessions acted on his own, announcing that he had ordered the FBI to open an investigation. On Oct. 12 the Justice Department's Office of Public Integrity announced that it had opened a criminal probe, too—a probe into anonymous allegations that Sessions had charged private phone calls and travel to the agency.

Sessions had earned a reputation as a straight-shooter since his appointment in 1986. Close associates were outraged and went public, charging that Sessions was being punished for his long-standing refusal to politicize the FBI for the current administration. Sessions has been in frail health since he was appointed. When he was made FBI director, he did not take his job for six weeks while he recuperated in hospital for a chronic bleeding ulcer.

But things had gone too far now to stop the great unraveling of the BNL scandal. Sen. Boren called on the Justice Department to step aside and appoint a special prosecutor. Last Friday, Oct. 16, Attorney General Barr held a news conference and announced that he would not appoint a special prosecutor, but did name retired federal Judge Frederick Lacey to conduct an independent investigation of the Justice Department's handling of the BNL case. This investigation would not be completed before the November election.

The presidential campaign and congressional recess have kept the Iraqgate scandal from exploding into full bloom. But once the dust settles in January, that will quickly change. First Drogoul's trial will be marked by sensational public testimony about how the Bush administration circumvented Congress to secretly fund Saddam Hussein's military buildup and the cover-up that followed.

Those revelations will in turn spark congressional hearings as Democrats, now in control of the White House for the first time in a dozen years, smell Republican blood. By piling this scandal atop the Iran/Contra affair, they will try to drive a final nail in the coffin of the Republican Party for many years to come.

But for George Bush and those he dragged into this sordid scheme, things look particularly bleak. Out of power, presumably, and no longer in control of the Department of Justice, Bush can no longer manipulate events. Even the shredder won't save him this time. Rep. Henry Gonzalez grabbed the incriminating documents confirming administration complicity in the scheme before they could be shredded—and if he should misplace his copies, he is welcome to mine.

Stephen Pizzo is co-author of Inside Job: The Looting of America's Savings and Loans, *and a regular contributor to* Mother Jones Magazine. *He lives in Sebastopol.*

6

The *New York Times/CBS News* poll records two periods during the last decade when public concern about drugs suddenly skyrocketed. In spring 1986, when the media "discovered" crack, the percentage of the public identifying "drugs" as "the No. 1 problem facing the nation" climbed from three percent to 13 percent in three months. A second shift occurred in 1989, when the number of people who identified drugs as the most serious problem leapt from 23 percent in June to 65 percent in September.

The statistics on actual drug use during the 1980s indicate no material basis for these increases in public concern. Annual reports by the University of Michigan on drug usage among U.S. high school and college students (the sectors of the population most likely to use drugs) show that most illegal drug use has been generally decreasing since the late 1970s. Powder and crack cocaine use peaked in 1985 and 1986, respectively.

So when the public suddenly became aware of the "drug crisis" in the spring of 1986, the use of all major drugs was declining. The media's role in prompting this public response can be extrapolated from the publishing record of the *New York Times*, whose lead is frequently followed by media around the nation.

Hype I: The Discovery of Crack

In May 1985, the *New York Times* published its first articles about crack, an inexpensive and easily smokable form of cocaine. Crack was presented in these stories as a highly addictive and destructive inner-city drug, which frequently compelled its users to violence. The image of poor mostly minority drug addicts, driven nearly insane by crack, mugging and murdering innocent (white) citizens was driven into the public imagination. Throughout 1985, the *Times* published an average of 36 articles per month on drug traffic and use. By November 1985, crack

had graduated to a front-page story, and the *Times* assigned a full-time reporter, Jane Gross, to cover the drug beat.

The drug story blossomed into a serious national issue in June 1986, after college basketball star Len Bias died from a cocaine overdose. Between July and October 1986, the *Times* printed a monthly average of 103 articles, hitting full stride in September with 169 articles.

Polls recorded a rapid shift in public anxiety about drugs following the heightened press coverage. On Sept.15, 1986, at the peak of coverage, Ronald and Nancy Reagan warned the nation in a televised address to "Just Say No" to drugs—a slogan that met with little public response when first coined in 1983. Congress, also eager to score some easy publicity points, responded two days later by hurriedly approving a $1.7 billion "anti-drug" package.

The passage of this legislation appeared to resolve the drug issue for both media and public, and press coverage of the drug issue and public concern decreased after October 1986 to a low but steady simmer.

Hype II: The Foreign Scourge

In 1989, drugs were again picked up by the national media, and again the *New York Times/CBS* poll showed a corresponding leap in public anxiety about drugs. This time, however, the public had already been primed by the 1988 presidential election, in which Bush's vow to "end the scourge of drugs" was a major campaign issue. By January 1989, when Bush took office, a full 16 percent of respondents said drugs were "the No. 1 problem facing the nation."

Throughout 1988, the *New York Times* ran an average of 65 drug stories each month (already twice the monthly average of 1985), and during 1989 this number again nearly doubled to a monthly average of 101 drug articles. The administration's "war on drugs" provided the foundation for the media's drug stories, focusing less on the addicts at home and more on the threat of international drug cartels and "narcoterrorists."

The media blitz was reinforced on Sept. 6, 1989, when Bush gave a special address from the Oval Office on the corrupting influence of drugs and foreign drug dealers. In September, the *Times* published 238 articles on drugs—almost seven articles a day. By the end of that month, 64 percent of the public believed that drugs were a more threatening problem than nuclear war, environmental degradation, toxic waste, AIDS, poverty or the national debt.

According to John Benson, the senior polling analyst at the Roper Center, "People responded with the first thing that came to mind, and as usual, that's what is appearing in the media."

Following the boom/bust pattern established in 1986, the public's anxiety about drugs began to fade after the U.S. invasion of Panama on Dec. 20, 1989, which was presented to the public as the drug bust of the century. After Manuel Noriega surrendered on Jan. 4 to the U.S. Drug Enforcement Agency, media interest in the drug issue melted away, as if Noriega's capture had solved the U.S.'s drug problems.

Hype III: The Hype Lives

Although public anxiety about drugs subsides after media attention to the drug issue fades, the periodic media crises have lasting effects. Strict laws for drug possession and distribution passed in 1986 have resulted in greatly increased arrest and incarceration rates, although drug use has been steadily decreasing since 1980. Drug arrests in the U.S. are now running at more than a million a year, more than two-thirds simply for possession.

Federal spending on drug policy has also been growing, increasing slowly until 1986, when it almost doubled. The federal anti-drug budget received another major boost in 1990, increasing from $6.4 billion to nearly $10 billion. This spending is primarily on interdiction and prison expansions, not on the treatment and rehabilitation programs that have been proven to reduce levels of addiction.

Today, the "drug issue" remains a blank screen of public concern upon which society's most profound fears—about the urban poor, or dark-skinned foreigners—can be easily focused. Although polls indicate that public concern about drugs is again at an ebb, it remains a small matter for the media or the administration to bring the issue back to life.

#7

Bush's Regulatory Chill: Immoral, Illegal and Deadly by Christine Triano and Nancy Watzman; *The Nation* • March 23, 1992

President Bush invoked the continuing recession during his State of the Union Message when he announced a ninety-day ban on nearly all new federal regulation. But not only will this regulatory moratorium do nothing for the economy, it is already having a profound adverse effect on health, safety and environmental programs. Numerous regulations, involving everything from nursing-home reform to worker exposure to cancer-causing chemicals, are at risk. And any delay of these regulations, even for ninety days, is quite simply a matter of life and death.

Bush's announcement—as election time approaches—is little more than a transparent pitch to corporate America's campaign contributors. Paving the way is Bush's designee to oversee the regulatory freeze, Vice President Quayle's Council on Competitiveness. In fact, the hidden agenda of the Bush plan is to expand radically the power of the Quayle council. A bastion of Reaganesque deregulatory zeal, the council is already responsible for weakening Clean Air Act provisions and other health, safety and environmental programs [see Jim Sibbison, "Dan Quayle, Business's Backdoor Boy," July 29/August 5, 1991]. In most cases, to insure that regulations are fair, government laws require federal agencies to allow all interested parties to contribute, on the record, during the drafting process. But the Quayle council refuses to operate with the same level of openness required of other agencies, thus providing backdoor access to businesses and high-priced lobbyists.

The council has already been accused of violating the law. The Bush moratorium raises further legal questions. Congress delegates authority to federal agencies to carry out laws through regulations. The executive branch can't arbitrarily put constraints on this process. Moreover, the Administrative Procedure Act bars "unreasonable delay" in rule making. Clearly, the President should not be able to halt this process unilaterally. Consumer groups, labor unions and others can be expected to challenge the moratorium in court.

Bush outlined his plan in a series of explicit memorandums to agency heads, stamped January 28, in which they are instructed to impose the moratorium on almost all regulations, save those subject to a statutory or judicial deadline. Perhaps worst of all, Bush has ordered a complete review of all *existing* regulations, which could delay needed protections well beyond ninety days. This means the whole universe of health, safety and environmental regulation is up for grabs.

Michael Boskin, chairman of the Council of Economic Advisers, and C. Boyden Gray, counsel to the President, will head a working group of the Council on Competitiveness that is charged with orchestrating the whole process. Gray is an old pro in the field of deregulation; he is former director of the Quayle council's predecessor, the Task Force on Regulatory Relief, which Bush headed when he was Vice President.

Public Citizen and OMB Watch have compiled a preliminary list of forty-four regulations across eleven agencies that could be affected by the moratorium and its accompanying "review." Contrary to Gray's bland pronouncements, it is not true that health and safety regulations are exempt from either the moratorium or the review. Bush's memo contains an exemption clause only for those regulations concerning "emergencies" that pose "an imminent danger to human health or safety." It is doubtful that the Administration will make the "emergency" claim for any of the forty-four regulations. Here are just a few that are likely to be labeled as threats to the economy:

• *Worker exposure to toxic chemicals.* The United States still lacks standards for workplace exposure to a variety of toxic chemicals, such as glycol ethers and formaldehyde. The Labor Department has identified fourteen safety regulations slated to be issued in 1992 under the Bush budget proposal, listing the "costs" (in dollars) and the "benefits" (in number of fatalities avoided) of each regulation on an annual basis. Divide these figures by four, and this standard agency worksheet starkly enumerates the possible impact of the prescribed ninety-day delay—approximately 289 workers' lives may be lost.

• *Labeling children's toys.* According to government figures, over the past decade at least 186 children have died by choking on small toys and toy parts. A regulation pending at the Consumer Product Safety Commission would require manufacturers to label toys that contain small parts and include an age recommendation for use. A C.P.S.C. review of technical literature, a survey of toy labeling and focus-group observations concluded that labels could effectively warn consumers about the risks posed by small toy parts.

• *Reporting of adverse effects from medical devices.* One of the reasons doubts about the safety of silicone breast implants took so long to surface was a lack of data. New regulations would force both manufacturers and hospitals to report adverse effects associated with such medical devices to the Food and Drug Administration.

• *Savings and loan redux.* Taxpayers will have to shell out at least $500 billion to pay for the greed and excess of S&L speculators. In an attempt to avoid the same sort of debacle with failing banks, a regulation pending at the Federal

Deposit Insurance Corporation would have banks, and not taxpayers, pay for their own bailout. The moratorium could affect this provision, which sets up a schedule for banks to pay back a $70 billion loan they have already received from the government.

Other regulations that could be affected by the moratorium and accompanying review include: nursing-home reforms; nutrition labeling for meat and poultry products; infant formula testing; an F.D.A. review of the safety and effectiveness of over-the-counter drugs such as diaper rash ointment and cold remedies; farm workers' protection from exposure to dangerous pesticides; and standards to insure that automobile safety belts adequately secure children's seats.

Requiring manufacturers to make sure that infant formula is safe hardly bogs down the economy. Like Jimmy Carter and Ronald Reagan before him, Bush is trying to paint himself as an outsider. But he is the one who hired the big-government bureaucrats he's now implicitly criticizing. If they really are suffocating the economy with regulation, how come it took Bush so long to notice?

Besides declaring war on his own Administration, the President is attempting to deprive the American people of something they not only want but expect—constructive government action in matters involving consumer protection, public health, worker safety and a clean environment. In a national poll conducted last November by Peter Hart Research Associates, Americans ranked "reduced government safety and environmental regulations" last among sixteen options as a way to help the economy.

For all that Americans shudder at the very mention of "red tape," they look to the government to protect them from unscrupulous and dangerous business practices. Just consider the kudos Bush's appointee to the F.D.A., David Kessler, has earned by cracking down on manufacturers who make false health claims on food packaging. Bush's own recent budget request to Congress has this to say about regu-

lations: "[They] are designed to result in public benefits—increased health and safety, reduced pollution, and reduced market imperfections."

The Bush moratorium is not a fresh idea. Reagan announced a similar, sixty-day ban on regulation in 1981, marking the beginning of a decade of unprecedented deregulation. We are still reeling from the results today; the S&L debacle, for example, propelled us toward the recession we are now struggling to overcome. If history bears any lesson, it is that the President's moratorium is ill advised and dangerous. As the ninety days tick by, this misconceived plan will certainly begin to take its toll, possibly in human lives.

Christine Triano is program associate at OMB Watch. Nancy Watzman is a policy analyst at Public Citizen's Congress Watch.

The Perils of Government Secrecy
by Steven Aftergood; *Issues in Science and Technology* • Summer 1992

Excessive classification of information wastes money, handcuffs innovation, and makes a mockery of democracy.

Last year the federal government classified 7,107,017 documents, an average of more than 19,000 documents per day. All of this information, along with countless volumes from past years, is withheld from the public ostensibly because its disclosure would damage national security. But classified files are increasingly overflowing with records of policy decisions, historical and budget documents, and reams of environmental data that could in no way compromise this nation's safety.

Government information policy is in disarray. Overclassification is widespread. The system has become intolerably inefficient and costly. The Department of Defense recently estimated, for example, that in 1989 the cost of protecting classified information in industry alone reached an astonishing $13.8 billion.

More important, at a time when economic security is far more at risk than military security, secrecy has prevented huge sectors of the nation's technology base from being applied to the commercial marketplace, hampering this country's economic competitiveness. It has also hindered scientific progress on issues critical to the world's health, such as global warming.

Worst of all, secrecy through classification is commonly abused by the president and the executive branch as a mechanism for avoiding congressional or public oversight. Secrecy has widened the gap between Americans and their government, retarding informed public debate on the major policy issues of our day.

It is time to look critically at what is being classified, reconsider national security needs in the wake of the Cold War, and reevaluate government secrecy practices in light of broad national economic and environmental as well as military goals.

A System Out of Control

No one disagrees that certain types of information, such as the design of weapons of mass destruction, must be protected against disclosure. It is clear, however, that government secrecy now extends far beyond the measures needed for reasonable protection of national security. Though the full scope of the classification system is itself classified, its contours can be deduced from the obstacles increasingly encountered by citizens trying to gain access to information.

Anyone who doubts that the system has grown out of control need only note a few examples of the absurdities that exist within it.

• *Secret historical documents.* Innumerable government documents from past decades remain locked away from historians, scholars, and the public. The recent controversy over withholding of documentation concerning the assassination of President Kennedy dramatizes the situation, and yet it is far from unique; such secrecy is systematic and perva-

sive. And it is by no means limited to recent events. At the National Archives the oldest classified military document as of last year was dated April 15, 1917, and concerns U.S. troop movements in Europe during World War I.

If classification of this document is to be taken seriously, we would have to infer that disclosure of the information could compromise national security. Such an inference is patently absurd. This suppression of history by the U.S. government is particularly ironic in view of the Russian government's great easing of access to historical documentation.

• *Secret presidential directives.* Classified presidential directives have been used for decades to establish U.S. policy in many diverse areas. Some of the National Security Directives (NSDs) issued by the Bush administration treat space policy, telecommunications, Soviet immigration policy, counter-narcotics (the war on drugs), and sundry other topics.

The very existence of these basic policy documents, never mind their contents, is consistently withheld from Congress and the citizenry, even though in many cases they commit government resources. Until May of this year not a single Bush administration NSD had ever been made public; at that time President Bush, under pressure, partially declassified NSD 26, which concerns the U.S. policy on Iraq. As a recent General Accounting Office report noted, "We do not know how many NSDs have been issued by the Bush administration... [I]t is impossible to satisfactorily determine how many NSDs... make and implement U.S. policy and what those policies are."

The secrecy imposed upon NSDs has little to do with their content. It is automatic. Classification in this case simply establishes an extra-Constitutional sphere for executive branch action that is unchecked by public awareness.

• *The "black" budget.* Public policy researchers estimate that in recent years approximately 15 percent of the Defense Department budget for weapons acquisition has been classified. Like all agencies, the Defense Department must present its annual budget to Congress and ask for an appropriation. However, money for classified work is handled separately, in an appendix, which is seen only by certain members of the Armed Services Committees and Defense Appropriations Subcommittees. In this way, extra money is slipped past full congressional oversight, and the way the money is subsequently spent is kept secret. The system allows secrecy to envelope the cost of a program, its purpose, even its existence.

Not surprisingly, abuses often result from this practice. Numerous program failures, cost overruns, and instances of fraud have been attributed to the black budget. Excessive secrecy was implicated by congressional investigators in the collapse of the A-12 naval attack aircraft program, which cost taxpayers several billions of dollars. The A-12 program, initiated in the 1980s, was canceled in 1991 by Defense Secretary Richard Cheney after he found out that he was being misinformed about it. The program had encountered significant cost overruns, schedule delays, and design problems that were allowed to persist unabated because its "special access" classification blocked responsible oversight.

What makes the black budget all the more galling is that in some cases it is only the American public that is kept in the dark. In April, while the Air Force maintained silence about a classified space launch, details of the launch were announced by *Tass* radio in Moscow two days in advance. *Tass* identified the launch date and location, launch vehicle, and purported mission. With subtle irony perhaps, the information was broadcast in English.

■*Secret environmental impact data.* The Department of Energy (DOE) has been notorious for withholding data on health effects at its nuclear weapons production facilities. Beyond that, however, few people are aware that the Departments of Defense and Energy can withhold environmental impact reports from the public. No matter how potentially dangerous a proposed project may be, information about its hazards can be concealed.

It is difficult to say how widespread this practice might be, though it is known to go beyond the occasional classified appendix. In one recent case, all environmental documentation concerning a proposed nuclear rocket ground-test facility in Nevada was classified at such a high level that the Energy Department in 1991 refused even to confirm or deny its existence. Similarly, the very existence of a Defense Department program on nuclear rocket propulsion would have remained classified but for the leak of documents to the media last year. According to one program official, secrecy was consciously motivated by the desire to avoid the public controversy often associated with nuclear programs.

■*Intelligence budget.* There are more than a dozen intelligence agencies within the government, of which the Central Intelligence Agency is only one. Others include offices in the Armed Services, the Defense Intelligence Agency, the National Security Agency, and the National Reconnaissance Office (NRO), which is responsible for satellite reconnaissance. In what may be the worst-kept secret in government, the very name and existence of the NRO are classified.

The total aggregate budget for these agencies is secret because, the CIA says, intelligence sources and methods would be revealed if the budget were disclosed. This strains credulity; merely indicating a budget figure would reveal nothing to compromise intelligence sources and methods.

Senator Daniel P. Moynihan, a former member of the Senate Intelligence Committee, recently stated that, "The American people would be baffled if they knew the true size and extent of the intelligence budget. Boggled."

In fact, the total budget is commonly estimated to be about $30 billion per year. How is it that official disclosure of such a number would jeopardize the lives of American agents or sensitive technologies? It wouldn't. What it would do is allow more Americans to ask whether the intelligence agencies have performed well enough to justify their enormous expenditures.

▪ *Intelligence product.* Not only is the amount of intelligence money a secret, the entire output of the massive intelligence bureaucracy is also secret. Most of its findings—its "product"—are provided to just a few individuals in the executive branch and even fewer in Congress. Yet the intelligence agencies collect whole categories of data, from economics to agriculture, that could be useful to the public sector.

More disturbing is that by virtue of its classification, intelligence information, which is often a fundamental driver of national policy, is exempt from independent critique, which prevents any check against mistaken information. Partially as a result, there have been serious government failures on the largest issues of our time.

Senator Moynihan attributes the recurring defects in intelligence analysis to the absence of an effective mechanism for self-correction. "The secrecy system got us to the point where in 1987, two years before the Berlin Wall came down, the CIA was reporting that per capita income in East Germany was higher than in West Germany. If you believed that, you will believe anything, and we did."

A more open intelligence program would help prevent such lapses. Indeed, late last year the CIA prepared a report on how the agency might achieve greater openness—and then classified the report. The vacuousness of this reflexive secrecy (and, in the author's opinion, the CIA's openness initiative itself) became evident when the report was eventually released as the result of public pressure. A pre-dominantly open intelligence program could be vigorously evaluated from many points of view, yielding a higher-quality, more reliable, and more useful product.

How It Got So Bad

Although there has always been some degree of secrecy in American government, it was only at the beginning of the Cold War that secrecy began to reach significantly beyond military information and to become an institutionalized part of the U.S. bureaucracy. In September 1951, President Truman issued Executive Order 10290, which for the first time established a classification system that encompassed civilian as well as military agencies. It authorized any executive branch agency to classify information and defined a vague standard for classified information as "official information the safeguarding of which is necessary in the interest of national security."

Significantly, the classification of security-related information is not founded on any statutory law. It is defined unilaterally by executive order. Nuclear weapons design information and related topics, in contrast, are protected by law under the Atomic Energy Act, first passed by Congress in 1946.

The classification system has been revised several times by succeeding presidents. Until the 1980s, the scope of information subject to classification gradually narrowed as the criteria were tightened. Commitment to openness peaked under the Carter administration. President Carter decreed that information could not be classified unless its disclosure could cause "identifiable" damage to national security; he instituted a "balancing test" by which even classified information would be disclosed if there was a substantial public interest in doing so; he stated that scientific information not clearly related to national security could not be classified; and he mandated a program of systematic declassification reviews by executive branch agencies.

But these evolutionary steps were undone by President Reagan. Reagan's 1982 Executive Order 12356, the basis for today's classification system, which eliminated the Carter-era threshold of identifiable damage, eliminated the balancing test, deleted the prohibition on withholding scientific information, and curtailed systematic declassification review, dictating that only the National Archives must conduct such review. The Reagan order makes it plain that, when in doubt, information is to be classified. And if there is a question about the level of classification, the higher level is to be adopted.

The executive order defines three increasingly stringent classification levels: confidential, secret, and top secret. The confidential level is supposed to be applied to "information, the unauthorized disclosure of which reasonably could be expected to cause damage to the national security." Secret information, the next highest level, is that which could be expected to cause "serious damage." And top secret information is defined as that which could cause "exceptionally grave damage." Restrictions on access to information are increased, as are protective measures for storage, communication, and handling, in accordance with the classification level. Before anyone can see information at any of the three levels, he or she must have the appropriate security clearance and must have an identifiable "need to know."

There is, in effect, a fourth level—special access—which carries a degree of secrecy beyond that of ordinary classification. In essence it means "this is only for those with a need to know, and we're not kidding this time." In many cases the very existence of a special access program is classified. Hence the commonly used, unofficial term "black program." Usually, special access is applied to certain weapons acquisition programs and intelligence and military operations.

One immediate problem with this scheme is its intrinsically subjective character. There is no comprehensive definition of "national security," much less a definition of "damage." One result, according to Steven Garfinkel, the Director of the federal Information Security Oversight Office, is a certain blurring among the classification levels. Garfinkel, whose office is nominally responsible for supervising implementation of the classification system, says, "The classification levels, especially secret and confidential, are almost interchangeable. For that reason, there's a lot of secret stuff that's not that sensitive, and there's a lot of confidential stuff that is."

Subjectivity is all the more problematic because classification authority is widely dispersed and is subject to little accountability. As of last year, there were about 6,500 individuals scattered across the executive branch who were authorized to classify information. The heads of most executive-branch agencies are given power by the president to classify; they in turn can delegate this authority throughout their departments. According to government statistics, by far the largest number of classification decisions were made last year by the Department of Defense (61 percent), followed by the CIA (26 percent), the Department of Justice (9 percent), the Department of State (3 percent), and others (1 percent).

To a large extent, these individuals have carte blanche to classify as they please. At a rate of 19,000 new classifications each day, no one even pretends that any substantial portion of these decisions are reviewed. Furthermore, the system encourages overclassification; the penalties for disclosing genuinely sensitive material can be severe, from official censure to imprisonment under the Espionage Act. The penalties for unnecessary classification are virtually nonexistent. Secrecy is further reinforced by the bureaucratic tendency to control information and to evade critical oversight.

The Need for Greater Openness
In science and technology, the need for openness is axiomatic. Without free and open communication, the cross-fertilization of ideas that

is essential to progress is inhibited and the peer-review process is crippled. A 1970 Report of the Defense Science Board's Task Force on Secrecy, a classic of sorts, declared that "more might be gained than lost if our nation were to adopt—unilaterally, if necessary—a policy of complete openness in all areas of information."

This radical notion, put forward by eminent and politically conservative scientists including physicists Frederick Seitz and Edward Teller, is rooted in the recognition that openness is a source of strength, not weakness. Yet at a time when economic security is far more at risk than military security, excessive government secrecy serves to impede one of the nation's most important economic strengths—its capacity for technological innovation.

Overclassification prevents the introduction of many advanced technologies into the commercial marketplace. Oblique reports in the trade press, notably *Aviation Week & Space Technology*, suggest that there are a number of emerging technologies developed in black programs that have commercial potential. Such reports refer, for example, to infrared sensors that do not require cryogenic cooling, which could improve by several orders of magnitude the sensitivity of environmental monitoring systems; electrostatic fields that condition air flow around aircraft, which could dramatically reduce fuel costs for commercial aviation; and advances in materials science that could improve aircraft control, propulsion, and other fields. These missed opportunities represent a "negative spinoff" phenomenon.

A defense contractor that develops a new technology within a black program can apply for a patent. But under the Invention Secrecy Act of 1951, a defense agency (today defined as any DOD entity, the DOE, or the National Aeronautics and Space Administration) can impose a "secrecy order" on the application and withhold the patent, if it believes that patent approval could have a "detrimental"

effect on national security. In FY 1991, a total of 5,893 secrecy orders were in effect, up from about 3,500 in 1980.

Remarkably, secrecy orders can also be applied to private individuals or businesses—referred to as "John Does"—that develop new technology independent of government support. The defense agencies routinely scrutinize patent applications, then tell the U.S. Patent and Trademark Office to inform an applicant that his invention must be kept secret and that a patent may not be granted. Even if a person or business withdraws the patent application, the prohibition against disclosure remains in effect.

The issuance of new John Doe orders has skyrocketed: in FY 1980 there were 43 new orders; in FY 1991 there were 506. The Patent and Trademark Office recently reported a "dramatic increase in the number of secrecy orders imposed upon privately owned patent applications."

Such intervention is often likely to be self-defeating. It renders some of the most talented engineers in the nation technologically and economically sterile, since their products can never be sold or even used unless a defense agency decides it wants to acquire the technology for its own classified needs.

The sole argument in favor of technological secrecy is that it can preserve lead time before an adversary can match or counter a particular advance. But proponents of this argument fail to acknowledge the easing of international security tensions and fail to recognize the limited effectiveness of even the most stringent security measures.

Not only does overclassification impede economic competitiveness, it also prevents scientists and policymakers from using high technology to address some of the greatest challenges to humanity in our time. Incredibly, with all the social and economic pressure that surrounds the greenhouse effect, the richest, most variegated sources of climatic information in the world—the extensive defense and intelligence data bases on global environmental conditions—remain largely inaccessible. Intelligence officials have been reluctant even to acknowledge that the United States has an overhead reconnaissance capability at all.

The classified "earth observing system" already in place is many times larger than NASA's proposed Earth Observing System (EOS), which would go into orbit in the late 1990s. For their own purposes, the Departments of Defense and Energy have conducted environmental monitoring from within the oceans, at the planet's surface, from the atmosphere, and, especially, from space. In some cases, data bases extend back several decades, offering the potential for inexpensively assessing long-term environmental trends as well as verifying various climatic models.

Yet secrecy in intelligence gathering is so hypertrophied that all this information has automatically been withheld without challenge, at least until recently. "What is totally stupid," observed Representative George E. Brown, Jr. (D-Calif.), last year, "is that we have a classification system which persists in perpetuating the fiction that this material is secret and that such a fiction contributes to our national security."

Some of the relevant limited-access data that have been publicly described are derived, for example, from the Defense Meteorological Support Program (DMSP) satellites, which produce visible and infrared data, and from optical sensors on the network of Global Positioning Satellites, which can provide information on cloud cover. Other systems, particularly intelligence satellites, are likely to have generated valuable yet inaccessible environmental data. Perhaps even more important, the intelligence agencies have unparalleled experience in data-base management, which could prove immensely useful in meeting the challenges faced by the Earth Observing System Data and Information System (EOSDIS), which is to process, archive, and distribute the data collected in NASA's EOS program.

Representative Brown, Senator Albert Gore (D-Tenn.), and others have long advocated a relaxation of restrictions on government environmental data, particularly within the framework of the Strategic Environmental Research and Development Program, a recent congressional initiative to direct some Defense Department resources to environmental problems. Their efforts have begun to bear fruit, and access to such data has begun to improve. Not long ago, Senator Gore got the U.S. Navy to agree to release its 30-year data base of sonar measurements of polar ice caps; given a more recent agreement between the U.S. Air Force and the National Oceanic and Atmospheric Administration, it appears that most of DMSP's data will be permitted into the public domain. A recent presidential directive may clear the way for more comprehensive access.

Toward Reform

The evolution of government secrecy proceeds in phases. In the beginning, it is threat-driven; it starts with the belief that disclosure of certain information could compromise national security. Controls are instituted to prevent that disclosure. But subsequently, the controls become bureaucratized and various categories of information are reflexively classified. In its latter, decadent phase, government secrecy bears little or no relation to any identifiable threat.

The classification system today has, for the most part, long since ceased to be threat-driven. Information is still routinely withheld from the public, accompanied by the statement that its disclosure "reasonably could be expected to cause damage to national security." But this is increasingly a ritualistic incantation devoid of content. It is simply not true to assert that disclosure of the number of presidential directives, or the movements of U.S. troops in World War I, or the $30 billion intelligence budget could in any way place the country in jeopardy.

What is to be done? The present Cold War classification system should be scrapped and replaced by an information policy that is founded on genuine national security requirements. A new consensus must be achieved on the types of information that legitimately need to be classified, and everything else should be released. In a democratic society, there must be a presumption in favor of openness.

What types of information should be classified? Morton H. Halperin, director of the American Civil Liberties Union's Washington office, has proposed four categories that make simple sense:

- Design and operational details of advanced weapons systems.
- Details of plans for military operations.
- Details of ongoing diplomatic negotiations.
- Intelligence methods, including codes, technology, and identity of spies.

The narrowed scope and renewed credibility of classification along these lines would have the beneficial effect of providing improved protection for information that could be truly vital to national security.

A new classification system will not come from within. Mounting financial costs will force some incremental changes, and periodic controversies like that concerning the Kennedy assassination will compel greater openness in highly specific areas, but more systematic change will not come voluntarily. Too many people have a vested interest in the status quo. As one State Department classification official put it, "No one is going to streamline himself out of a job."

Because classification is still entirely based on executive order, adoption of new criteria could come simply with the arrival of a new administration that has a different concept of national security and democracy. But a new administration might be tempted by the realization that the classification system serves its political interests by enabling it to shield programs from congressional and public scrutiny.

In that case, substantive changes are likely to require congressional action. The executive branch jealously guards its classification activities and argues, implicitly or explicitly, that classification is solely its prerogative. A submissive Congress in recent years has tended to agree. And yet there is no question that Congress has all the power it needs to legislate a government-wide information policy, including new classification criteria. The passage of the Atomic Energy Act, which dictates the control of nuclear weapons design information, for example, would seem to provide sufficient proof of that.

There have already been some tentative forays in Congress toward easing secrecy restrictions. In 1991, Congress included a provision in the State Department Authorization bill to expand the scope and accuracy of the publication of the Foreign Relations of the United States series (the official history of U.S. foreign policy) by mandating new procedures for declassification of pertinent documents. Currently, legislation is pending on disclosure of certain files concerning the Kennedy assassination, and of some information concerning nuclear weapons stockpiles.

Any comprehensive attempt to recast the classification system should include measures such as the following:

Reduce classification at the source. A critical step in achieving a policy based on openness is to drastically curtail the production of new classified documents. Before dealing with the abundant residue of the past, the continuing flow of classified materials should be stanched.

This will require the elaboration of new classification criteria, along the lines of the limited topics noted above, which can logically be traced to identifiable national security threats. While the executive branch would remain free to handle information internally as it sees fit, the categories of information that could be withheld from the public must be drastically diminished. Furthermore, no information, regardless of its classification, should be withheld from the Congress on national security grounds.

Another way to reduce classification at the source would be to sharply cut the number of individuals authorized to classify information. A reduction of the 6,500 classification authorities by perhaps 90 percent would go a long way toward imposing discipline on the process. Additional benefits would be lower costs and improved protection for truly sensitive information.

Implement bulk declassification of older documents. Once a new standard has been established, it will be necessary to undo the abuses of the past.

The review and processing required to declassify documents is costly and time-consuming. As much as possible, automatic "bulk declassification" of broad categories of old information should be practiced. This could be mandated by either executive order or legislation.

A related measure is the establishment of what federal officials call a "drop-dead date" policy. This would be a systematic declassification of documents, with certain exceptions, once they reached a certain age. According to Steven Garfinkel, director of the Information Security Oversight Office, adoption of a drop-dead date is under consideration in the executive branch. But this idea has been kicked around before, and it is likely to remain "under consideration" indefinitely. Furthermore, Garfinkel says, if a drop-dead date is ever voluntarily implemented by the executive branch, the term "is not going to be at the 20-year level and it's not going to be at the 30-year level," but some longer period.

Given the pivotal changes in international politics in the last several years, a period of perhaps five years would seem in order.

Remarkably, the 1970 Defense Science Board Report on Secrecy advised that, "As a general guideline, one may set a period between one and five years for complete declassification."

Eliminate the special-access classification system. Another important interim step toward open government would be to eliminate the special-access category altogether.

In 1985, the General Accounting Office reported that there were between 5,000 and 6,000 active special-access contracts with industry. The Senate Armed Services Committee reported in 1991 that, "Over time, the vast expansion in the number of special access programs...[has] led to serious negative consequences." According to the report, these have included failures of internal management (as was the case with the A-12 aircraft program); the shielding of numerous small programs from congressional oversight by placing them under a larger "umbrella" program that is blithely classified; and refusal to provide access necessary for proper oversight.

If thwarting oversight is the goal, special access is a success. A 1990 study by the House Armed Services Committee revealed that only 5 to 10 percent of all special-access programs are actually reviewed in depth by Congress. The prospect of evading congressional attention serves as an ongoing incentive for the executive branch to place even more programs in the special-access category. This temptation to fraud and abuse led the House Armed Services Committee to conclude in 1991 that special access "is now adversely affecting the national security it is intended to support." It should be abolished.

Failure to rein in government secrecy will result in enormous financial costs and constraints on scientific and technological ventures, and in damage to the democratic process. When secrecy is unnecessarily applied in important policy areas, the result is the corruption of the nation's political discourse and the stupefaction of its members.

Another result is a *de facto* information policy based on unauthorized disclosures of classified information, or "leaks." The problem with such an approach is that it presents a distorted picture of events, since individuals that breach their commitment to protect secret information generally do so selectively to advance some parochial interest. Already, leaked documents are the currency of national security reporting in Washington.

One way or another, those who implement the classification system need to come to grips with the realities of the present day. Secrecy is no longer an unfortunate necessity, it has become a destructive habit. Openness in government is not a threat to national security, or a concession to political opposition, it is the foundation of the nation's political way of life and the source of much of its strength.

Recommended reading

General Accounting Office, "The Use of Presidential Directives to Make and Implement U.S. Policy." GAO/NSIAD-92-72, January 1992.

Morton H. Halperin and Daniel N. Hoffman, *Top Secret: National Security and the Right to Know*. New Republic Books, 1977.

William B. Scott, " 'Black World' Engineers, Scientists Encourage Using Highly Classified Technology for Civil Applications," *Aviation Week & Space Technology* (March 9, 1992): 66.

Frederick Seitz, chairman, "Report of the Defense Science Board Task Force on Secrecy." Office of the Director of Defense Research and Engineering, The Pentagon, July 1, 1970.

Steven Aftergood is a senior research analyst at the Federation of American Scientists (FAS), where he directs the FAS Project on Secrecy & Government.

Excerpt from "Dictating Content: How Advertising Pressure Can Corrupt a Free Press" by Ronald K.L. Collins; Center for the Study of Commercialism • 1992

How robust can media freedom be when those who subsidize it seek to dictate or influence its content? Print and electronic journalists are confronting that question as they strive to keep press freedom alive in recessionary times.

Example: Northwest Airlines apparently does not like the way that the *Star Tribune* and the *St. Paul Pioneer Press* covered a recent $759-million state financing story pertaining to it. So it yanked its ads from both papers for several months. "There are many explanations," a Northwest spokesman told the *Tribune*, "that can fit that set of facts." One explanation, formally denied by the airline, appears plain—press freedom does not include the right to scrutinize advertisers.

The example is not aberrational. According to a new study of 250 newspapers, conducted by University of Minnesota Department of Journalism Professors Lawrence Soley and Robert Craig, 89 percent of those responding reported that advertisers removed ads in retaliation of news stories they deemed objectionable. Similarly, in a survey of real-estate editors published last November in the *Washington Journalism Review*, American University journalism Professor Wendy Swallow Williams found that 80 percent of those surveyed said advertisers had threatened to pull ads because of negative coverage.

These kinds of advertising demands can take on new meaning in a sluggish media economy. Newspaper ad revenue, which began to fall sharply in mid-1990, fell another 5 percent in 1991. Magazine ad revenue was down about 2.5 percent in 1991. Among the big three networks, only ABC reported a profit in 1991; overall the networks saw a drop in ad revenues from $5 billion in 1990 to $4.7 billion in 1991. While there have been some slight upswings more recently, the economic climate remains chilly—the *L.A. Times*, for example, is currently feeling the cold winds of drops in ad revenue.

So how are the advertisers' demands being answered? While difficult to discover, "the problem is very deep" opines media expert and Berkeley journalism Professor Ben Bagdikian. William Woo, editor of the *St. Louis Post-Dispatch* and chair of the ethics committee of the American Society of Newspaper Editors (ASNE), told a *Wall Street Journal* reporter that "[t]he assumption is that journalism is becoming increasingly vulnerable" to ad pressure.

After reviewing some 100 magazines, a 1992 report in the *New England Journal of Medicine* found statistical evidence of a clear correlation between the amount of cigarette advertising in a magazine and the likelihood that it will carry an article on the dangers of smoking. Similarly, the Soley-Craig University of Minnesota study revealed that 37 percent of the 250 papers polled (60 percent responded) reported that advertising pressure had affected editorial content in some way.

Anecdotal evidence is mountain high. For example, John Robert Star, the managing editor of the *Arkansas Democrat*, doesn't mince words, "Our policy is no different from every other paper I know about: People hired as columnists by the paper don't trash advertisers." A spokesperson for *Time* Magazine said: "*Time*, as does *Newsweek*, has a lot of cigarette advertising. Do you carry material that's insulting to your advertiser?" And in February of 1992 a "Saturday Night Live" skit was changed to appease a sensitive advertiser (General Motors) who had "previewed" the show and objected to its satirical premise about job layoffs.

Stressing media economics, Beverly Klein, senior vice president of marketing at the *Milwaukee Journal/Sentinel*, told an *Inside Media* reporter that the heads of newsrooms need to comprehend "the whole picture, where the revenue is coming from" so as to help them "understand how an advertiser reacts" to various news reports. Echoing a similar point about special ad-friendly sections in papers, Don Flores, publisher of the *Iowa City Press Citizen*, admitted to the same reporter that newspapers "haven't found a better way to get sections out that won't be offensive" to advertisers.

Such troubling signs of real or potential compromise, however economically understandable, are incompatible with the ideal of a free and uninhibited press. It is imperative that journalism retain its critical edge if it is to preserve its own integrity and honor the public's right to know.

Steps must be taken to increase public information and decrease advertising pressure and its negative effects. First, the problem must continue to be publicized and a major conference should be convened to examine the character and extent of this problem. Second, voluntary media guidelines must be formulated, with due input from interested groups. The guidelines should address the ethics of a variety of practices ranging from advertising contracts demanding friendly coverage to the fairness of punishing reporters for disclosing conflicts of interest at their own place of employment.

The American press must stand up to advertising pressure in all its various forms. Failing that, no press deserves to be labeled free.

The Pentagon's Secret Stash by Tim Weiner; *Mother Jones* • March/April 1992

A special report about the "Black Budget," hidden accounts that suck up $36 billion a year—much of it for weapons designed to fight the Russians. Don't they know the cold war is over?

President Franklin D. Roosevelt sat in the Oval Office fifty years ago and listened in wonder as Vannevar Bush, the dean of engineering at the Massachusetts Institute of Technology, described a twenty-five-pound bomb that could explode with the force of 3.6 million pounds of dynamite. The best guess was that $100 million would be needed to build the secret weapon. The president told Bush that he would deliver a blank check for the Manhattan Project, to be funded by a "special source," a hidden reservoir of cash. On that day, October 9, 1941, the black budget was born. Four years later, its first brainchild exploded over Hiroshima.

Today, every day, close to $100 million flows through underground pipelines from the Treasury to the Pentagon to fuel the national-security machinery of the United States. The black budget—"black" in the sense of being unseen, covert, hidden from light—is the secret treasury of the nation's military and intelligence agencies. It is appropriated and spent with the barest public debate or scrutiny.

The black budget began its sharp ascent in the 1980s. As the Pentagon's budget doubled, the secret budget quadrupled to an estimated $36 billion a year. It financed wonder weapons for World War III, billion-dollar nuclear bombers, and space-based brains to win six-month nuclear wars. And now, in the 1990s, though the prospect of nuclear Armageddon between the United States and the Soviet Union has evaporated, the secret projects still grind on. Billions are still being spent covertly to build nuclear bombers that can fly at eight times the speed of sound, underground nuclear-war command posts for the president and his peers, nuclear-powered engines for Star Wars rockets, and a hundred more highly classified military machines.

Classified: Top Secret

The secret budget grew exponentially during the cold war. In 1947, the United States, then the world's sole superpower, began to build an enormous national-security system to preserve and extend its might. The system demanded secret funds, so the weaponry for fighting cold war was built with money taken surreptitiously from the Pentagon's budget.

First came the Central Intelligence Agency in 1947. Next, the Pentagon's National Security Agency, with its global web of wiretaps and other electronic eavesdropping equipment, was formed in 1952. Then, in 1960, came the National Reconnaissance Office, the spy-satellite service still so secret that the Pentagon denies its existence. Providing the billions to run these agencies became a great game, played behind closed doors by the Pentagon, the CIA, and one or two senior members of Congress. Almost no one in Congress—and no one in the public or the press—could account for these funds. Back in the early 1960s, when the CIA sought to build its present-day headquarters in Langley, Virginia, Richard Russell of Georgia, then head of the Senate Armed Services Committee, simply created a fictitious new aircraft carrier and let the CIA siphon off the cash. The money for the ghost ship built the spooks' shop.

All along, money to finance the search for strategies to fight and win a nuclear war has been buried in the Pentagon's budget. But even at the height of the cold war, the secret budget for nukes and spooks never exceeded $9 billion a year—until Ronald Reagan took over. Key member of the Reagan administration really believed, as one of its Pentagon strategists, Colin Gray, put it, that "the United States may have no practical alternative to waging a nuclear war." Their search for newer and better nuclear-war-fighting weapons created a critical mass in the subterranean dynamo of secret Pentagon spending. The covertness that had been confined to the nation's intelligence agencies soon also enshrouded the most complex—and least sensible—of the weapons on the Pentagon's drawing boards and assembly lines. Extraordinary secrecy, like that surrounding the Manhattan Project, became everyday practice inside the Pentagon.

Of the roughly $36 billion in the secret budget today, about $30 billion is consumed by the Pentagon's intelligence services, the CIA, the Justice Department's counterintelligence programs, and small intelligence branches within the State, Energy, and Treasury departments. About $5 billion goes to build and develop weapons programs, many of which remain so highly classified that only the two most senior members of the congressional armed-services and appropriations committees know anything about them.

There have been a few open protests about this secrecy from several Congress members and Pentagon outsiders. Les Aspin, chairman of the House Armed Services Committee, has been saying for years that most of the secret budget for weaponry should be brought into the light and that "it is simply bad public policy to hide amounts of government spending." Robert Costello, who was in charge of buying weapons at the Pentagon during the last years of the Reagan administration, believes that the secret budget hides billion-dollar programs from oversight and criticism. "[Inside the Pentagon] the mindset is, 'I'm going to use secrecy to build my nice isolated little cocoon,'" Costello says. And when the cocoons came under attack, when the secrecy was criticized by skeptics inside the Pentagon, "they fired the bastards that wanted to put screws on them."

Secrecy about the nation's nuclear-war plans still provides a steely cover—until a small number of programs become too costly or too haywire to survive. In the five years that I've been trying to ferret out information about the black budget, as a reporter for the *Philadelphia Inquirer* and while researching a book, only a handful of the twenty-first-century wonder weapons financed by the secret treasury have come to light. Public pressure and congressional anger forced the lid off the now famous B-2 bomber, and reporters and public-policy advocates uncovered strange programs with eerie names such as Timberwind, MILSTAR, and Island Sun. The relatively few secret programs made public so far raise questions about the entire enterprise—and its relevance to a post-cold-war world. For, almost without exception, these black projects have proved wildly expensive, technologically dubious, or arguably insane.

Timberwind

Timberwind, a program to build a nuclear-powered rocket engine, is a secret component of Star Wars. Still highly classified, its overall costs are estimated at $8 billion. Although Strategic Defense Initiative and Pentagon officials refuse to confirm or deny the project's existence, Timberwind tests are scheduled to take place sometime later in the decade in the Nevada desert. According to one armed-service-committee staff member, SDI officials only briefed those in Congress who they thought would be sympathetic to the program and kept Timberwind secret from the majority of the members of the armed-services committees.

Why a nuclear-powered engine? To build faster, more powerful rockets to shoot down incoming Soviet nukes. The United States is still set on constructing a nest of one hundred antiballistic missiles, the maximum-size force permitted by ABM treaties, at a proposed site in the Dakotas.

The Timberwind engine, which is supposed to provide a bigger boost for the ABMs and other delivery systems, has been considered a possible key to fielding an ABM force to protect U.S. military posts from a nuclear attack by our old adversary, the Evil Empire. The idea that the Russians no longer seem set on nuking the U.S. heartland has not yet stilled Timberwind, which has already chewed up more than $185 million in research funds.

MILSTAR: Still Classified

The Military Strategic and Tactical Relay system was designed to be the ultimate war machine: a network of space satellites and blast-hardened ground stations that would endure a six-month nuclear war. The fact that the Pentagon planned to fight and win a nuclear war of that duration suggests how far removed from reality the nation's nuclear strategists were in the 1980s. In their vision, MILSTAR would weave together the communications links of U.S. nuclear forces so that they could keep launching missiles at the Soviets long after the White House and the Pentagon were blown to smithereens.

For a cost of up to $40 billion, MILSTAR was to pierce the ferocious electronic static of nuclear war, to keep relaying the go-codes and launching orders to the surviving missilemen in their submarines and silos—for six months, until the last warhead screamed across the sky.

Sounds like a technological fantasy, impossible to accomplish at any price? It is. But the Pentagon and the White House "consistently sent the signal" that such a system was needed, according to John Steinbruner, director of foreign-policy studies at the Brookings Institution and one of the nation's top civilian experts on nuclear-war strategy. "They want an enduring system. They've told the weapons and systems designers to do it. And they've driven the designers crazy. The designers don't know how to build a system capable of surviving a protracted nuclear war, even spending tens or hundreds of billions of dollars. But the money's being spent, no question about it."

Due to immense cost overruns, MILSTAR's architecture has been scaled back; the Pentagon now emphasizes the program's "conventional" role in some future global war. In the first—and to date, the only—public report ever listed on MILSTAR, the Senate Armed Services Committee revealed in November 1990 that "the Department of Defense has not justified the extraordinary expense of this over-designed system."

Despite the relaxation of forty years of nuclear tension between Washington and Moscow, the money for MILSTAR continues to flow: $1.6 billion in the 1992 Pentagon budget alone. And MILSTAR's nuclear-war-fighting mission remains. Bruce Blair, a former Strategic Air Command missileman who has studied the nation's nuclear-war plans for the Pentagon and Congress, argues that the mission arose from an "illicit evasion of the adversarial process," sparked by the Pentagon's "loss of faith in the democratic system."

Support for MILSTAR would not have survived the rigors of open debate in the planning stages, Blair says. "By hiding the specific means to goals like MILSTAR, you're hiding the goals themselves," he concludes. "That's sabotaging our form of government."

The Doomsday Project

Though MILSTAR may not ever serve the space-based brain for World War III, many related secret projects grind on, as if nuclear Armageddon were still around the bend. One set of these programs, managed by a secret White House agency called the National Program Office, is known less formally around the Pentagon as the "Doomsday Project."

The project, which originated in the early 1980s as Lieutenant Colonel Oliver North's first major White House assignment, aims to keep the White House and Pentagon running during and after a nuclear war or some other major crisis. This apocalyptic concoction has swallowed at least $7.5 billion in secret funds. But its fantastically elaborate communications links cannot withstand dry-run tests, even without nuclear bombs exploding right and left around them, according to a senior army officer familiar with the scenario.

The Doomsday Project is actually an amalgam of secret programs such as Island Sun, which involves a convoy of generals hurtling down interstate highways in lead-laced tractor-trailer trucks, dodging nuclear detonations and barking commands through scramblers. Other major program components feature a network of underground bunkers for the surviving military and civilian leaders—a Dr. Strangelove-style dream.

Among the many open questions about the Doomsday Project is a constitutional one: whether those elite survivors would assume executive powers. A superb CNN investigation broadcast last November revealed that the National Program Office, headed by Vice-President J. Danforth Quayle, had drawn up a list of unelected nation-security wizards who could assume command of the country if the constitutional successors to the presidency were vaporized or otherwise unavailable after a nuclear attack. Not a comforting thought for the day after World War III: You're driving frantically away from a looming mushroom cloud, and Al Haig's voice crackles over the car radio, "I'm in control here at the White House. . . ."

The Solid-Gold Bomber

The Stealth bomber—the fantastically expensive B-2 nuclear bomber, the poster child of the black budget, the bat-winged behemoth built to blast the Kremlin to rubble and the rubble into dust during World War III—was developed in secret in the name of national security. The B-2 was a done deal before a word of public debate on its costs and capabilities was spoken. Now $32 billion has been spent on the plane. Three planes have been built, and twelve or thirteen more are on the production line. There's $4.4 billion in the 1992 Pentagon budget just to keep the lines open. But if production stops after 16 Stealth bombers, that's more than two billion bucks a plane. At such a price, you could build the B-2, which weighs seventy tons, out of solid gold—and still have more than a billion in leftover cash to stuff in the bomb bays. But the Pentagon has even topped that: two highly classified programs to build stealth weapons for the B-2 and other bombers—the Advanced Cruise Missile and the Tri-Service Standoff Attack Missile—will cost up to $22 billion, according to air-force officials.

A third stealthy missile, a drone code-named Tacit Rainbow, has been canceled. Tacit Rainbow was supposed to hunt down and kill enemy radars and air defenses. But due to what the Pentagon politely called "quality-control problems" at the Northrop Corporation (the same folks who brought you the B-2 bomber), the drone couldn't find its own backside with both hands and a road map. Unfortunately, it burned up a billion dollars before that fact came out; the program, like many of its counterparts in the black budget, had been kept so secret that its failures were hidden until the money was gone.

Attack Planes

At $2 billion apiece, the B-2 would still be a bargain compared to the A-12 attack plane. Three billion dollars went into this secret program, but no planes were built, and none ever will be. The Pentagon discovered too late that the design for the plane was impossible; the A-12 would crack in two if a pilot tried to land it on an aircraft carrier. Navy officers and officials at contractors General Dynamics Corporation and McDonnell-Douglas Aerospace Corporation allegedly kept the plane's problems secret from civilian overseers—and even from Pentagon auditors—for a year, in order to keep the secret money flowing. (Both General Dynamics and McDonnell-Douglas deny any wrongdoing.) Now that the secret is out, the program has been canceled as a dismal failure. The navy's deputy general counsel wrote in an executive report that the excessive secrecy, which he called an "abiding cultural problem" in the world of black programs, had concealed the A-12's fundamental flaws.

When the contractors covered up their mistakes and kept them secret from the navy, the navy told Secretary of Defense Dick Cheney that all was well with the A-12. That was a lie that, like a virus, was passed on by Cheney to Congress. When he discovered he'd been had, Cheney went off like a ballistic missile, fuming, "No one can tell me exactly how much it will cost to keep this program going." In January 1991, he finally killed the A-12. Such is the price of secrecy: all the navy has to show for the $3 billion spent under cover on the A-12 is six stacks of useless drawings gathering dust in a top-secret file cabinet.

Challenge to the Black Budget

The above-mentioned programs are but a handful of the major secret projects that the military financed under the shroud of national security in the 1980s. But the fact that this list can be compiled at all—the fact that you're reading this article—is a measure of the success achieved by watchdog groups and the press.

When public pressure forced the B-2, the A-12, MILSTAR, Tacit Rainbow, and other secret programs into the open, the projects were scaled back or canceled outright. They could not survive the light. If that pressure for public debate continues, the black budget—a story that may become a classic saga of the life and slow death of an unconstitutional system— might be seeing its last days. For six years now, cracks have begun to show in the black budget's secret superstructure.

Back in 1985, when the costs and the true nature of all black programs were still state secrets, the Center for Defense Information, a Washington-based public watchdog group run by a retired admiral and staffed by dogged young investigators, published the first-ever analysis of any part of the secret budget. By picking apart the list of all Pentagon research-and-development programs, adding up the costs of all unclassified development programs, and comparing the total to the bottom line of the R & D budget, the Center was able to show that the price tag for all classified research programs was growing fast, from $600 million a year under Jimmy Carter to $9 billion a year under Ronald Reagan. Soon, researchers at the Federation of American Scientists became intrigued and started doing their own analyses. A 1985 editorial in *Defense News*, a trade publication started up to capitalize on the Pentagon's boom times, warned that "it is only a matter of time before the public gets a peek inside the rat's maze and is repelled by what is there."

In early 1986, a handful of elected representatives decided to challenge the system. Les Aspin, then the new head of the House Armed Services Committee, wrote to Reagan's defense secretary, Caspar Weinberger, protesting that 70 percent of the money that the Pentagon was seeking for secret weaponry

had been classified for reasons having nothing to do with national security. Congressman John Dingell of Michigan, head of the House Energy and Commerce Committee, also wrote Weinberger: "The Air Force has been hiding virtually all relevant data on 'black' programs from the Congress." He wanted information.

Nothing doing, replied Weinberger. The Pentagon steadfastly refused to acknowledge the existence of secret programs through the 1980s. Nor did the first newspaper and magazine stories about the black budget have much impact.

What first began to erode the monolith was the revelation that a handful of White House soldiers, retired military men, and CIA operatives had set up a highly profitable weapons dealership with branches in Tehran, Tegucigalpa, and Tel Aviv. Iran-contra exploded the notion that the nation could tolerate the level of secrecy that the White House and the Pentagon had demanded. The congressional investigation of Iran-contra, though badly botched, showed that the whole fiasco never could have happened without the machinery of the secret budget. The Pentagon and the CIA had worked "to avoid complying with an established law by going black," in the words of Senator William Cohen of Maine. They ginned up their covert Central America networks, funded them with profits from the Iran arms sales, and lied when asked by Congress or the media to explain what they were doing. The constitutional nightmare of Iran-contra was the perfect distillation, the quintessence, of the secret budget. As Ronald Reagan was packing up his memorabilia and preparing to turn the White House over to his loyal underling George Bush, a scattershot assault on this system had begun.

Among a few members of Congress, it has become an article of faith that the "executive branch keeps too many things classified, and classified at too high a level, and classified for too long," says Jim Currie, a former spokesperson for the Senate intelligence committee. But

Congress has also acted largely by default—declassifying the Pentagon's billion-dollar drawing-board blunders after the fact, harrumphing loudly after discovering what the CIA's been doing behind its back, moaning when the White House ignores its laws.

Today, after half a century of black budgets, the secret cache largely remains inviolate. The wall surrounding it has proven more durable than the one that divided Berlin. "Basically the whole government secrecy apparatus is still in cold-war mode. The inherited structures of the last forty years are still in place and still provide for great latitude in government secrecy," says Steven Aftergood of the Federation of American Scientists. Aftergood, a self-taught expert on the secret budget, was the first to uncover the Timberwind program last year.

"Some of the largest classified programs have come out of the black," Aftergood adds. "There have been a number of scandalous failures involving excessive secrecy, like the A-12. There have been gestures by Congress in the direction of greater openness. And above all, there is a growing skepticism and concern among more and more members of the public about government secrecy. Sooner or later, I hope that will bring a fundamental change....But right now, it's difficult to discern the fundamental change that will be required to create a truly open and democratic system."

Concrete changes, even symbolic ones, have been few and feeble. Congress has the power to relegate the black budget to the cold war's graveyard, to place it in the national-security museum along with fallout shelters and loyalty oaths. Congress could demand the disclosure of data on the cost and the character of secret programs. But it has done so only in a piecemeal way, allowing most of its thrusts to be parried by the sword and shield of Pentagon secrecy. It has not confronted the underlying fact that the secrecy system itself defies the Constitution, which requires that the government publish a complete and accurate account of all federal spending. "The fault lies with the Congress," says Congresswoman Pat Schroeder of Colorado. "If we forced the release of this information, there would be no issue. As long as the Congress goes along with the Pentagon's secrecy program, we have no [legitimate] complaint."

Two case studies in congressional action and inaction culminated last November. They point to ways in which the secrecy of the black budget can be eroded—but very slowly. In the summer of 1991, Congress discovered a slew of undisclosed programs with operating funds for secret military intelligence units that the Pentagon had clandestinely built and sustained. "There are dozens of these programs that we knew nothing about," one senior congressional staff member tells me. "The Pentagon's been stonewalling us," says another.

These supersecret projects were never subjected to the limited oversight required of such programs as the A-12 and Timberwind. At most, 8 or 9 members of Congress—the Speaker of the House and the senior members of the armed-services and appropriations committees—were allowed to go to the Pentagon and be briefed in lead-lined rooms. These few were at the mercy of the briefers' completeness and accuracy. The other 140 members of the committees voting on the Pentagon's budget had to operate in the dark. Now Congress, in secret language incorporated in the classified annex of the 1992 Pentagon budget, has demanded more information on these "deep black" programs.

Separately, the Senate intelligence committee voted ten-to-five last July to change a long-standing practice of secrecy by publishing the bottom line of the intelligence budget—the money that goes to the CIA and the Pentagon's intelligence agencies, such as the National Security Agency, the National Reconnaissance Office, and the Defense Intelligence Agency. The new director of central intelligence, Robert M. Gates, pleased the committee during his October confirmation hearings by supporting the idea as a symbolic gesture showing that post-coldwar glasnost had come to the CIA. I heard Gates make that statement, and it sounded like a promise to me. But in November, after President Bush threatened to veto the entire intelligence bill unless the committee's measure was watered down, Congress caved in. The members of the intelligence committees changed their order to a powerless "sense of Congress" resolution.

There is pertinent history in the difficult struggle to unveil the intelligence budget. Back in April 1976, the Church Committee, the only congressional panel ever to publish a detailed investigation of the CIA, voted eight-to-three to disclose the sum total of classified spending for espionage, counterespionage, and intelligence analysis. The committee said that "publication of the aggregate figure for national intelligence would begin to satisfy the constitutional requirement [for a public budget] and would not damage the national security."

The movement for openness that time around was beaten back. And the point man for the counterattack was the head of the CIA, George Bush. As president fifteen years later, Bush fought the same battle—and won again. Meanwhile, Congress continues to protest that Bush treats its secret military and intelligence appropriations as mere suggestions to spend the black budget as he sees fit, to regard the black budget enacted by Congress as simply a sketch, not a legal blueprint, and to ignore congressional orders and limitations on secret funds. To permit this sleight of hand to continue is a sweeping abdication of authority by Congress, the Senate Appropriations Committee reported last September.

The issue here is not some run-of-the-mill power struggle between Congress and the White House; it is the heart of U.S. constitutional government. It's easy to make a joke of the fact that spending money is the only real power that Congress holds. But "this power of the purse," wrote James Madison, the Constitution's principal author, is "the most complete and effectual weapon with which

any Constitution can arm the immediate representatives of the people." By allowing the Pentagon and the nation's intelligence agencies to have a secret purse, Americans are ceding a portion of their political power to unelected and unaccountable national-security soldiers.

Tim Weiner is a Pulitzer Prize-winning Washington correspondent for the Philadelphia Inquirer. *He is the author of* Blank Check *(Warner Books), a book about secret programs.*

For more information about two watchdog groups mentioned in this story, contact:
- Center for Defense Information, 1500 Massachusetts Ave. N.W., Washington, DC 20005; (202)862-0700.
- Federation of American Scientists, 307 Massachusetts Ave., N.E., Washington, DC 20002; (202)546-3300.

Behind the Story
When Tim Weiner arrived in Washington, D.C., in 1986 as an investigative reporter for the *Philadelphia Inquirer*, he had no idea that he was about to plunge into a six-year effort to uncover the nation's secret intelligence and weapons programs.

"I was originally assigned to get to the bottom of the spare-parts pricing scandal then heating up. You know, the story about the ten-thousand-dollar wing nuts and so on," Weiner says.

Step one in covering that story was a close study of the country's military budget. "The first time I looked at it, I was struck by the proliferation of code words and blank spaces," he remembers. "I wondered about programs with names like OMEGA, OLYMPIA, BELL WEATHER, and BERNIE. But even more startling than the fact that the purpose of the programs was not revealed was that the cost was not reported—to Congress or the public. I couldn't understand how in the world the Pentagon could get away with blanking out the costs."

In pursuit of more information about this "black budget," which has quadrupled during the Reagan-bush era, Weiner met with Pentagon whistle-blowers, citizen watchdog groups, members of Congress, and their assistants. He plowed through classified and unclassified government documents. But what he was finding generated more questions than answers.

Then Weiner got a break. An insider who knew the big picutre agreed to talk and provide both information and guidance. "He thought that the whole system was out of control—and he was in the middle of it," recalls Weiner. "He thought the secret budget was being used to mask the biggest, most costly, and least sensible weapons programs in the Pentagon."

Weiner's newspaper stories received virtually no acknowledgment from top administration officials. Once, he put a series of questions to Caspar Weinberger, Ronald Reagan's secretary of defense. "He glared at me and said, 'This is funding which we believe it is better for us not to publicize on the very sound premise that we don't see the purpose of giving additional information to the enemy," Weiner says. "That may have been well and good back in the dark days of the Evil Empire. But the secrecy no longer makes any sense."

For his 1987 series of newspaper stories about secret military programs, Weiner received the Pulitzer Prize in 1988. The articles, the prize, and a book he authored called *Blank Check* (published in 1990) drew some attention on Capitol Hill. But Weiner says he's not surprised that little has changed in the intervening years.

"It has had remarkably little impact," he says. "Almost every effort at reform failed last year. There was no limit placed on the amount of black money a program can consume. And the Congress even allowed President Bush to beat it back from publishing the bottom line on the intelligence budget."

Weiner remains obsessed by the story, saying he's only scratched the surface so far. "There's a host of multibillion-dollar programs," he adds, "just churning away, secretly and in defiance of what the Constitution says. These secret programs are like an enormous ship churning through the night. Even if an order was to come down from the bridge tomorrow to reverse course, it would take years to make a difference. And tragically, that order has not come."

Note: If you'd like to obtain reprints of the articles cited in Stories #11–#25 in Chapter 3, "The Top 25 News Stories of 1992," please send $7.50 to CENSORED Reprints, Shelburne Press, P.O. Box 2468, Chapel Hill, NC 27515. (Some articles not available due to lack of permission to reprint.)

The *CENSORED!* Resource Guide

K nowing where to direct concerns, compliments, ideas or even offers to help is a question many people have of both the alternative and establishment media.

With this in mind, Project Censored assembled a simple, easy-to-use and dependable resource guide for anyone who wants to follow up on these stories or get actively involved in doing something about the issue or the media.

Following is a collection of names, addresses, phone and fax numbers, when available, to a variety of organizations, individuals, and electronic and print media outlets that might prove useful.

Although this information was current as of early 1993, you may want to double-check to ensure the names, addresses, etc., are still accurate. If you are aware of any changes and/or corrections to the list, please send them to Censored Resource Guide, Sonoma State University, Rohnert Park, CA 94928.

We plan to update the list in the 1994 edition of *CENSORED!* And, if you have any additions that should be included, please send them to the same address.

TABLE OF CONTENTS
Censored Resource Guide

Alternative Broadcast Media Producers & Organizations

ALTERNATIVE RADIO
2129 Mapleton
Boulder, CO 80304
Tel: 303/444-8788

ALTERNATIVE VIEWS
Box 7297
Austin, TX 78713
Tel: 512/477-5148
Fax: 512/471-4806

COMMON GROUND
Stanley Foundation
216 Sycamore Street, Ste. 500
Muscatine, IA 52761
Tel: 319/264-1500

EMPOWERMENT PROJECT
1653 18th Street, Ste. 3
Santa Monica, CA 90404
Tel: 310/828-8807
Fax: 310/829-2305

GLOBALVISION
1600 Broadway
New York, NY 10019
Tel: 212/246-0202

MEDIA NETWORK/
ALTERNATIVE MEDIA INFORMATION
CENTER
39 W. 14th Street, #403
New York, NY 10011
Tel: 212/929-2663
Fax: 212/929-2732

NATIONAL ASIAN AMERICAN
TELECOMMUNICATIONS ASSOCIATION
346 9th Street, 2nd Fl.
San Francisco, CA 94103
Tel: 415/863-0814
Fax: 415/863-7428

NATIONAL FEDERATION OF COMMUNITY
BROADCASTERS
666 11th Street NW, Ste. 805
Washington, DC 20001
Tel: 202/393-2355

PACIFICA (PROGRAM SERVICE)
3729 Cahuenga Blvd. West
North Hollywood, CA 91604
Tel: 818/506-1077

PACIFICA NATIONAL NEWS BUREAU
702 H Street NW, Ste. 3
Washington, DC 20001
Tel: 202/783-1620

PAPER TIGER TV/DEEP DISH
339 Lafayette Street
New York, NY 10012
Tel: 212/420-9045

RADIO FOR PEACE INTERNATIONAL
World Peace University
Box 10869
Eugene, OR 97440
Tel: 503/741-1794
Fax: 503/741-1279

SECOND OPINION
Erwin Knoll (host)
c/o The Progressive
409 E. Main Street
Madison, WI 53703
Tel: 608/257-4626
Fax: 608/257-3373

VIDEO DATABANK
37 S. Wabash
Chicago, IL 60603
Tel: 312/899-5172
Fax: 312/263-0141

THE VIDEO PROJECT: FILMS AND VIDEOS
FOR A SAFE AND SUSTAINABLE WORLD
5332 College Avenue, Ste. 101
Oakland, CA 94618
Tel: 510/655-9050
Fax: 510/655-9115

WINGS
Women's Int'l News Gathering Service
P.O. Box 5307
Kansas City, MO 64131
Tel: 816/361-7161

Alternative & Electronic News Services

ALTERNET
2025 Eye Street NW, Ste. 1118
Washington, DC 20006
Tel: 202/887-0022

INSIGHT FEATURES
Networking for Democracy
3411 W. Diversey, Ste. 1
Chicago, IL 60647
Tel: 312/384-8827
Fax: 312/384-3904

INTERPRESS
Global Infomation Network
777 United Nations Plaza
New York, NY 10017
Tel: 212/286-0123
Fax: 212/818-9249

LATIN AMERICA DATA BASE
Latin American Institute
University of New Mexico
801 Yale Blvd. NE
Albuquerque, NM 87131-1016
Tel: 800/472-0888
or 505/277-6839
Fax: 505/277-5989

NEW LIBERATION NEWS SERVICE
P.O. Box 41
MIT Branch
Cambridge, MA 02139
Tel: 617/492-8316

PACIFIC NEWS SERVICE
450 Mission Street, Rm. 506
San Francisco, CA 94105
Tel: 415/243-4364

PEACENET; ECONET; CONFLICNET
INSTITUTE FOR GLOBAL
COMMUNICATIONS
18 DeBoom Street
San Francisco, CA 94107
Tel: 415/442-0220
Fax: 415/546-1794

PEOPLE'S NEWS AGENCY
1354 Montague Street NW
P.O. Box 56466
Washington, DC 20040
Tel: 202/829-2278
Fax: 202/829-0462

Alternative Periodicals & Publications

ACTION FOR CULTURAL SURVIVAL
Cultural Survival, Inc.
215 First Street
Cambridge, MA 02142
Tel: 617/621-3818
Fax: 617/621-3814

THE ADVOCATE
6922 Hollywood Boulevard, 10th Fl.
Los Angeles, CA 90028
Tel: 213/871-1225
Fax: 213/467-6805

AFRICA NEWS
P.O. Box 3851
Durham, NC 27702
Tel: 919/286-0747
Fax: 919/286-2614

AGAINST THE CURRENT
Center for Changes
7012 Michigan Avenue
Detroit, MI 48210
Tel: 313/841-0161
Fax: 313/841-8884

AKWESASNE NOTES
Mohawk Nation
P.O. Box 196
Rooseveltown, NY 13683-0196
Tel: 518/358-9531
Fax: 613/575-2064

ALERT: Focus on Central America
CISPES
P.O. Box 12156
Washington, DC 20005
Tel: 202/265-0890
Fax: 202/265-7843

ALTERNATIVES
Lynne Rienner Publishers
1800 30th Street, Ste. 314
Boulder, CO 80301-1032
Tel: 303/444-6684
Fax: 303/444-0824

AMERICA'S CENSORED NEWSLETTER
P.O. Box 310
Cotati, CA 994931

AMICUS JOURNAL
40 W. 20th Street
New York, NY 10011
Tel: 212/727-2700
Fax: 212/727-1773

BLACK SCHOLAR
P.O. Box 2869
Oakland, CA 94609
Tel: 510/547-6633
Fax: 510/547-6679

COMMON CAUSE
2030 M Street NW
Washington, DC 20036
Tel: 202/833-1200
Fax: 202/659-3716

COVERT ACTION INFORMATION
BULLETIN
1500 Massachusetts Ave. NW, #732
Washington, DC 20005
Tel: 202/331-9763
Fax: 202/331-9751

DEFENSE MONITOR
1500 Massachusetts Ave. NW
Washington, DC 20005
Tel: 202/862-0700
Fax: 202/862-0708

DISSENT
521 Fifth Avenue
New York, NY 10017
Tel: 212/595-3084

DOLLARS AND SENSE
1 Summer Street
Somerville, MA 02143
Tel: 617/628-8411
Fax: 617/628-2025

E: THE ENVIRONMENTAL MAGAZINE
P.O. Box 5098
Westport, CT 06881
Tel: 203/854-5559
Fax: 203/866-0602

EARTH ISLAND JOURNAL
300 Broadway, Ste. 28
San Francisco, CA 94133-3312
Tel: 415/788-3666
Fax: 415/788-7324

ENVIRONMENTAL ACTION
6930 Carroll Avenue, Ste. 600
Takoma Park, MD 20912
Tel: 301/891-1106
Fax: 301/891-2218

ENVIRONMENTAL IMPACT REPORTER
P.O. Box 1834
Sebastopol, CA 95473
Tel: 707/823-8744

THE HUMAN QUEST
Churchman Co., Inc.
1074 23rd Avenue N.
St. Petersburg, FL 33704
Tel: 813/894-0097

HURACAN
P.O. Box 7591
Minneapolis, MN 55407

IN CONTEXT
P.O. Box 11470
Bainbridge Island, WA 98110
Tel: 206/842-0216
Fax: 206/842-5208

IN THESE TIMES
2040 N. Milwaukee Avenue, 2nd Fl.
Chicago, IL 60647-4002
Tel: 312/772-0100
Fax: 312/772-4180

ISSUES IN SCIENCE & TECHNOLOGY
National Academy of Sciences
2101 Constitution Avenue, NW
Washington, DC 20418
Tel: 202/334-3305
Fax: 202/334-1290

LATIN AMERICAN PERSPECTIVES
2455 Teller Road
Newbury Park, CA 91320
Tel: 805/499-0721
Fax: 805/499-0871

LEFT BUSINESS OBSERVER
250 W. 85th Street
New York, NY 10024-3217
Tel: 212/874-4020

MOTHER JONES
1663 Mission Street, 2nd Fl.
San Francisco, CA 94103
Tel: 415/558-8881
Fax: 415/863-5136

MS. MAGAZINE
230 Park Avenue
New York, NY 10169
Tel: 212/551-9595

MUCKRAKER
Center for Investigative Reporting
568 Howard Street, 5th Fl.
San Francisco, CA 94105-3007
Tel: 415/543-1200

MULTINATIONAL MONITOR
P.O. Box 19405
Washington, DC 20036
Tel: 202/387-8034
Fax: 202/234-5176

THE NATION
72 Fifth Avenue
New York, NY 10011
Tel: 212/242-8400
Fax: 212/463-9712

NATIONAL CATHOLIC REPORTER
115 E. Armour Boulevard
Kansas City, MO 64111
Tel: 816/531-0538
Fax: 816/531-7466

NATIONAL REVIEW
150 E. 35th Street
New York, NY 10016
Tel: 212/679-7330
Fax: 212/696-0309

NEW DIRECTIONS FOR WOMEN
108 W. Palisade Avenue, 2nd Fl.
Englewood, NJ 07631
Tel: 201/568-0226
Fax: 201/568-6532

NEWSLETTER ON INTELLECTUAL
FREEDOM
American Library Association
50 E. Huron Street
Chicago, IL 60611
Tel: 312/944-6780
Fax: 312/440-9374

NORTHERN SUN NEWS
P.O. Box 581487
Minneapolis, MN 55458-1487
Tel: 612/729-8543

THE PAPER
540 Mendocino Avenue
Santa Rosa, CA 95401
Tel: 707/527-1200

THE PROGRESSIVE
409 E. Main Street
Madison, WI 53703
Tel: 608/257-4626
Fax: 608/257-3373

PROPAGANDA REVIEW
Media Alliance
Fort Mason, Bldg. D, 2nd Fl.
San Francisco, CA 94123
Tel: 415/441-2557

PUBLIC CITIZEN
2000 P Street NW, Ste. 610
Washington, DC 20036
Tel: 202/833-3000

ROLLING STONE
1290 Ave. of the Americas, 2nd Fl.
New York, NY 10104
Tel: 212/484-1616
Fax: 212/767-8203

THE SAN FRANCISCO BAY GUARDIAN
520 Hampshire
San Francisco, CA 94110
Tel: 415/255-3100

SECRECY & GOVERNMENT BULLETIN
Federation of American Scientists
307 Massachusetts Avenue NE
Washington, DC 20002
Tel: 202/675-1012

SF WEEKLY
425 Brannan Street
San Francisco, CA 94107
Tel: 415/541-0700
Fax: 415/777-1839

SOJOURNERS
P.O. Box 29272
Washington, DC 20017-5290
Tel: 202/636-3637
Fax: 202/636-3643

SOUTHERN EXPOSURE
P.O. Box 531
Durham, NC 27702
Tel: 919/419-8311
Fax: 919/419-8315

THE SPOTLIGHT
300 Independence Avenue SE
Washington, DC 20003
Tel: 202/544-1794

STRATEGIES
Strategies for Media Literacy
1095 Markst Street, Ste. 410
San Francisco, CA 94103
Tel: 415/621-2911

TIKKUN
5100 Leona Street
Oakland, CA 94619
Tel: 510/482-0805
Fax: 510/482-3379

UNCLASSIFIED
Association of National Security Alumni
2001 S Street NW, Ste. 740
Washington, DC 20009
Tel: 202/483-9325

URGENT ACTION BULLETIN
Survival International
310 Edgeware Road
London W2 1DY
England
Tel: 071/723-5535
Fax: 071/723-4059

UTNE READER
1624 Harmon Place, Ste. 330
Minneapolis, MN 55403
Tel: 612/338-5040

VILLAGE VOICE
36 Cooper Square
New York, NY 10003
Tel: 212/475-3300
Fax: 212/475-8944

WAR AND PEACE DIGEST
War and Peace Foundation
32 Union Square E.
New York, NY 10003
Tel: 212/777-6626
Fax: 212/995-9652

THE WASHINGTON SPECTATOR
London Terrace Station
P.O. Box 20065
New York, NY 10011

WHOLE EARTH REVIEW
27 Gate Five Road
Sausalito, CA 94965
Tel: 415/332-1716
Fax: 415/332-3110

WORLD PRESS REVIEW
200 Madison Avenue, Ste. 2104
New York, NY 10016
Tel: 212/889-5155
Fax: 212/889-5634

WORLD WATCH
Worldwatch Institute
1776 Massachusetts Avenue NW
Washington, DC 20036
Tel: 202/452-1999
Fax: 202/296-7365

Z MAGAZINE
116 Botolph Street
Boston, MA 02115
Tel: 617/787-4531
Fax: 508/457-0626

Free Press/Right-to-Know Publications & Organizations

AMERICAN LIBRARY ASSOCIATION
INTELLECTUAL FREEDOM COMMITTEE
50 E. Huron Street
Chicago, IL 60611
Tel: 312/944-6780 or
800/545-2433
Fax: 312/440-9374

ARTICLE 19: INTERNATIONAL
CENTRE AGAINST CENSORSHIP
90 Borough High Street
London SE1 1LL England
Tel: 071/403-4822
Fax: 071/403-1943

BILL OF RIGHTS JOURNAL
175 Fifth Avenue, Rm. 814
New York, NY 10010
Tel: 212/673-2040
Fax: 212/460-8359

CALIFORNIA FIRST AMENDMENT
COALITION
2218 Homewood Way
Carmichael, CA 95608
Tel: 916/485-2912
Fax: 916/485-3442

CIVIL LIBERTIES
American Civil Liberties Union
132 W. 43rd Street
New York, NY 10036
Tel: 212/944-9800
Fax: 212/869-9065

COALITION ON GOVERNMENT
INFORMATION
American Library Assn.
110 Maryland Avenue NE
Washington, DC 20002
Tel: 202/547-4440
Fax: 202/547-7363

COMMITTEE TO PROTECT JOURNALISTS
16 E. 42nd Street, 3rd Fl.
New York, NY 10017
Tel: 212/983-5355
Fax: 212/867-1830

DATACENTER
Right-to-Know Project
464 19th Street
Oakland, CA 94612
Tel: 510/835-4692
Fax: 510/835-3017

FIRST AMENDMENT CONGRESS
1445 Market Street, Ste. 320
Denver, CO 80202
Tel: 303/820-5688
Fax: 303/534-8774

FREE PRESS ASSOCIATION
P.O. Box 15548
Columbus, OH 43215
Tel: 614/291-1441

FREEDOM OF EXPRESSION FOUNDATION
5220 S. Marina Pacifica
Long Beach, CA 90803
Tel: 310/985-4301
Fax: 310/985-2369

FREEDOM OF INFORMATION CENTER
20 Walter Williams Hall
University of Missouri at Columbia
Columbia, MO 65211
Tel: 314/882-4856
Fax: 314/882-9002

FREEDOM OF INFORMATION
CLEARINGHOUSE
P.O. Box 19367
Washington, DC 20036
Tel: 202/833-3000

INDEX ON CENSORSHIP
Fund for Free Expression
485 Fifth Avenue
New York, NY 10017
Tel: 212/972-8400
Fax: 212/972-0905

INTER AMERICAN PRESS ASSOCIATION
2911 NW 39th Street
Miami, FL 33142
Tel: 305/634-2465

MEDIA COALITION/AMERICANS
FOR CONSTITUTIONAL FREEDOM
1221 Avenue of the Americas, 24th Fl.
New York, NY 10020
Tel: 212/768-6770
Fax: 212/391-1247

MEIKLEJOHN CIVIL LIBERTIES INSTITUTE
P.O. Box 673
Berkeley, CA 94701
Tel: 510/848-0599
Fax: 510/848-6008

NATIONAL COALITION AGAINST
CENSORSHIP
275 7th Avenue
New York, NY 10001
Tel: 212/807-6222
Fax: 212/807-6245

NATIONAL COMMITTEE AGAINST
REPRESSIVE LEGISLATION
3321 12th Street NE
Washington, DC 20017
Tel: 202/529-4225

PEOPLE FOR THE AMERICAN WAY
2000 M Street NW, Ste. 400
Washington, DC 20036
Tel: 202/467-4999
Fax: 202/293-2672

REPORTERS' COMMITTEE FOR
FREEDOM OF THE PRESS
1735 Eye Street NW, Ste. 504
Washington, DC 20006
Tel: 202/466-6312

STUDENT PRESS LAW CENTER
1735 I Street NW, Ste. 504
Washington, DC 20006
Tel: 202/466-5242
Fax: 202/466-6326

WORLD PRESS FREEDOM COMMITTEE
C/O THE NEWSPAPER CENTER
11600 Sunrise Valley Drive
Reston, VA 22091
Tel: 703/648-1000
Fax: 703/620-4557

WOMEN'S INSTITUTE FOR FREEDOM
OF THE PRESS
3306 Ross Place NW
Washington, DC 20008
Tel: 202/966-7783

Journalism/Media Analysis Publications & Organizations

ACCURACY IN MEDIA
1275 K Street NW, Ste. 1150
Washington, DC 20005
Tel: 202/371-6710
Fax: 202/371-9054

ADBUSTERS: A Magazine of Media and
Environmental Strategies
The Media Foundation
1243 W. Seventh Avenue
Vancouver, British Columbia
Canada V6H 1B7
Tel: 604/736-9401
Fax: 604/737-6021

AMERICAN JOURNALISM REVIEW
4716 Pontiac Street, Ste. 310
College Park, MD 20740-2493
Tel: 301/513-0001
Fax: 301/441-9495

AMERICAN SOCIETY OF JOURNALISTS
AND AUTHORS
1501 Broadway, Ste. 302
New York, NY 10036
Tel: 212/997-0947
Fax: 212/768-7414

AMERICAN SOCIETY OF NEWSPAPER
EDITORS
P.O. Box 17004
Washington, DC 20041
Tel: 703/648-1144
Fax: 703/620-4557

ASIAN AMERICAN JOURNALISTS
ASSOCIATION
1765 Sutter Street, Rm. 1000
San Francisco, CA 94115
Tel: 415/346-2051
Fax: 415/931-4671

ASSOCIATION OF AMERICAN PUBLISHERS
220 E. 23rd Street
New York, NY 10010
Tel: 212/689-8920
Fax: 212/696-0131

ASSOCIATION OF HOUSE DEMOCRATIC
PRESS ASSISTANTS
House of Representatives
2459 Rayburn Bldg.
Washington, DC 20515
Tel: 202/225-1554
Fax: 202/225-4951

BLACK PRESS INSTITUTE
2711 E. 75th Place
Chicago, IL 60649
Tel: 312/375-8200
Fax: 312/375-8262

BLACK WOMEN IN PUBLISHING
P.O. Box 6275
FDR Station
New York, NY 10150
Tel: 212/772-5951

CENTER FOR INVESTIGATIVE REPORTING
568 Howard Street, 5th Fl.
San Francisco, CA 94105-3007
Tel: 415/543-1200
Fax: 415/543-8311

CENTER FOR MEDIA AND PUBLIC AFFAIRS
2101 L Street NW, Ste. 405
Washington, DC 20037
Tel: 202/223-2942
Fax: 202/872-4014

CENTER FOR THE STUDY OF
COMMERCIALISM
1875 Connecticut Avenue NW, Ste. 300
Washington, DC 20009-5728
Tel: 202/797-7080
Fax: 202/265-4954

CHRISTIC INSTITUTE
8773 Venice Boulevard.
Los Angeles, CA 90034
Tel: 310/287-1556
Fax: 310/287-1559

COLUMBIA JOURNALISM REVIEW
700 Journalism Bldg.
Columbia University
New York, NY 10027
Tel: 212/854-1881
Fax: 212/854-8580

COMMUNICATIONS CONSORTIUM
1333 H Street NW, 11th Fl.
Washington, DC 20005
Tel: 202/682-1270
Fax: 202/682-2154

CULTURAL ENVIRONMENT MOVEMENT
P.O. Box 31847
Philadelphia, PA 19104

DEADLINE
Center for War, Peace and the News Media
New York University
10 Washington Place, 4th Fl.
New York, NY 10003
Tel: 212/998-7960
Fax: 212/995-4143

EDITOR AND PUBLISHER
11 W. 19th Street
New York, NY 10011
Tel: 212/675-4380
Fax: 212/929-1259

ESSENTIAL INFORMATION
P.O. Box 19405
Washington, DC 20036
Tel: 202/387-8030
Fax: 202/234-5176

EXTRA!
Fairness and Accuracy in Reporting
130 W. 25th Street
New York, NY 10001
Tel: 212/633-6700
Fax: 212/727-7668

FUND FOR INVESTIGATIVE JOURNALISM
1755 Massachusetts Avenue NW
Washington, DC 20036
Tel: 202/462-1844

GAY AND LESBIAN PRESS ASSOCIATION
P.O. Box 8185
Universal City, CA 91608
Tel: 818/902-1476

GLAAD
Gay and Lesbian Alliance Against
Defamation
150 W. 26th Street, Ste. 503
New York, NY 10001
Tel: 212/807-1700
Fax: 212/807-1806

GLOBAL INFORMATION NETWORK
777 United Nations Plaza
New York, NY 10017
Tel: 212/286-0123
Fax: 212/818-9249

INDEPENDENT
625 Broadway, 9th Fl.
New York, NY 10012
Tel: 212/473-3400
Fax: 212/677-8732

INSTITUTE FOR ALTERNATIVE
JOURNALISM
100 E. 85th Street
New York, NY 10028
Tel: 212/799-4822
Washington Office:
Tel: 202/887-0022

INVESTIGATIVE JOURNALISM PROJECT
Fund for Constitutional Government
122 Maryland Avenue NE, Ste. 300
Washington, DC 20002
Tel: 202/546-3732
Fax: 202/543-3156

INVESTIGATIVE REPORTERS & EDITORS
100 Neff Hall
University of Missouri
School of Journalism
Columbia, MO 65211
Tel: 314/882-2042
Fax: 314/882-5431

JOURNALISM QUARTERLY
George Washington University
Journalism Program
Washington, DC 20052
Tel: 202/994-6226

LIES OF OUR TIMES
Institute for Media Analysis
145 W. 4th Street
New York, NY 10012
Tel: 212/254-1061
Fax: 212/254-9598

MEDIA ACCESS PROJECT
2000 M Street NW, 4th Fl.
Washington, DC 20036
Tel: 202/232-4300
Fax: 202/293-2672

MEDIA ALLIANCE
Fort Mason Center, Bldg. D, 2nd Fl.
San Francisco, CA 94123
Tel: 415/441-2557

THE MEDIA INSTITUTE
1000 Potomac Street NW, Ste. 204
Washington, DC 20007
Tel: 202/298-7512
Fax: 202/337-7092

MEDIA WATCH
P.O. Box 618
Santa Cruz, CA 95061-0618
Tel: 408/423-6355
Fax: 408/423-9119

NATIONAL ALLIANCE OF THIRD WORLD
JOURNALISTS
1325 G Street NW
Washington, DC 20005
Tel: 202/737-6225
Fax: 202/737-6824

NATIONAL ASSOCIATION OF BLACK
JOURNALISTS
P.O. Box 17212
Washington, DC 20041
Tel: 703/648-1270
Fax: 703/476-6245

NATIONAL ASSOCIATION OF HISPANIC
JOURNALISTS
National Press Bldg., Ste. 1193
Washington, DC 20045
Tel: 202/662-7145
Fax: 202/662-7144

NATIONAL CONFERENCE OF EDITORIAL
WRITERS
6223 Executive Boulevard.
Rockville, MD 20852
Tel: 301/984-3015

NATIONAL NEWSPAPER ASSOCIATION
1627 K Street NW, Ste. 400
Washington, DC 20006
Tel: 202/466-7200
Fax: 202/331-1403

NATIONAL WRITERS UNION
873 Broadway, Rm. 203
New York, NY 10003
Tel: 212/254-0279

NEWSPAPER ASSN. OF AMERICA
11600 Sunrise Valley Drive
Reston, VA 22091
Tel: 703/648-1000
Fax: 703/620-4557

NEWSPAPER GUILD
8611 Second Avenue
Silver Spring, MD 20910
Tel: 301/585-2990
Fax: 301/585-0668

NEWSPAPER RESEARCH JOURNAL
Scripps Hall School of Journalism
Ohio University
Athens, OH 45701
Tel: 614/593-2590
Fax: 614/593-2592

ORGANIZATION OF NEWS OMBUDSMEN
c/o Art Nauman
Sacramento Bee
P.O. Box 15779
Sacramento, CA 95852
Tel: 916/442-8050

PROJECT CENSORED
Communications Studies Dept.
Sonoma State University
1801 E. Cotati Avenue
Rohnert Park, CA 94928
Tel: 707/664-2500
Fax: 707/664-2505

PUBLIC MEDIA CENTER
446 Green Street
San Francisco, CA 94133
Tel: 415/434-1403
Fax: 415/986-6779

THE QUILL
Society of Professional Journalists
16 S. Jackson
Greencastle, IN 46135
Tel: 317/653-3333
Fax: 317/653-4631

ST. LOUIS JOURNALISM REVIEW
8380 Olive Boulevard
St. Louis, MO 63132
Tel: 314/991-1699
Fax: 314/997-1898

TIMES MIRROR CENTER
FOR THE PEOPLE & THE PRESS
1875 Eye Street NW, Ste. 1110
Washington, DC 20006
Tel: 202/293-3126

TYNDALL REPORT
135 Rivington Street
New York, NY 10002
Tel: 212/674-8913
Fax: 212/979-7304

WOMEN IN COMMUNICATIONS
2101 Wilson Boulevard, Ste. 417
Arlington, VA 22201
Tel: 703/528-4200
Fax: 703/528-4205

Library & Reference Sources

THE ACTIVIST'S ALMANAC:
The Concerned Citizen's Guide to the
Leading Advocacy Organizations in America
by David Walls, 1993
Simon & Schuster Fireside Books
New York

ALTERNATIVE PRESS INDEX
Alternative Press Center, Inc.
P.O. Box 33109
Baltimore, MD 21218
Tel: 301/243-2471

DIRECTORY OF ELECTRONIC JOURNALS,
NEWSLETTERS AND ACADEMIC
DISCUSSION LISTS
by Kovacs and Strangelove
Association of Scientific and Academic
Publishing
1527 New Hampshire Avenue NW
Washington, DC 20036

ECOLINKING: EVERYONE'S GUIDE TO
ONLINE INFORMATION
by Don Rittner, 1992
Peachpit Press, Berkeley, CA

ENCYCLOPEDIA OF ASSOCIATIONS
1993 ed., 4 vols.
Gale Research Inc., Detroit and London

FROM RADICAL TO EXTREME RIGHT
A bibliography of current periodicals of
protest, controversy, advocacy and dissent
by Gail Skidmore and Theodore Jurgen
Spahn, 1987, 3rd ed.
Scarecrow Press, Inc.
Metuchen, NJ, and London

GALE DIRECTORY OF PUBLICATIONS AND
BROADCAST MEDIA
1992 ed., 3 vols. plus supplement
Gale Research Inc., Detroit and London

THE INTERNATIONAL DIRECTORY OF
LITTLE MAGAZINES AND SMALL PRESSES
Len Fulton, ed., 26th ed., 1990/91
Dustbooks
P.O. Box 100
Paradise, CA 95967

THE LEFT INDEX: A QUARTERLY INDEX
TO PERIODICALS OF THE LEFT
Reference and Research Services
Santa Cruz, CA

MACROCOSM USA: POSSIBILITIES FOR A
NEW PROGRESSIVE ERA
Sandi Brockway, ed., 1992
Macrocosm USA, Inc.
P.O. Box 185
Cambria, CA 93428-0185
Tel: 805/927-8030
Fax: 805/927-1987

MEDIA GUIDE — 1992
Jude Wanniski, ed.
Polyconomics, Inc., Morristown, NJ
Tel: 800/633-4288

PROGRESSIVE PERIODICALS DIRECTORY
by Craig T. Canan
2nd ed., 1989
Progressive Education
P.O. Box 120574
Nashville, TN 37212

ULRICH'S INTERNATIONAL PERIODICALS
DIRECTORY
1992/93, 3 vols.
R.R. Bowker, New Providence, NJ

THE WORKING PRESS OF THE NATION
1991 ed.
National Research Bureau
225 W. Wacker Drive, Ste. 2275
Chicago, IL 60606-1229
Tel: 312/346-9097

National Broadcast Media

ABC WORLD NEWS TONIGHT
47 W. 66th Street
New York, NY 10023
Tel: 212/456-4040

ASSOCIATED PRESS RADIO NETWORK
1825 K Street NW, Ste. 710
Washington, DC 20006
Tel: 202/955-7200

CBS EVENING NEWS
524 W. 57th Street
New York, NY 10019
Tel: 212/975-3693

CBS THIS MORNING
524 W. 57th Street
New York, NY 10019
Tel: 212/975-2824

CNN
One CNN Center
Box 105366
Atlanta, GA 30348
Tel: 404/827-1500

CNN
Washington Bureau
820 First Street NE
Washington, DC 20002
Tel: 202/898-7900

C-SPAN
400 N. Capitol Street NW, Ste. 650
Washington, DC 20001
Tel: 202/737-3220
Fax: 202/737-3323

CROSSFIRE
CNN
820 First Street NE
Washington, DC 20002
Tel: 202/898-7951

PHIL DONAHUE SHOW
30 Rockefeller Plaza
New York, NY 10019
Tel: 212/975-2006

FACE THE NATION
CBS News
2020 M Street NW
Washington, DC 20036
Tel: 202/457-4481

GOOD MORNING AMERICA
ABC News
147 Columbus Avenue
New York, NY 10023
Tel: 212/456-5900
Fax: 212/456-7290

LARRY KING SHOW (RADIO)
Mutual Broadcasting
1755 S. Jefferson Davis Highway
Arlington, VA 22202
Tel: 703/685-2000
Fax: 703/685-2142

LARRY KING LIVE TV
CNN
820 First Street NE
Washington, DC 20002
Tel: 212/898-7900

MACNEIL/LEHRER NEWSHOUR
New York Office:
WNET-TV
356 W. 58th Street
New York, NY 10019
Tel: 212/560-3113

Washington Office:
3620 S. 27th Street
Arlington, VA 22206
Tel: 703/998-2870

MEET THE PRESS
NBC News
4001 Nebraska Avenue NW
Washington, DC 20016
Tel: 202/885-4200
Fax: 202/362-2009

MORNING EDITION/ALL THINGS
CONSIDERED
National Public Radio
2025 M Street NW
Washington, DC 20036
Tel: 202/822-2000
Fax: 202/822-2329

BILL MOYERS
Public Affairs Television
356 W. 58th Street
New York, NY 10019
Tel: 212/560-6960

NBC NIGHTLY NEWS
30 Rockefeller Plaza
New York, NY 10112
Tel: 212/664-4971

NIGHTLINE
ABC News
47 W. 66th Street
New York, NY 10023
Tel: 212/456-7777

NIGHTLINE
ABC News
1717 DeSales Street NW
Washington, DC 20036
Tel: 202/887-7364

PBS
1320 Braddock Place
Alexandria, VA 22314-1698
Tel: 703/739-5000
Fax: 703/739-0775

RADIO FREE EUROPE/RADIO LIBERTY
1201 Connecticut Avenue NW, Ste. 1100
Washington, DC 20036
Tel: 202/457-6900
Fax: 202/457-6997

RUSH LIMBAUGH
WABC Radio
2 Penn Plaza, 17th Fl.
New York, NY 10121
Tel: 212/613-3800
Fax: 212/563-9166

60 MINUTES
CBS News
524 W. 57th Street
New York, NY 10019
Tel: 212/975-2006

THIS WEEK WITH DAVID BRINKLEY
ABC News
1717 DeSales Street NW
Washington, DC 20036
Tel: 202/887-7777

TODAY SHOW
NBC News
30 Rockefeller Plaza
New York, NY 10112
Tel: 212/664-4249

20/20
ABC News
147 Columbus Avenue
New York, NY 10023
Tel: 212/456-2020
Fax: 212/456-2969

OPRAH WINFREY
Harpo Productions
P.O. Box 909715
Chicago, IL 60690
Tel: 312/633-1000

National Columnists

RUSSELL BAKER
The New York Times
229 W. 43rd Street
New York, NY 10036
Tel: 212/556-1234

DAVID BRODER
The Washington Post
1150 15th Street NW
Washington, DC 20071
Tel: 202/334-6000

ALEXANDER COCKBURN
The Nation
72 Fifth Avenue
New York, NY 10011
Tel: 212/242-8400
Fax: 212/463-9712

ROWLAND EVANS AND ROBERT NOVAK
Chicago Sun Times
401 N. Wabash Avenue
Chicago, IL 60611
Tel: 312/321-3000
Fax: 312/321-3084

ELLEN GOODMAN
The Boston Globe
P.O. Box 2378
Boston, MA 02107
Tel: 617/929-2000

NAT HENTOFF
The Village Voice
36 Cooper Square
New York, NY 10003
Tel: 212/475-3300
Fax: 212/475-8944

MOLLY IVINS
Fort Worth Star-Telegram
P.O. Box 1870
Fort Worth, TX 76101
Tel: 817/390-7400
Fax: 817/390-7520

JAMES KILPATRICK
Universal Press Syndicate
4900 Main Street, 9th Fl.
Kansas City, MO 64112
Tel: 800/255-6734
or 816/932-6600

MORTON KONDRACKE
The New Republic
1220 19th Street NW
Washington, DC 20036
Tel: 202/331-7494
Fax: 202/331-0275

MAX LERNER
New York Post
210 South Street
New York, NY 10002
Tel: 212/815-8000
Fax: 212/732-4241

MARY MCGRORY
The Washington Post
1150 15th Street NW
Washington, DC 20071
Tel: 202/334-6000

CLARENCE PAGE
Chicago Tribune
435 N. Michigan Avenue
Chicago, IL 60611
Tel: 312/222-3232

ANNA QUINDLEN
New York Times
229 W. 43rd Street
New York, NY 10036
Tel: 212/556-1234

A.M. ROSENTHAL
New York Times
229 W. 43rd Street
New York, NY 10036
Tel: 212/556-1234

MIKE ROYKO
Chicago Tribune
435 N. Michigan Avenue
Chicago, IL 60611
Tel: 312/222-3232

WILLIAM SAFIRE
New York Times
229 W. 43rd Street
New York, NY 10036
Tel: 212/556-1234

GEORGE WILL
Newsweek
444 Madison Avenue
New York, NY 10022
Tel: 212/350-4000

National Publications & News Services

ASSOCIATED PRESS
50 Rockefeller Plaza
New York, NY 10020
National Desk: 212/621-1600

BRITISH MEDICAL JOURNAL
B.M.A. House
Tavistock Square
London WC1H 9JR
England
Tel: 071/387-4499

CHICAGO TRIBUNE
435 N. Michigan Avenue
Chicago, IL 60611
Tel: 312/222-3232

CHRISTIAN SCIENCE MONITOR
One Norway Street
Boston, MA 02115
Tel: 800/225-7090
or 617/450-2000

FORTUNE
Time Warner, Inc.
Time & Life Bldg.
Rockefeller Center
New York, NY 10020
Tel: 212/586-1212

HARPER'S MAGAZINE
666 Broadway
New York, NY 10012-2317
Tel: 212/614-6500
Fax: 212/228-5889

KNIGHT-RIDDER NEWS SERVICE
790 National Press Building
Washington, DC 20045
Tel: 202/383-6080

LOS ANGELES TIMES
Times-Mirror Square
Los Angeles, CA 90053
Tel: 800/528-4637

MCCLATCHY NEWS SERVICE
P.O. Box 15779
Sacramento, CA 95852
Tel: 916/321-1895

THE NEW REPUBLIC
1220 19th Street NW
Washington, DC 20036
Tel: 202/331-7494
Fax: 202/331-0275

NEW YORK TIMES
229 W. 43rd Street
New York, NY 10036
Tel: 212/556-1234

Washington Bureau:
1627 Eye Street NW, 7th Fl.
Washington, DC 20006
Tel: 202/862-0300

NEWSWEEK
444 Madison Avenue
New York, NY 10022
Tel: 212/350-4000

RUETERS INFORMATION SERVICES
1700 Broadway
New York, NY 10019
Tel: 212/603-3300
Fax: 212/603-3446

SAN FRANCISCO EXAMINER
110 Fifth Street
San Francisco, CA 94103
Tel: 415/777-2424
Fax: 415/512-1264

SCRIPPS/HOWARD NEWS SERVICE
1090 Vermont Avenue NW, Ste. 1000
Washington, DC 20005
Tel: 202/408-1484

TIME MAGAZINE
Time Warner, Inc.
Time & Life Building
Rockefeller Center
New York, NY 10020-1393
Tel: 212/522-1212

TRIBUNE MEDIA SERVICES
64 E. Concord Street
Orlando, FL 32801
Tel: 800/332-3068
or 305/422-8181

UNITED PRESS INTERNATIONAL
1400 Eye Street NW
Washington, DC 20005
Tel: 202/898-8000

U.S. NEWS & WORLD REPORT
2400 N Street NW
Washington, DC 20037
Tel: 202/955-2000
Fax: 202/955-2049

USA TODAY
1000 Wilson Boulevard.
Arlington, VA 22229
Tel: 703/276-3400

WALL STREET JOURNAL
200 Liberty Street
New York, NY 10281
Tel: 212/416-2000

WASHINGTON POST
1150 15th Street NW
Washington, DC 20071
Tel: 202/334-6000

An Eclectic Chronology of Censorship From 605 B.C. to 1993

> "What experience and history teach is this—that people and governments never have learned anything from history, or acted on principles deduced from it."
> —*Georg Wilhelm Friedrich Hegel*

The following eclectic chronology culls information and events from a variety of sources, both traditional and nontraditional. It also reflects the alternative definition of censorship offered in Chapter 1 ("Project Censored: Raking Muck, Raising Hell"), one that is free of the restrictions of traditional definitions.

Normally, a chronology plots a series of events, dating from the earliest to the most recent. For example, a popular chronology of photography could start in 1888 with George Eastman's invention of the first true, hand-held camera designed to use roll film, and continue forward to 1992's "contribution"—Madonna's photographic book *Sex*.

However, this eclectic chronology of censorship departs from the traditional date-based events listing to include comments, insights and even a poem, as well as events. I hope it provides you with insights not readily apparent in the more traditional form.

A thorough reading of this chronology should make it clear that censorship is not merely an occasional social aberration but rather a threat that has been with us from the earliest recorded times. As A. Holmes said, "If history without chronology is dark and confused, chronology without history is dry and insipid." At the very least, I hope you find this neither dry nor insipid.

In addition, this chronology should provide you with insights into how we as a society have supported rules, regulations, leaders and institutions that have fostered censorship.

I hope the following persuades you that freedom of expression is never permanently secured; it must be fought for and won each day. Project Censored is but one of many combatants who have fought against censorship. While the battle is never-ending, it is truly worthy.

A Censored Chronology

605 B.C. Perhaps the earliest recorded case of censorship occurred when Jehoiakim, the king of Judah, burned Jeremiah's book of prophecies. This prescient event, found in the Bible (Jer. 36:1-32), may also be the first example of self-censorship, since Jeremiah had written the book at Jehoiakim's bidding.

Fifth century B.C. While we revere the ancient Greeks for respecting freedom of speech, censorship was not unknown. In the fifth century B.C., poets, philosophers, musicians, authors and others were subject to bans, persecution and exile.

443 B.C. Most dictionaries trace censorship back to ancient Rome, when two magistrates, called "censors," were appointed to conduct an annual census to register citizens and assess their property for taxation and contract purposes. The censors also were authorized to censure and penalize offenders thought to be guilty of vice and immorality by removing their voting rights and tribe membership. This form of censorship was discontinued in 22 B.C., when the emperors took over the censorial powers.

399 B.C. The ultimate form of censorship is death, and Socrates—one of the first philosophers to express a rational defense of freedom of speech— became an early victim of it. After he was tried and convicted of impiety and of corrupting youth, Socrates was put to death. Ironically, his best-known pupil, Plato, outlined the first comprehensive system of censorship, particularly of the arts. In *The Republic*, Book II, Plato warned against allowing children to hear casual tales by casual persons and called for the establishment of a censorship system for fiction writers.

221 B.C. About two centuries after the appointment of censors in Rome, the Chinese launched their own office of censorship under the Ch'in dynasty (221-206 B.C.). Although originally designed to critique the emperor's performance, the office soon was used by the emperor to investigate and punish official corruption and misgovernment. The institution eventually became a huge bureaucracy that effectively ended with the overthrow of the Ch'ing dynasty in 1911.

213 B.C. One of China's most famous monarchs, Tsin Chi Hwangti, built the Great Wall of China (214-204 B.C.). He also exercised a most impressive act of censorship in 213 B.C., by ordering all books in China destroyed, except those concerning science, medicine and agriculture. In addition, he executed 500 scholars and banished thousands of others.

A.D. 58 In Acts 19:19 of the Bible, the apostle Paul praised converts who burned books (worth 50,000 pieces of silver) in the purifying fires of orthodoxy, providing modern-day Christian censors with scriptual authorization for their book burnings.

A.D. 95 Following up on Paul's advice, the Apostolic Constitutions, written by St. Clement of Rome, warned Christians that the Scriptures provided everything a true believer needed to read.

A.D. 499 Under Pope Gelasius, the concept of the Papal Index, a list of books unsuitable for Roman Catholics, first appeared. It was formalized in 1564 and still exists to this day.

A.D. 642 Another major loss of recorded history, comparable to events in China in 213 B.C., took place when Omar, head of the Moslem religion, ordered the great Alexandrian Library destroyed. Some 700,000 rolls of manuscripts were lost forever.

1215 King John of England, under pressure from English barons, sealed the Magna Carta at Runnymede, guaranteeing certain civil and political liberties to the English people.

1231 The Inquisition, an open season for censors, was launched by the Roman Catholic Church as a formal way of discovering heresy and punishing heretics. Thousands of scriptures were inspected, reviewed and often destroyed by the Inquisitors—self-described defenders of the Truth of the Sacred Text—from 1231 to 1596. For almost four centuries, book burners also were empowered to burn authors at the stake.

1450 Johann Gutenberg invented the printing press, with its movable type, thereby providing the technological breakthrough for the intellectual revolution of the Renaissance and its challenge to the institution of censorship. It also threatened the tight control secular and religious leaders exercised over the production and distribution of information.

1501 In an effort to protect the Church of Rome against heresy, Pope Alexander VI issued an edict banning the printing of books. Not unlike their colleagues in the Roman Catholic Church, Protestant Reformation leaders (including John Knox, Martin Luther and John Calvin) persecuted heretics and papists. In England, Henry VIII burned copies of William Tyndale's New Testament and had Thomas More beheaded for refusing to acknowledge the king's power over religion. In 1529, Henry VIII issued an official list of banned books, some 30 years before the widely known Papal Index was institutionalized. By 1586, prior restraint was running rampant in England, where all books had to be read and approved by the Archbishop of Canterbury or the Bishop of London prior to publication.

1512 Nicolaus Copernicus publishes *Commentarious*, his hypothesis on the revolutions of the heavenly bodies. It stated that the earth was not the center of the universe but revolved around the sun. The theory, which totally contradicted the geocentric theory favored by the Catholic Church, was condemned and placed on the Papal Index in 1616.

1517 Protesting papal censorship, the sale of indulgences and other expedients, Martin Luther, an ordained priest, posted his 95 theses on the door of the Palast Church in Wittenberg, laying the foundation for the German Reformation and the Lutheran Church.

1541 Concerned about nude figures in Michelangelo's fresco, *The Last Judgment*, in the Sistine Chapel, Pope Paul IV ordered artists to paint over the more provocative parts to protect the innocent. The pope may have been the first to "sanitize" Michelangelo, but censors in the last decade of the 20th century continue to be indignant over reproductions of Michelangelo's *David*.

1564 After abortive attempts dating back more than a thousand years, the papacy successfully issued the formal *Index Librorum Prohibitorum* (Index of Prohibited Books), as authorized by the Council of Trent. Approximately 500 pages in length, it listed books and authors condemned by the Roman Catholic Church. While it survived until 1774 in France and 1834 in Spain, the Index (as it's known colloquially) remains in force for Roman Catholics up to the present day. It's the longest running, and possibly most effective, example of censorship in world history.

1633 Galileo Galilei was forced by the Inquisition to renounce and reject *Dialago*, published in 1632, which supported the theories of Copernicus. *Dialago* was added to the infamous Index, where it remained until 1822.

1643 The British Parliament reintroduced the Licensing Act, ending a brief respite from censorship that began in 1640 with the abolishment of the Court of Star Chamber. It was this renewal of book licensing that instigated John Milton's eloquent plea for free speech a year later.

1644 The *Areopagitica* was published. Subtitled a "Speech of Mr. John Milton For the Liberty of Unlicenc'd Printing, To the Parliament of England," this work was considered to be the English-speaking world's first and most powerful statement urging freedom of expression. Some of its better known excerpts include the following:

> *"Who kills a man kills a reasonable creature, God's image; but he who destroys a good book, kills reason itself."*
>
> *"Give me the liberty to know, to utter, and to argue freely according to conscience, above all liberties."*
>
> *"Though all the winds of doctrine were let loose to play upon the earth, so Truth be in the field, we do injuriously, by licensing and prohibiting to misdoubt her strength. Let her and Falsehood grapple; whoever knew Truth put to the worse in a free and open encounter."*

While Milton's eloquent statement is rightfully credited with being the genesis of press freedom in America, his treatise actually dealt with *prior restraint* (the right to license), not with post-publication censorship. The latter finally was resolved by the First Amendment to the Constitution of the United States in 1787.

1690 A small, three-page newspaper, entitled "Numb. 1, PUBLICK OCCURRENCES Both FOREIGN and DOMESTICK, Boston, Thursday Sept. 25th, 1690," is generally agreed to be the first newspaper published in America. There was no "Numb. 2," because the governor and council issued a statement four days after its publication declaring their "high resentment and Disallowance of said Pamphlet, and order that the same be Suppressed and called in." They found that the editor, Benjamin Harris, had printed "Reflections of a very high nature: As also sundry doubtful and uncertain Reports." While this was an inauspicious beginning for a free press in the New World, there remain many reflections of a high nature that continue to be subject to censorship today.

1695 Because of increasing resistance, partially generated by Milton's *Areopagitica*, the Licensing Act was not renewed in 1695, a date that has come to signify the establishment of freedom of the press in England. However, this did not mark the end of censorship in that country. Prior censorship, through licensing, was replaced with punitive (or post-publication) censorship, a form that, though preferable to prior censorship, is still found in most societies to this day. This is not to say that prior censorship is no longer attempted: consider the case of *The*

Progressive Magazine, the target of the first case of press prior restraint in America (*U.S. v. Progressive*, 1979). Again, in 1987, the Supreme Court's *Hazelwood* decision gave school administrators prior restraint control over student newspapers.

1735 The John Peter Zenger case provided a classic example of an attempt at punitive, or post-publication, censorship in America; it established that truth was a defense against charges of libel. Zenger was arrested and charged with seditious libel for criticizing New York Governor William Cosby in his *New York Weekly Journal.* At the age of 80, Andrew Hamilton, one of the leading attorneys in the colonies, took on the case *pro bono*, considering the issue to be critical to the future of liberty. Putting Milton's *Areopagitica* at the core of the defense, Hamilton won the case with the presumption that truth could not be libel. The case is often referred to as the birth of freedom of the press in America.

1765 The British Stamp Act of 1765 taxed all printed materials circulated in the colonies; the Taunted Acts of 1766 placed duties on American imports of glass, lead, paint, tea and paper. These historic documents outraged colonial journalists and encouraged press protests until all duties, except those on tea, were removed in 1770. The famed Boston Tea Party followed in 1773 (planned at the home of a *Boston Gazette* editor). Then, in rapid succession, the British reacted with the Intolerable Acts of 1774, the First Continental Congress met in 1774, and the first shot of the War of Independence was fired in 1775.

1776 In Philadelphia, on July 4, the Declaration of Independence was signed by representatives from the 13 states of America. It opened with these words: "When in the Course of human events it becomes necessary for one people to dissolve the political bonds which have connected them with another...."; and it continued, "We hold these truths to be self-evident, that all men are created equal, that they are endowed by their Creator with certain unalienable Rights, that among these are Life, Liberty and the pursuit of Happiness...." These eloquent words, with their emphasis on liberty and equality, paved the way for a free society granting free speech and a free press.

1787 The Constitution of the United States was drafted in 1787, ratified in 1788 and went into effect on the first Wednesday of March 1789, thereby formally establishing the United States of America.

1789 The French Revolution of 1789 specifically enshrined the freedoms of "speech, thought, and expression" in Clause 11 of its Declaration of the Rights of Man.

1791 On December 15, the first ten amendments, known collectively as the Bill of Rights, were added to the Constitution. These provisions established a formal contractual agreement between the government and its citizens, encompassing specific concerns not addressed in the Constitution. Foremost among these is Article I, dealing with the freedoms of religion, speech, the press and the right of petition: "Congress shall make no law respecting an establishment of religion, or prohibiting the free exercise thereof; or abridging the freedom of speech, or of the press; or the right of the people peaceably to assemble, and to petition the Government for a redress of grievances." What might be most remarkable about this extraordinary document isn't what it does say but what it doesn't say. It has no restrictions, contingencies, exclusions or other provisos dealing with heresy, blasphemy, pornography, obscenity, defamation, national security, sedition, public morals, racism, sexism, libel, slander or a host of other social concerns that have threatened to dilute the strength of the First Amendment for 200 years.

1798 The ink was barely dry on the Bill of Rights when Congress enacted the Alien and Sedition Acts of 1798. The legislation would punish anyone who spoke, wrote or published "any false scandalous and malicious [speech] against the government of the United States" or used speech that would bring the President or Congress "into contempt or disrepute." Although the acts expired in 1801, it wasn't until 1964 that the Supreme Court declared them "inconsistent with the First Amendment."

1802 The English Society for the Suppression of Vice was launched in England, paving the way for similar groups in the United States later in the 19th century.

1818 Dr. Thomas Bowdler, an early British version of Jerry Falwell, was an unsuccessful physician consumed with cleansing the language of any indelicate words or phrases. Specifically, he wanted to eliminate from Shakespeare "whatever is unfit to be read aloud by a gentleman in the company of ladies." In 1818, in London, he published his *Family Shakespeare*, which was also widely distributed in the United States. The expurgated version of Shakespeare led to the term "bowdlerized," referring to this form of censorship.

1841 Ralph Waldo Emerson published his famed essay, "Self-Reliance." In this tribute to free expression, he wrote, "The virtue in most request is conformity. Self-reliance is its aversion.... Whoso would be a man must be a non-conformist.... A foolish consistency is the hobgoblin of little minds, adored by little statesmen and philosophers and divines."

1842 At the age of 24, Karl Marx began his career as a working journalist with an essay titled "Remarks on the Latest Prussian Censorship Instruction." Censored by German authorities, it was published a year later by a German-exile press in Switzerland. Marx went on to decry censorship for protecting the interests of the elite and perpetuating the domination of the powerless by the powerful. Ironically, communist societies subsequently used censorship to protect the interest of the elite and to dominate the powerless.

1842 While Marx was being censored in Germany, the U.S. Congress passed the Tariff Law of 1842, prohibiting "all indecent and obscene prints, paintings, lithographs, engravings and transparencies" from being imported. In 1857, the law was expanded to include images, figures and photographs, in order to prevent the importation of Greek statues of "questionable" taste into the U.S.

1857 In England, the Obscene Publications Act of 1857 led to an early definition of obscenity. It was also known as the Campbell Act, named for its proponent, the Lord Chief Justice. To assure passage of his bill, Campbell defined an obscene work as one written for the single purpose of corrupting the morals of youth and designed to shock the sense of decency in any well-regulated mind.

1859 In his famous essay "On Liberty," John Stuart Mill, who believed every man is competent to choose what he will read or hear, expressed his thesis: "Who can compute what the world loses in the multitude of promising intellects combined with timid characters, who dare not follow out any bold, vigorous, independent train of thought, lest it should land them in something which would admit of being considered irreligious or immoral?... No one can be a great thinker who does not recognize that as a thinker it is his first duty to follow his intellect to whatever conclusions it may lead.... There is always hope when people are forced to listen to both sides. It is when they attend only one that errors harden into prejudices and truth itself ceases to have the effect of truth, by being exaggerated into falsehood."

1861 During the Civil War, the U.S. War Department warned journalists against providing any military information that would aid the enemy. The order was generally disregarded, though, leading to casualties. The better correspondents and editors proved able to report on the war, while still concealing information of value to the enemy. In the North, the greatest censorship came from angry mobs who attempted to destroy newspapers with which they disagreed.

1873 The New England Watch and Ward Society and the New York Society for the Suppression of Vice were founded for the purpose of pressuring publishers, editors and news agents into rejecting controversial writers.

1873 Anthony Comstock was America's answer to England's Thomas Bowdler. In 1873, Comstock, a religious fanatic whose motto was "Morals, Not Art or Literature," joined with the YMCA to found the New York Society for the Suppression of Vice. As head of this organization, he was given a monopoly by New York to eliminate vice in the state. He also succeeded in getting Congress to pass what was known as The Comstock Act of 1873, which consolidated various statutes and regulations dealing with "obscene, lewd, and lascivious" publications and specifically barred birth-control material from the mail.

Comstock was extraordinarily successful in "fighting vice." In 1874, he reported that in a two-year period, his society had seized 130,000 pounds of bound books, along with 60,300 "articles made of rubber for immoral purposes." When he retired in 1915, he estimated that he had destroyed over 160 tons of obscene literature.

One of his great successes was the suppression of Paul Chabas's *September Morn,* a romantic painting of a young, nude girl bathing on the shore of a lake. The censored painting led to a controversy over the distinction between "nude" and "naked" that persisted for nearly 120 years. Finally, in 1992, Anne-Imelda Radice, acting head of the National Endowment for the Arts in the United States, announced her personal ability to differentiate between "nude" and "naked."

1896 A simple kiss in the play *The Widow Jones*, when seen magnified to a larger-than-life scale on a screen in the May Irwin-John C. Rice film *Kiss*, resulted in the first known attempt at film censorship.

1900 The turn of the century marked the Golden Age of Muckraking—a brief, glowing uncensored moment in history when journalists exposed the ills of society, publishers gave them the soapbox, people reacted with indignation, and politicians responded with legislation. The first two decades of the 20th century were distinguished by the clamorous, sometimes sensationalized, efforts of investigative writers like Rheta Child Doss, Finley Peter Dunne, Frank Norris, Upton Sinclair, Lincoln Steffens and Ida Tarbell. President Theodore Roosevelt applied the term "muckrakers" to journalists in a pejorative manner, but today it's considered a mark of distinction among some reporters. Unfortunately, except for the contributions of a few notable commentators like Drew Pearson, George Seldes and I.F. Stone, late 20th-century America hasn't enjoyed a comparable period of socially aware, concerned and effective journalism.

1909 Appearing before the Select Committee of both Houses of Parliament, which was considering censoring stage plays in 1909, George Bernard Shaw opened his testimony by citing his qualifications as a witness: "I am by profession a playwright.... I am not an ordinary playwright in general practice. I am a specialist in immoral and heretical plays. My reputation has been gained by my persistent struggle to force the public to reconsider its morals.... I object to censorship not merely because the existing form of it grievously injures and hinders me individually, but on public grounds." The statement, titled "The Necessity of Immoral Plays," was rejected by the committee. Shaw subsequently published it as part of the Preface to *The Shewing-Up of Blanco Posnet*. Shaw pointed out in *The Rejected Statement*, Part I, that "Assassination is the extreme form of censorship."

1911 From 1911 to 1926, the Hearst media empire used its various propaganda techniques to persuade the U.S. to declare war against Mexico; the public would have had a better understanding of the message if it had known Hearst's real motivation: to protect his family's Mexican landholdings—some 2,500 square miles—against possible expropriation.

Apparently impressed by Hearst's endeavors, Col. Robert Rutherford McCormick, owner of the *Chicago Tribune*, sent reporter George Seldes to Mexico in 1927 to cover the "coming war" with the United States. Seldes never did find a "war," but did write a series of ten columns on the situation in Mexico. The first five echoed the official State Department line, supporting American business interests; the second five reported the other side of the issue, which Seldes observed or verified himself. Despite promises to publish all ten columns, the *Tribune* ran only the first five. Disgusted with this obvious act of censorship, Seldes quit the *Tribune*.

1912 The first radio-licensing law was passed by Congress and signed by William Howard Taft. It authorized the Secretary of Commerce and Labor to assign wave lengths, time limits and broadcast licenses. The only control at the time was a loose form of self-censorship by the stations, whose taboos included lewd jokes and any discussion of birth control.

H.V. Kaltenborn, who lectured on current events over WEAF in New York, became one of the first broadcasters to become embroiled in a controversy over the content of a talk. Kaltenborn had criticized Secretary of State Charles Evans Hughes regarding the way he had dealt with the Russians. This led to a request from Washington, through the American Telephone and Telegraph Company, which leased the telephone lines to WEAF, that Kaltenborn be taken off the air. Recognizing the threat to its own best interests, WEAF acquiesced, and Kaltenborn left the station. AT&T saw nothing wrong with its actions; in fact, it acknowledged that it had "constant and complete" cooperation with governmental agencies and had indulged in censorship to maintain this cooperative relationship. The government's first attempt at electronic censorship was a resounding success. Nevertheless, undaunted by the threat of censorship, radio expanded rapidly; by 1927 there were 733 stations and considerable interference on the broadcast bands. The near-chaotic situation ended with the passage of the Federal Radio Act of 1927, establishing the Federal Radio Commission (FRC). The Federal Communications Commission (the FCC) was later established, with passage of the Federal Communications Act of 1934.

1914 *The Woman Rebel*, a feminist newspaper edited by Margaret Sanger, advocated the practice of birth control. After five issues it was stopped by the U.S. Post Office, which had the authority to censor the press at the time.

1917 The National Civil Liberties Bureau was founded and renamed the American Civil Liberties Union (ACLU) in 1920. The organization was created to address civil liberties problems arising out of World War I, including the Espionage and Sedition Acts, conscientious objectors and political prisoners. It gained national recognition in the mid-1920s by defending the accused individuals in the Scopes trial, the Sweet case and the Sacco-Vanzetti case. In 1988, it attracted national attention when presidential candidate George Bush resorted to Red-baiting by referring derisively to "card-carrying members" of the ACLU.

1917 World War I kept Congress busy churning out legislation designed to prevent any conceivable sign or sound of disloyalty from occurring. First, the Espionage Act of June 15 provided heavy fines and imprisonment for anyone encouraging disloyalty or obstructing recruitment; in essence, it made it easier to jail Wobblies, communist sympathizers and radicals. Soon after, on October 6, came the Trading-with-the-Enemy Act, censoring all messages sent abroad and requiring domestic media containing articles in a foreign language to file sworn translations with local postmasters.

1918 Following on the heels of the two paranoia-induced decrees discussed above came the Sedition Act of May 16. This document made it unlawful to "utter, print, write, or publish any disloyal, profane, scurrilous, or abusive language about the form of the government of the United States, of the Constitution of the United States, or the uniform of the Army or Navy of the United States." As if this weren't sufficient, President

Woodrow Wilson authorized the formation of the Committee on Public Information (CPI), a propaganda machine headed up by journalist George Creel.

Now, for the first time, the brute forces of censorship were buttressed by the slick techniques of propaganda, self-censorship and disinformation, in what Creel called "a fight for the mind of mankind." It worked. While the press ultimately rejected CPI's manipulative efforts, most newspapers reportedly published all 6,000 press releases sent out by the CPI News Division.

In late November, *The Nation* Magazine warned of the apparent control of the press not merely by the government and its legislation but also by the patriotic desire of the press itself to support the government. This cheerleading function of the press was most recently observed during the Gulf War in 1991.

1918 Lenin reintroduced censorship in the Soviet Union as a temporary emergency measure to protect the incipient Bolshevik regime against hostile propaganda, demonstrating how censorship is often rationalized as necessary for self-protection.

1918 The biggest censored story of World War I started on November 11, Armistice Day, when journalist George Seldes and three colleagues broke the Armistice regulations and drove into Germany to see for themselves what was happening. Through luck and bravado, they managed to get an interview with Field Marshal Hindenburg. When Seldes asked what ended the war, Hindenburg replied it was the American infantry attack in the Argonne; without it, Germany would have held out much longer. As a form of punishment for breaking regulations, Seldes's story of Hindenburg's confession was suppressed by military censors, with the support of other U.S. journalists angry because they'd been scooped.

The historic interview was never published, except by Seldes, who believed it could have altered the course of history. Hitler built Nazism on what Seldes called a total lie—i.e., that Germany did not lose the war on the battlefield but rather because of the *Dolchstoss*, or stab-in-the-back "by civilians," "by the Socialists," "by the Communists" and "by the Jews." Had the world known of Hindenburg's confession, Hitler might not have so easily manipulated German citizens into supporting his cause. We'll never know what might have been because of a military censor.

1918 While there were many victims of the repressive censorship laws of World War I, Eugene V. Debs was one of the most famous. Founder of the Social Democratic Party in the United States, and five-time presidential candidate (between 1900 and 1920), Debs was tried for espionage, for opposing the war effort. His citizenship was revoked, and he was sentenced to ten years in prison. While in jail, he ran for president in 1920 as the Socialist candidate and received nearly a million votes. President Harding commuted his sentence on Christmas Day 1921.

1919 In a Supreme Court ruling in the espionage case *Schenck v. United States*, Justice Oliver Wendell Homes, delivering the unanimous opinion of the Court, supported the ruling with the now-famed example of a clear and present danger: "The most stringent protection of free speech would not protect a man in falsely shouting fire in a theatre and causing a panic."

1920 Walter Lippmann, an outstanding journalist, author and ethicist of the time, issued an early warning about latter-day journalists and media moguls in his essay, "Journalism and the Higher Law": "Just as the most poisonous form of disorder is the mob incited from high places, the most immoral act the immorality of a government, so the most destructive form of untruth is sophistry and propaganda by those whose profession it is to report the news. The news columns are common carriers. When those who control them arrogate to themselves the right to determine by their own consciences what shall be reported and for what purpose, democracy is unworkable. Public opinion is blockaded."

1922 The Motion Picture Producers and Distributors of America (MPPDA) was formed as a self-censoring response to outside critics. The MPPDA, chaired by Will Hays, former Postmaster General and Chairman of the Republican National Committee, paved the way for creating a formal motion picture code in 1930.

1924 In *Literature and Revolution*, Leon Trotsky established the role of art in a revolutionary society as a service to the revolutionary state, with artists creating with relative freedom but, of course, under "watchful revolutionary censorship."

1925 John T. Scopes, a young high school teacher, was convicted of violating Tennessee's law prohibiting the teaching of biological evolution (Darwin's theory). In one of the most famous courtroom confrontations in American history, famed liberal attorney Clarence Darrow defended Scopes, and William Jennings Bryan assisted the state with the prosecution. Scopes later was released on a technicality by the Tennessee State Supreme Court.

1927 The seeds for repressive censorship measures in Germany were sown when the Reichstag passed a morality law to protect young people from indecent prints and pictures. The law was used by the police to enter private homes, to supervise dancing in homes and to protect children from parents. By the time the National Socialists came to power in 1933, with the appointment of Adolph Hitler as chancellor, modern art was banned and leaders of the Expressionist movement were exiled.

1929 Boston earned its "Banned in Boston" epithet in late 1929 when a wave of censorship swept through the city, resulting in what was called a "memorable wholesale book holocaust." Among the 68 books by prominent authors banned during that period were *What I Believe*, by Bertrand Russell; *Oil,* by Upton Sinclair; *An American Tragedy,* by Theodore Dreiser; *Elmer Gantry,* by Sinclair Lewis; *The Sun Also Rises,* by Ernest Hemingway; and *Antic Hay,* by Aldous Huxley.

1930 The MPPDA adopted its first Motion Picture Production Code (also known as the Hays Code, after the head of the MPPDA). At first, adhering to it was strictly voluntary. Then, in 1933, in response to the National Legion of Decency—founded by the Catholic Church, which had started to review movies—the MPPDA established a stronger code and began to review all scripts. Acceptable films were given a Hays Office seal of approval.

In 1968, again in reaction to outside efforts at censorship, the Motion Picture Association of America (MPPDA became MPAA in 1948) developed a formal, but still voluntary, rating system of four categories: G for general audiences; PG for parental guidance suggested; R for restricted (children under 17 must be accompanied by a parent or guardian); and X for no one under 17 admitted. In 1984, the MPAA added a fifth category: PG-13, parental guidance suggested for children under 13. In 1990, the X rating was revised to NC-17 (no children under 17 admitted). The X rating had become so popular among promoters of hardcore pornography, it was no longer suited for general use by the theaters.

Finally, in mid-1992, the MPAA revamped its ratings once again, this time to include explanations as to why films are given ratings other than G. For example, the MPAA gave the film *Christopher Columbus— The Discovery*, a PG-13 rating, noting that it included "some action violence" and "nudity."

Since its inception in 1930, the MPAA has claimed that the ratings code is not designed to censor but rather to warn parents about the content of a film.

1933 James Joyce's celebrated novel *Ulysses* broke the historic barrier of customs censorship when the New York Federal District Court and the Circuit Court of Appeals ruled that it was not obscene within the meaning of federal statutes. Judge John Woolsey of the District Court said, "Although it contains...many words usually considered dirty, I have not found anything that I consider to be dirt for dirt's sake."

1934 The Federal Communications Act established the Federal Communications Commission (the FCC) to succeed the Federal Radio Commission, granting it the right to renew a license as long as the broadcaster operated in the "public interest, convenience, and necessity." It was explicitly stated that the FCC would not have the authority to censor; however, it did have the authority to withhold a license from a broadcaster not operating in the "public interest." Thus, while the FCC couldn't prohibit liquor advertising, it could emphasize that a station advertising liquor, which children could hear, would have to prove it was acting in the public interest when its license came up for renewal. Not surprisingly, stations haven't accepted liquor advertising since. The ban on cigarette advertising was also voluntary.

Although the FCC was not allowed to practice censorship, it wasn't long before advertisers discovered they weren't subject to the same restrictions. Cream of Wheat, which sponsored best-selling author Alexander Woollcott on CBS, received some complaints from listeners that Woollcott had made derogatory remarks about Adolph Hitler. When the author refused the advertiser's request to refrain from such remarks, his series was canceled.

1937 Automobile safety, essentially, has been a censored subject since the 1930s. Auto manufacturers haven't liked to acknowledge that driving can be hazardous to your health. Yet, in January 1937, Clair Straith, a plastic surgeon who specialized in treating facial injuries from auto accidents, published an article in the *American Medical Association Journal* warning of the dangers and suggesting ways the industry could make cars safer. Nonetheless, Detroit continued to stress power and speed. Only in recent years have they started to talk about and promote safety features.

Nearly three decades later, Ralph Nader, in *Unsafe at Any Speed*, wrote, "It is more than coincidental that radio, television, newspapers and magazines have so long ignored the role of vehicle design in producing...collisions." Not one out of 700 newspapers accepted the offer to run a serialization of his book. Even now, automobiles continue to be a major killer. In 1990, 44,531 Americans were killed in motor-vehicle accidents, more than three times as many as were murdered by guns that year. The total cost of these accidents to the nation was $137.5 billion—more than two percent of the 1990 gross domestic product.

1938 Information concerning the hazards of cigarette smoking was available as early as 1938 but was ignored, censored or played down by the media to such an extent that, even two decades later, only 44 percent of the people thought smoking was a cause of lung cancer. Today, more than half a century after the hazards of smoking were first known, tobacco manufacturers continue to deny such health hazards. Moreover, in the face of declining market share (owing to an informed populace that now understands the dangers), the tobacco industry targets more vulnerable audiences, including young people and residents of the Third World.

1938 The infamous House Un-American Activities Committee (HUAC) was founded, under the chairmanship of Congressman Martin Dies, Jr. (D-TX), to "expose communist infiltration" in the CIO union and in FDR's New Deal administration. This powerful congressional body was particularly successful in using the principle of guilt by association.

1938 *Fortune* Magazine sent a copy of an editorial it wrote about hunger in America to six New York City daily newspapers; it warned of the dangers to a democracy when a third of its citizens are starving. The New York *Post* featured the editorial on its front page and noted that four of the six dailies, including the *New York Times*, had completely ignored the story.

The issue continued to attract media attention even three years later, when Senator Robert M. La Follette addressed the Senate, saying that 45 million people were below the safety line in nutrition; in addition, "Twenty million families must live on not more than eight or nine cents per person per meal. About 14 percent of all American families must live on an average of five cents per person per meal." Again, the *New York Times*, which proudly claims it prints "all the news that's fit to print," failed to report a word of this the next day.

1939 Communist dictator Joseph Stalin required the active participation of Soviet artists in the political guidance of the country. To accomplish this, they were expected to practice self-censorship in the interest of the state; those who didn't cooperate often vanished suddenly.

1940 On May 20, George Seldes—America's journalist *emeritus*, and the most censored journalist in history—published Volume I, Number 1, of *In Fact*, a biweekly newsletter for "the millions who want a free press." The premiere issue exposed a secret meeting of 18 prominent American leaders dedicated to supporting the British war effort, reprimanded the press for their failure to reveal how a major soap manufacturer had been caught "fooling the American people through fake advertising," and warned his readers about Father Coughlin and his anti-Semitic hate campaign. George Seldes, hailed as the grandfather of the alternative press and the creator of modern investigative journalism, celebrated his 102nd birthday in September 1992. He is a former Project Censored judge and the inspiration for *America's CENSORED Newsletter*.

1940 Morris Ernst, one of the nation's leading crusaders against censorship, compiled and categorized a comprehensive list of works censored in the United States. The list included some of the world's greatest classics, including works by Homer, Shakespeare, Whitman and Darwin.

1940 The American Library Association (ALA) established the Committee on Intellectual Freedom, one of the nation's leading advocates of the First Amendment and free speech. Part of the committee's responsibility is to guard, protect, defend and extend intellectual freedom.

1940 *The Outlaw*, a sexy western starring a sultry Jane Russell in a push-up bra designed by Howard Hughes, was denied the film industry's "seal of approval" because, as one judge put it, Jane Russell's breasts "hung over the picture like a thunderstorm spread out over a landscape." While the film is now available in the 95- and 103-minute versions, no one appears to have a copy of the original uncensored 117-minute version.

1941 The Manhattan Project, the research effort that led to the atomic bomb, was launched in total secrecy. Within a few years, more than a half-million people across the U.S. were involved in one of the most secretive scientific projects in history. The successful information-control practices employed by the Manhattan Project paved the way for managing, manipulating and obfuscating the news that has since characterized the nation's nuclear research, in times of peace as well as war.

1941 An extraordinary, two-year U.S. Senate investigation of the concentration of economic power in the U.S. concluded that the National Association of Manufacturers (representing large corporations) and the U.S. Chamber of Commerce were getting favored treatment from the press. Although similar charges often have been made since then, America's corporate elite and the press deny such favored treatment exists.

1941 World War II censorship was initiated when President Franklin Delano Roosevelt created the U.S. Office of Censorship, appointing Byron Price, former executive news editor of the Associated Press, director. Price had the authority to censor all international communications, including mail, cable and radio. At its peak, the postal section of his office had more than 10,000 employees. Nonetheless, there was little public outrage over censorship during World War II, the result of Price's efforts to encourage publishers to practice "voluntary cooperation" with the censorship program. That effort, along with the Office of War Information (OWI), a propaganda organization headed up by Elmer Davis, formerly with CBS News and the *New York Times*, co-opted the traditional negative reaction to information control. The fact that American citizens were more united behind the nation during World War II than during World War I also aided the censorship effort. The Office of Censorship closed on August 15, 1945, a few hours after the surrender of Japan. Shortly after the end of the war, the OWI was succeeded by the United States Information Service, under the auspices of the State Department.

1947 "A Free and Responsible Press," a comprehensive and critical report on the status of the media, was issued by the Commission on Freedom of the Press, headed by Dr. Robert M. Hutchins, chancellor of the University of Chicago. The study, funded by a $200,000 grant from Henry Luce, owner of *Time* and *Life*, found free speech to be in grave danger—not so much from the government as from those who controlled access to the media. The report warned that "One of the most effective ways of improving the press is blocked by the press itself. By a kind of unwritten law, the press ignores the errors and misrepresentation, the lies and scandals, of which its members are guilty." Not surprisingly, the landmark report was given a lukewarm reception by the press.

1947 The Dead Sea Scrolls, dating from approximately 22 B.C. to A.D. 100, were discovered in Wadi Qumran. They were almost immediately subjected to censorship by controlled access, which continued until 1991, when biblical scholars forced official researchers to share the information.

1947 Charlie Chaplin's *Monsieur Verdoux*, a satirical film criticizing munitions makers and military leaders and espousing a more humanistic morality, drew protests and pickets by veterans and religious groups. The outcry resulted in the film being withdrawn from distribution. Chaplin, one of America's greatest filmmakers, whose impersonation of "the little tramp" created laughter everywhere it was shown, left the U.S. for a self-imposed exile in Switzerland.

1947 Prompted by allegations that the government was infiltrated by communist spies, President Harry S. Truman issued an executive order establishing a loyalty-security program for government employees. The program paved the way for one of the nation's most repressive political periods, from 1949 to 1953, which came to be known as the McCarthy era, named after Senator Joseph McCarthy (R-Wisconsin). McCarthy, who charged incessantly that "card-carrying communists" infiltrated our government from top to bottom, was one of the most feared and contro-versial men in U.S. Senate history. He was eventually censured by the U.S. Senate on a vote of 67-22, and died a discredited disgrace in 1957.

1948 The Library Bill of Rights was adopted by the American Library Associa-tion to resist "all abridgment of the free access to ideas and full freedom of expression." With the First and Fourteenth Amendments to the Constitution as its foundation, the Bill takes an unequivocal stand on the freedom to read and supports democracy in full measure, stating, "There should be the fullest practicable provision of material presenting all points of view concerning the problems and issues of our times, interna-tional, national, and local." America's librarians are the nation's first line of defense in the ongoing battle against censorship.

1948 Alfred Kinsey published *Sexual Behavior in the Human Male*, first of the "Kinsey Reports," which influenced public attitudes toward sex, helped promote sexual freedom and expression—and provided a major target for censors. The second report, *Sexual Behavior in the Human Female*, was published in 1953.

1948 The Universal Declaration of Human Rights was adopted by the General Assembly of the United Nations as Article XIX. It holds that freedom of expression is not the property of any political system or ideology but is, rather, a universal human right, now defined and guaranteed in interna-tional law. Article 19 also became the name of an international human rights organization founded in 1986.

1949 Apparently seeing a threat of communism in certain murals on the walls of public buildings, Richard Nixon, then a Republican Congressman from California, wrote, "...I believe a committee should make a thorough investigation of this type of art in government buildings with the view of obtaining removal of all that is found to be inconsistent with American ideals and principles." Nixon went on to even greater efforts at censor-ship as his career progressed.

1952 The Television Code, adopted by the National Association of Broadcast-ers, spoke eloquently about commercial television's responsibility to augment the "educational and cultural influence of schools, institutions of higher learning, the home, the church, museums, foundations, and other institutions devoted to education and culture." It also addressed the medium's specific responsibilities toward children and the commu-nity. The Code has been subject to a number of interpretations and revisions since. Potential dangers of censorship from the networks, affiliates, advertisers and the government have yet to be addressed.

1953 On January 17, I.F. Stone published the first issue of *I.F. Stone's Weekly* in Washington, DC. Following in the footsteps of George Seldes, whom he cited as a mentor, Stone used his extraordinary investigative skills to criticize the U.S. government and its policies. The *Weekly* was an early and clamorous opponent of U.S. involvement in the Vietnam War. Stone's wit and wisdom had attracted more than 70,000 subscribers by the time its final issue was published in December 1971.

1953 President Dwight D. Eisenhower, warned of censorship during a talk at Dartmouth College: "Don't join the book burners. Don't think you are going to conceal faults by concealing evidence that they ever existed. Don't be afraid to go into your library and read every book as long as it does not offend your own ideas of decency. That should be the only censorship." In June 1953, in a letter to the ALA Convention, President Eisenhower wrote, "As it is an ancient truth that freedom cannot be legislated into existence, so it is no less obvious that freedom cannot be censored into existence."

1954 The evening of March 9, 1954, has been called television's finest hour. It was the night Edward R. Murrow, on his weekly program "See It Now," permitted Sen. Joseph R. McCarthy to destroy himself in front of millions of viewers. Murrow concluded his program saying, "The actions of the junior senator from Wisconsin have caused alarm and dismay amongst our allies abroad and given considerable comfort to our enemies. And whose fault is that? Not really his; for he didn't create this situation of fear, he merely exploited it and rather successfully. Cassius was right. 'The fault, dear Brutus, is not in our stars but in ourselves.'"

Referring to the years the press had permitted McCarthy to decimate Americans' civil rights, Murrow later said, "The timidity of television in dealing with this man when he was spreading fear throughout the land is not something to which this art of communication can ever point with pride. Nor should it be allowed to forget it." McCarthy was surely not the first demagogue to intimidate the press; nor was he the last.

1957 The Supreme Court made its first significant effort to define obscenity. Until now it had worked with what was known as the Hicklin Rule, a carry-over description of obscenity from British law, which ruled that obscenity had a tendency to deprave and corrupt those whose minds are open to such immoral influences (such as children) and into whose hands it might fall. In 1957, the Supreme Court replaced this extraordinarily strict interpretation of obscenity with what came to be known as the Roth-Memoirs test. This ruling established three tests, or standards, for ruling a work obscene: 1) The dominant theme of the material, taken as a whole, appeals to an average person's prurient interest in sex; 2) the material is patently offensive because it affronts contemporary community standards, assuming a single national standard, relating to sexual matters; and 3) the material is utterly without redeeming social value. This test for obscenity, while less restrictive than Hicklin, permitted a wide range of legal maneuvering and remained in effect until 1973.

1958 William O. Douglas, Supreme Court Justice, wrote: "The First Amendment does not say that there is freedom of expression provided the talk is not 'dangerous.' It does not say that there is freedom of expression provided the utterance has no tendency to subvert. It does not put free speech and freedom of the press in the category of housing, sanitation, hours of work, factory conditions, and the like, and make it subject to regulation for the public good. Nor does it permit legislative restraint of freedom of expression so long as the regulation does not offend due process. All notions of regulation or restraint by government are absent from the First Amendment. For it says in words that are unambiguous, 'Congress shall make no law...abridging the freedom of speech, or of the press.'"

1959 D. H. Lawrence's novel, *Lady Chatterly's Lover*, first published in Italy in 1928, was banned by the Federal Post Office Department when published in New York in 1959. The New York City Postmaster withheld some 200,000 copies of a circular announcing the new Grove Press edition of the book. The Federal Courts subsequently ruled that the book was not hard-core pornography and dismissed the banning restriction. This book and James Joyce's *Ulysses* were among the most important contemporary censorship cases. Both books, by noted literary artists, were subjected to obscenity charges; both were tried, appealed and approved in federal courts; and both remain controversial to this day.

1959 Clarifying the distinction between freedom and pornography in a capitalist system versus a communist system, Soviet premier Nikita Khrushchev said, "This is a dance [the Can-Can] in which girls pull up their skirts.... This is what you call freedom—freedom for the girls to show their backsides. To us it's pornography. The culture of people who want pornography. It's capitalism that makes the girls that way.... There should be a law prohibiting the girls from showing their backsides, a moral law."

1960 A classic example of the misguided foolishness of news media self-censorship was provided by events surrounding the Bay of Pigs disaster. In November 1960, editors of *The Nation* Magazine tried to interest major news media in an article charging that the U.S. was preparing to invade

Cuba, but none took the story. While reports of the impending invasion were widely known throughout Central America, the American press followed the lead of the *New York Times*, which dismissed the reports as "shrill... anti-American propaganda." Following the tragic, ill-fated invasion, President John F. Kennedy, who had persuaded the *Times* to withhold the story, acknowledged that had the press fulfilled its traditional watchdog role and reported the pending invasion, it would have saved the nation from a disastrous decision. He told the *Times*: "If you had printed more about the operation, you could have saved us from a colossal mistake."

1960 *The New York Times v. Sullivan*—a landmark case in libel law, introduced the concept of malice in journalism. On March 29, the *New York Times* published a full-page ad signed by some 64 people who charged that thousands of black Southern students engaging in nonviolent protests had been deprived of their constitutional rights. The ad specifically cited an event that occurred in Montgomery, Alabama. L.B. Sullivan, the commissioner of public affairs in Montgomery at the time, filed a libel suit against the New York Times Company and others. In finding for the *Times*, Supreme Court Justice William J. Brennan, Jr., said, "We are required in this case to determine for the first time the extent to which the constitutional protections for speech and press limit a State's power to award damages in a libel action brought by a public official against critics of his official conduct." In doing so in this case, the court ruled that it would be more difficult, under law, for a public official to win a libel suit than it would be for a private citizen. The ruling now requires that the public official would have to prove that the statement was made with "actual malice"—that is, with knowledge that it was false, or with reckless disregard as to whether it was false. The 1981 movie *Absence of Malice*, starring Sally Field and Paul Newman, popularized this court decision regarding libel.

1963 Whatever the truth may be behind the assassination of President John F. Kennedy, the news media cannot justify their early and uncritical endorsement of the Warren Commission Report. Their initial attempts to silence the critics of the official version smacked of raw censorship. When a leading scholar offered to write an analysis of the commission's operations, the *New York Times* rejected the offer, saying "the case is closed." Mark Lane's book on the same subject, *Rush to Judgment*, was not rushed to print. Lane couldn't find a publisher for 15 months, and it was published only after the media decided the issue was acceptable for coverage as a "controversy."

Lane's second book, *Citizen's Dissent*, published in early 1968, records how his pleas for a national examination of the evidence was rejected by *Look*, *Life*, the *Saturday Evening Post* and others. This book provides what may be the most exhaustive and documented study ever undertaken of the mass media's use of hidden bias on one issue. Not surprisingly, three years after publication, Lane reported that he hadn't been able to discover "one newspaper story in the mass media noting that the book had been published." Lane said that several media representatives told him: "We will bury that book with silence." And they did.

Incredibly, the media's conspiracy-like efforts to attack anything critical of the original Warren Commission Report's interpretation of the assassination was still in evidence in 1991. The press, in what appeared to be a well-orchestrated campaign, left no stone unturned in its criticism of film producer Oliver Stone and his movie *JFK*, which did not support the commission's findings. The effort was so exceptional, Stone had to hire one of the nation's leading public relations firms, Hill & Knowlton, to counteract the attacks and defend himself.

Indicative of the extent of censorship surrounding the Kennedy assassination was the way the Abraham Zapruder eight-millimeter film was handled. This extraordinary bit of footage, which recorded the actual assassination, raised serious questions about the Warren Commission's version of the event. The film, originally purchased by Time, Inc., and later resold to Zapruder, was never shown on national television until 1975, when it was aired on Tom Snyder's late-night "Tomorrow" show.

1966 In passing the Freedom of Information Act (FOIA), Congress established the American public's "right to know." It was signed into law by President Lyndon Johnson and went into effect on July 4, 1967. Unfortunately, years of information control and manipulation, as well as disdain for the FOIA by the Reagan/Bush administrations, encouraged federal agencies to find ways to circumvent it. Today it's extremely time-consuming and expensive for the public—as well as the press—to use it.

1966 At 10 AM, on February 10, the U.S. Senate Foreign Relations Committee began hearings on the Vietnam War with the testimony of Ambassador George F. Kennan. Over the objections of Fred W. Friendly, president of CBS News, the network aired a fifth CBS rerun of "I Love Lucy" instead of the hearings. Because of that decision, Friendly quit CBS and subsequently wrote *Due to Circumstances Beyond Our Control....* to tell what happened. The book begins with a quotation: "What the American people don't know can kill them." And it did. More than 58,000 Americans died in Vietnam, and tens of thousands of returned Vietnam veterans have died from war-related problems since.

1968 Dr. Paul Ehrlich's book *The Population Bomb* created a stir with its prediction that mass famines would plague the world within 20 years. Ehrlich warned that to avoid the tragedy of overpopulation, birth rates must be curbed. In 1971, media critic Robert Cirino, referring to Ehrlich's book, was prescient with his warning that "Experts have been making urgent pleas for controlling population and pollution for the last twenty-five years. But did the news media alert us in time?" Ehrlich's prediction has been tragically fulfilled by the African famines of the 1980s and 1990s, yet his warning continues to go unheeded. The earth's population is now growing at a rate of more than 100 million a year, and few people, including the press, seem to be aware that this is indeed a problem.

1968 The Columbia University Center for Mass Communications in New York offered all three networks a documentary using U.S. Army footage that depicted the horrifying effects of the atomic bomb on individual Japanese victims. The Army had suppressed the film since 1945 and finally released it at the insistence of the Japanese government. The film was described by Columbia professor Sumner J. Glimcher as "perhaps the best argument for people to live in peace." All three networks rejected the offer to run the documentary, nor did they use the Army's film, which also was available to them, to produce a documentary of their own.

1968 On March 16, some 570 South Vietnamese civilians were slaughtered in Mylai by the U.S. military. Although the massacre was reported over the radio in South Vietnam and in French publications, neither the U.S. press nor that of any other country challenged the official Pentagon version: that 128 "Reds" had been killed. Ronald Ridenhour, a former soldier, spent six months investigating the tragedy and talking to witnesses before trying to interest the media in the story. He contacted the President, Secretary of State, Secretary of Defense, numerous congressmen, *Life*, *Look*, *Newsweek*, *Harper's*, major newspapers, two wire services and at least one of the networks. Neither the politicians nor the media were interested.

By September, nearly 18 months after the tragedy, David Leonard, a reporter for the *Columbus Enquirer*, followed up on a lead about Lt. William Calley, Jr., and published a front-page article about him. The media ignored it, and the story died. In October, Seymour Hersh, then a freelance writer in Washington, DC, investigated the report, and tried to sell his version to several publications, including *Life* and *Look*. Again, they weren't interested. He finally sold the story to the Dispatch News Service, which released it on November 13; the issue was put on the national agenda at last.

1968 The critical need for mass media coverage of social problems, and the potential impact such coverage can have, was made clear when CBS News broadcast a documentary titled "Hunger in America." The documentary stirred a public debate, made hunger a national issue overnight and had a lasting impact. The U.S. Department of Agriculture expanded its food program to more counties, increased its monthly surplus of food going to the poor and called for an expansion of the food stamp program.

1968 "The Final Report: The President's Task Force on Communications Policy," published December 7, was highly critical of the nation's commercial television system. It strongly recommended creating a television communications system that would ensure a diversity of ideas and tastes, so that all minorities and majorities could be represented on television. President Johnson refused to make the report public before he left office, and the new President, Richard Nixon, delayed its release for another four months, until May 1969. Neither Johnson nor Nixon should have been worried; when the media finally did get the report, they essentially suppressed the potentially explosive information. The *Los Angeles Times* "covered" the report in a two-inch article on Page 2, under the daily news roundup; the *New York Times* reported it under a small headline in the middle of Page 95.

1969 In a letter to the *New York Times*, Charles Tower, chairman of the National Association of Broadcasters Television Board, proposed an interesting new definition of censorship. Tower criticized the *Times* for attacking CBS for "censoring" social commentary on the Smothers Brothers show (see below). He wrote, "There is a world of difference between the deletion of program material by Government command and the deletion by a private party (such as a broadcaster).... Deletion by Government command is censorship.... Deletion of material by private parties...is not censorship."

1969 "The Smothers Brothers Comedy Hour," a weekly entertainment program, was canceled by CBS for failing to cooperate with the network's program-previewing policies. According to the brothers, the program was often censored by CBS, with up to 75 percent of a program being edited out before being aired.

In one classic case of broadcasting censorship, as cited by Robert Cirino in his book *Power to Persuade*, CBS asked Pete Seeger, the famed folk singer who was blacklisted by broadcasters for 17 years, to drop the following verse from one of his songs on the Smothers Brothers program. It referred to the position in which the U.S. found itself in Vietnam in 1967:

> *But every time I read the papers*
> *That old feeling comes on;*
> *We're waist-deep in the Big Muddy*
> *And the big fool says to push on.*©

When Seeger refused to drop the verse, CBS censored the entire song, leading Seeger to say, "It is wrong for anyone to censor what I consider my most important statement to date.... I think the public should know that the airwaves are censored for ideas as well as for sex."

1969 In August, the outrageous but historic three-day Woodstock Music and Art Fair in New York State paved the way for future rock festivals by showing it was possible to overcome censorship rules and regulations created by local authorities to prevent such festivals.

1969 On November 13, during a speech in Des Moines, Iowa, Vice President Spiro Agnew launched a series of scurrilous and unsubstantiated attacks on the nation's media, accusing them of favoring liberals. His stand was applauded by the vast majority of media owners, who shared Agnew's opinion. These accusations are still used today to support the pervasive myth of "the liberal American media."

1970 Agnew continued his verbal assault, attacking the underground press, rock music, books and movies for luring American youth into a drug culture. He told his audience, "You need a Congress that will see to it that the wave of permissiveness, the wave of pornography, and the wave of moral pollution never become the wave of the future in our country." In a speech in Las Vegas, he specifically criticized radio stations for playing songs that contain "drug culture propaganda." On March 5, 1971, the FCC issued a notice to broadcasters, holding them responsible for airing songs that would "promote or glorify the use of illegal drugs" and made it abundantly clear that any station ignoring this notice could lose its license.

1970 On May 4, four students protesting the Cambodian incursion during the Vietnam War were killed by the National Guard on the Kent State University campus in Ohio.

1970 *How to Talk Back to Your Television Set*, a strident criticism of television by Nicholas Johnson, a former member of the FCC, cites a series of CBS documentaries that were "shelved, turned down, or killed," including "a 'hard-hitting' documentary on homosexuals, gutted, before showing, by the management...an 'in-depth investigation of Saigon corruption, also tabled...film footage of North Vietnam rejected for broadcast...an hour [-long] production on [the] black middle class, dumped...a project on 'Police Brutality,' turned into 'an industrial promo film for sponsor IBM'... a probe of the military industrial complex, ultimately devoted to 'the nomenclature of military rockets.'" Johnson also noted that CBS had pending for several years a project on "Congressional ethics"; he wondered whether we'd ever see it.

1970 The President's Commission on Obscenity and Pornography failed to find evidence linking obscene materials to criminal behavior, a conclusion that led both President Richard M. Nixon and the U.S. Senate to reject the report. The lesson was not lost on President Ronald Reagan, who later appointed Attorney General Edwin Meese to direct his own Commission on Pornography in 1985.

1971 Robert Cirino, a secondary school teacher in San Fernando, California, published an extraordinary book, *Don't Blame the People: How the news media use bias, distortion and censorship to manipulate public opinion*. After being rejected by mainstream publishers, Cirino published the book himself. Following its success as a college textbook, it was picked up and published by Random House in 1972. Cirino's closing paragraph sums up the role of the American press and suggests a solution:

"The effort to improve the quality of life in America has to be first the fight to save America from the distorted view of reality presented by the communication industry. It is a fight to restore the average man's participation in government by really letting him decide important questions. It is the average man, the man who doesn't have large corporate interests to protect, that is the strength of a democracy. His reasoning ability and sense of justice enacted into decisions and policies constitute the type of government envisioned by those who wrote America's Declaration of Independence. There has never been a better idea of governing a nation. Our major mistakes have not been the result of democracy, but of the erosion of democracy made possible by mass media's manipulation of public opinion. This erosion could only be stopped in the unlikely event that the Courts, the Congress and the American people were to demand that all political viewpoints have equal control over access to a mass communication system that is not for sale to anyone."

1971 On June 13, the *New York Times* started to print the Pentagon Papers, part of a top-secret, 47-volume government study of decision-making on Vietnam. Two days later, the *Times* was barred from continuing the series. In pleading its right to publish the papers before the Supreme Court, the *Times*, in effect, appeared to abandon the First Amendment in proposing the establishment of guidelines for prior restraint. Supreme Court Justice William O. Douglas warned the *Times*: "The First Amendment provides that Congress shall make no laws abridging the freedom of the press. Do you read that to mean that Congress can make some laws abridging freedom of the press?" It was, added Justice Douglas, "a very strange argument for the *Times* to be making." On June 30, the Supreme Court, by a 6-3 vote, told the *Times* it could go ahead and print the rest of the material.

1971 In December, I.F. Stone, marking the end of a special era in journalism, published the last issue of *I.F. Stone's Weekly*. In the essay, "Notes on Closing, but Not in Farewell," Stone wrote: "To give a little comfort to the oppressed, to write the truth exactly as I saw it, to make no compromises other than those of quality imposed by my own inadequacies, to be free to follow no master other than my own compulsions, to live up to my idealized image of what a true newspaperman should be and still be able to make a living for my family—what more could a man ask?"

1971 *The Selling of the Pentagon*, a hard-hitting CBS documentary, told the American people how much money the Pentagon was spending to buy a favorable public image for itself. Congress, particularly Rep. F. Edward Hebert, chair of the House Armed Services Committee, and members of the Nixon administration were outraged. When CBS rebroadcast the film about a month later, it had to add 15 minutes of rebuttal from Hebert (who called it "un-American"), Vice President Spiro Agnew (who called it a "vicious broadside against the nation's defense establishment") and Secretary of Defense Melvin Laird (often caricatured with a missile head). The House Committee on Interstate and Foreign Commerce unsuccessfully attempted to subpoena all copies of the film, and a committee vote to request a contempt citation against CBS was voted down.

1972 The break-in of the Democratic National Committee offices in the Watergate complex by the Republican CREEP (Committee to Re-elect the President) in June sparked one of the biggest political cover-ups in modern history. And the press, to its lasting shame, was an unwitting, if not willing, partner in the cover-up. The break-in, by CREEP employees known as the "plumbers," was described as a "two-bit burglary" not worthy of press attention. It didn't rate the national news agenda until after November, when Richard Nixon was re-elected by a landslide.

Carl Bernstein of the *Washington Post*, along with Bob Woodward, eventually made it a national story. Bernstein noted that out of some 2,000 full-time reporters for major news organizations, just 14 were assigned to the story on a full-time basis, even six months after the break-in. When Walter Cronkite tried to do an extraordinary two-part series on Watergate, on the "CBS-TV Evening News" *before* the election, a phone call from the Nixon White House to Bill Paley, chair of CBS, resulted in Cronkite's scheduled program being reduced. The power of a President to directly intervene and censor the nation's leading broadcast news organization was revealed.

1972 The Supreme Court ruled that dancing, even topless dancing, is a type of expression entitled to protection under the First Amendment. This judicial ruling encouraged the growth of topless, and eventually bottomless, dancing in bars throughout America.

1972 The Supreme Court ruled that the CIA could preview its employees' speeches and publications to protect against any disclosure of classified information. In 1980, this ruling was expanded to include prepublication review of all materials, including unclassified information. This decision was based on the case of a former CIA agent who published a book criticizing U.S. actions during the Vietnam War. The book contained no classified information.

1972 The first issue of *Index on Censorship* was published, acknowledging that "the need for such a magazine would become clear in the next few years"—and it has. The *Index*, an international advocate of free expression, focuses on the censorship, banning and exile of writers and journalists throughout the world.

1973 Beginning with the case of *Miller v. California*, the Supreme Court refined the Roth-Memoirs 1957 definition of obscenity, replacing national standards with local community standards. What is known as the Miller Test for obscenity is used today by American courts to determine whether a work is, by law, obscene. Written material is legally obscene under the following three conditions: 1) An average person, applying contemporary local community standards, finds that the work, taken as a whole, appeals to prurient interest; 2) the work depicts, in a patently offensive way, sexual conduct specifically defined by applicable state law; and 3) the material lacks serious literary, artistic, political or scientific value.

Sticks and Bones—a dramatic, filmed version of an award-winning stage drama about the homecoming of a blind Vietnam veteran and his callous reception—was scheduled to be shown on CBS on March 9. Four days before air date, CBS executives postponed the program, saying it would be "unnecessarily abrasive to the feelings of millions of Americans whose lives or attention were dominated at the time by the returning POWs and other veterans." Joseph Papp, producer of the film, called the postponement "a cowardly cop-out, a rotten affront to freedom of speech." When the drama was finally shown five months later, only 91 stations carried it. Many advertisers canceled their commercials.

1975 Ruling on the constitutionality of a Tennessee ban on the rock musical *Hair*, the U.S. Supreme Court ruled that live theater has legal protection against prior restraint, as is the case with books, movies and other forms of expression.

1976 Project Censored, the national media research project focusing on news media censorship, was founded. The top ten Censored stories of 1976 were the following:

> 1. Jimmy Carter and the Trilateral Commission
> 2. Corporate Control of DNA
> 3. Selling Banned Pesticides and Drugs to Third World Countries
> 4. The Oil Price Conspiracy
> 5. The Mobil Oil/Rhodesian Connection
> 6. Missing Plutonium and Inadequate Nuclear Reactor Safeguards
> 7. Workers Die for American Industry
> 8. Kissinger, the CIA, and SALT
> 9. Worthless or Harmful Non-prescription Drugs
> 10. The Natural Gas "Shortage"

1977 The FCC outlawed a monologue, "Seven Words You Can't Say on Radio" by comedian George Carlin, from being broadcast on radio or television. While the words still have shock value in print, they're surely not strangers on television, particularly on cable. The seven words that assured Carlin of lasting fame were "shit," "piss," "fuck," "cunt," "cocksucker," "motherfucker" and "tits."

1977 When the ACLU defended the rights of the Nazis to demonstrate in Skokie, near Chicago, 15 to 20 percent of ACLU members dropped their membership in protest. While the Illinois Appellate Court gave the Nazis permission to demonstrate but not to wear the swastika, the Illinois Supreme Court subsequently ruled that the Nazis had a right to display the swastika.

1977 The problem of decommissioning nuclear power plants—one of Project Censored's top ten Censored stories of 1977—was discovered when some of the original plants and reactors had to be shut down. In two cases, the costs for dismantling the plant ran almost as high as the original construction costs. Decommissioning nuclear power plants remains an unresolved issue in 1993.

1978 The specter of sterility was raised when researchers discovered that the average sperm count among American men had dropped substantially since a landmark study done less than 30 years earlier. The research revealed that the probable causes were industrial and agricultural chemicals similar to the DBCP pesticide (which, earlier, had led to male sterility at a chemical plant), and that the trend may represent a potential sterility threat to the entire male population. The threat, one of the top ten Censored stories of the year, wasn't dramatic enough to attract the attention of the mass media at the time. However, in mid-September 1992, a new study made front-page news when a growing number of scientists concluded that changes in sexuality, including reduced fertility, may have occurred in humans exposed to chemical pollution.

1979 The longest period of government censorship by prior restraint of a publication in U.S. history began March 9. A Federal District Court in Wisconsin imposed a temporary restraining order on *The Progressive*, a Wisconsin-based monthly magazine, censoring publication of the article, "The H-Bomb Secret: How We Got It, Why We're Telling It." The government claimed that the description of how a hydrogen bomb is designed would help foreign countries produce H-bombs more swiftly. But the government finally acknowledged the meaning of the First Amendment on September 17, when it ruled that the magazine could publish the article.

1979 To find cheap labor and escape U.S. health and safety regulations, increasing numbers of major American corporations set up branches or contracted jobs under "sweatshop" conditions in Third World countries. This story—one of the top ten Censored stories of 1979—attracted national attention during the 1992 Presidential election year, as unemployment plagued workers in the U.S., and health problems and environmental pollution plagued workers in the Third World.

1980 The top Censored story of 1980, "Distorted Reports of the El Salvador Crisis," launched more than a decade of top ten Censored stories dealing with underreported or biased reports of U.S. intervention in Central America.

1981 The American people were told that the overregulation of business and the "declining moral fiber of the American worker" had caused the worst economic crisis since the Depression. But Maurice Zeitlin, a UCLA economic sociologist, testifying before the California Senate Committee on Industrial Relations, charged that we no longer had a competitive economy, and that monopoly, militarism and multinationalization were at the root of our economic crisis. His testimony, cited as the top Censored story of 1981, also suggested that we could expect more of the same until the root causes are examined and changed.

1982 President Reagan established an oppressive system of security classification with his Executive Order 12356. It reversed a trend toward openness on the part of previous administrations by eliminating what was known as the balancing test. Now it was no longer necessary to weigh the public's need to know against the need for classification. In addition, the Executive Order reduced the threshold standard for classification. That same year, Project Censored cited Reagan as "America's Chief Censor" for his efforts to reduce the amount of information available to the public about the operation of the government, the economy, the environment and public health, and for his attempts to weaken the Freedom of Information Act.

1982 *The Media Monopoly*, by Ben Bagdikian, was published, revealing that just 50 corporations control half or more of the media in America.

1983 National Security Decision Directive 84 (NSDD 84), issued by the Reagan Administration in March, required all government personnel with access to classified materials to sign a lifetime secrecy pledge.

1984 Fulfilling the Orwellian expectations of the year, President Reagan implemented NSDD 84—the largest censoring apparatus ever known in the United States. For the first time in history, all federal employees were required to submit their speeches, articles and books for prepublication review by their superiors for the rest of their lives. Under pressure from Congress, the administration suspended the prepublication review provision in September 1984, but a 1986 General Accounting Office report on its impact concluded that the suspension had little effect, and that prepublication review was alive and well in America.

1984 On September 14, CBS reporter Mike Wallace appeared on "The Phil Donahue Show," predicting that one of the segments he was working on for "60 Minutes" could possibly change the course of the presidential election. The story focused on one of Ronald Reagan's closest friends, Nevada Senator Paul Laxalt, who was high on Reagan's list of potential

Supreme Court nominees. Journalists investigating Laxalt found he had accepted political contributions from supporters linked to organized crime, received highly questionable loans, tried to limit FBI investigations into Nevada gaming operations and owned a Carson City casino that engaged in illegal skimming operations. After being contacted by Laxalt and his attorney, CBS decided not to run the story. Although the story didn't have a chance to change the course of the 1984 election, as predicted by Wallace, Reagan never nominated Laxalt to the Supreme Court.

1985 President Ronald Reagan appointed Attorney General Edwin Meese to head his Commission on Pornography. The members, reportedly hand-picked for their support of censorship, spent considerable time investigating erotic films, books and magazines protected by the First Amendment. Based on the testimony of the Rev. Donald Wildmon, executive director of the National Federation of Decency, the commission sent a letter to 26 major corporations, including K-mart, Southland (7-Eleven stores) and Stop N Go Stores, that accused them of selling and distributing pornography by selling publications such as *Playboy* and *Penthouse*. A U.S. District Court subsequently ruled that the commission had threatened the First Amendment rights of magazine publishers and distributors and ordered the letter withdrawn.

1985 The drive for profits, coupled with the apparent collapse of the FCC, led to a frenzy of media mergers and paved the way for an international information monopoly. Consumer advocate Ralph Nader warned of the increased threat of censorship resulting from conglomerate self-interest: "Self-censorship is alive and well in the U.S. media."

1986 The American Library Association (ALA) charged the Reagan administration with efforts to eliminate, restrict and privatize government documents; with launching an official new "disinformation" program that permitted the government to release deliberately false, incomplete and misleading information; and with developing a new category of "sensitive information," restricting public access to a wide range of previously unclassified data. While the ALA charges were accurate and well documented, they were ignored by the major news media.

1986 FAIR, Fairness & Accuracy in Reporting, an anti-censorship organization based in New York, was established to shake up the establishment-dominated media. It draws attention to important news stories that have been neglected and defends working journalists when they are muzzled.

1986 Article 19, an international human rights organization named after Article XIX of the Universal Declaration of Human Rights (see 1948), was founded in London to document and fight censorship on an international basis. The UN declaration holds that "Everyone has a right to freedom of opinion and expression; this right includes freedom to hold opinions without interference and to seek, receive and impart information and ideas through any media regardless of frontiers."

1986 The Final Report of the Attorney General Edwin Meese's Commission on Pornography was released. As expected, it simply ignored the First Amendment. But what can you expect from Edwin Meese, the subject of a 1984 Censored story that charged him with directing a secret operation involving a variety of illegal and unconstitutional activities while a California state official in the late '60s and early '70s. The effort was aimed at subverting the anti-war movement in California.

1987 In what many consider to be an unconstitutional ruling, the Supreme Court's *Hazelwood* decision provided renewed support for censorship through the use of prior restraint. In essence, the court gave high school administrators the power to censor student publications in advance. The ruling reversed a long-time trend of First Amendment support for freedom of expression issues on high school campuses. Oddly enough, this violation of the First Amendment has been ignored by the major news media. Despite widespread student protest, it is still unchallenged in 1993.

1987 The continuing centralization of media ownership raised critical questions about the public's access to a diversity of opinion when Ben Bagdikian updated his 1982 book, *The Media Monopoly*. He found that just 26 corporations now controlled half or more of America's media enterprise. Bagdikian also predicted that by the 1990s, a half-dozen giant firms would control most of the world's media.

1988 Top Censored story of this election year revealed how the major mass media ignored, overlooked or undercovered at least ten critical stories reported in America's alternative press that raised serious questions about the Republican candidate, George Bush, dating from his reported role as a CIA "asset" in 1963 to his Presidential campaign's connection with a network of anti-Semites with Nazi and fascist affiliations in 1988.

1989 Fulfilling his 1987 predictions about world media conglomerates, Ben Bagdikian revealed in a well-documented article in *The Nation* that five global media lords already dominated the fight for hundreds of millions of minds throughout the world. Further, these media monopolies conceded they may control most of the world's important newspapers, magazines, books, broadcast stations, movies, recordings and video cassettes by the turn of the century. The Big 5 of 1989 were:

- Time Warner Inc., the world's largest media corporation
- German-based Bertelsmann AG, owned by Reinhard Mohn
- Rupert Murdoch's News Corporation Ltd., of Australia
- Hatchette SA, of France, the world's largest producer of magazines
- U.S.-based Capital Cities/ABC Inc.

1990 In April, for the first time in history, an American museum and its director faced criminal charges for pandering obscenity. Their crime was a display of erotic photographs by Robert Mapplethorpe. The director, Dennis Barrie, and the Contemporary Arts Center in Cincinnati were both acquitted of pandering in October. Cincinnati earned its name "Censornati."

1990 The flawed coverage of events leading up to the Persian Gulf crisis was the top Censored story of the year. Traditional press skepticism of government/military activities was the first casualty in the days immediately following Iraq's invasion of Kuwait as the U.S. media became cheerleaders for the Bush administration.

1991 For the second year in a row, the top Censored story of the year focused on the Gulf War. It revealed how the networks rejected uncensored videotape footage of the heavy Iraqi civilian damage, the result of American-led bombing campaigns. Instead, the networks continued to feed the Pentagon-approved, high-tech, smart-bomb, antiseptic, nonthreatening version of the war. The second overlooked story of the year revealed a number of specific Gulf War issues that didn't receive the coverage they deserved; while the #6 Censored story provided photographic evidence that challenged President Bush's original explanation for our rapid deployment in the Gulf.

1991 On May 24, the Supreme Court, in a ruling as unconstitutional as its earlier *Hazelwood* decision, upheld a Reagan administration interpretation of Title X, the Public Health Services Act, that prohibited abortion counseling at federally funded family planning clinics. The 1987 interpretation suggested that Title X "required physicians and counselors to withhold information about abortion even from patients who were at medical risk from continuation of the pregnancy." The Court ruled that the word "abortion" could not be uttered in any of America's 4,500 federally supported clinics that provide aid and counseling to millions of poor women. In essence, the U.S. Supreme Court ruled that First Amendment free speech rights are a function of federal funding.

1991 The introduction to the *Article 19 Yearbook of 1991* (see 1986) provided some sobering statistics about censorship on an international scale. In 62 of the 77 countries surveyed for the report, people were detained for peacefully expressing their opinions. In 27 of the countries, people, including journalists, were reportedly tortured, killed or otherwise maltreated because of their opinions.

1991 In the introduction to Volume IV of *The Right to Know*, published in 1992 by the DataCenter in Oakland, California, Zoia Horn, a long-time champion of intellectual freedom, made the following comments about how we "celebrated" the 200th anniversary of the Bill of Rights in 1991. "The 200th anniversary of the Bill of Rights should have been the occasion for a reaffirmation of democratic principles. Unfortunately, it fizzled into just another public relations campaign profiting Philip Morris, Inc., the sponsor of a widely viewed exhibit. Many people polled during the Persian Gulf war saw no contradiction between the censorship and manipulation of the media by the Pentagon and the Bill of Rights. Indeed, previous polls have revealed that people on the street, asked to read the Bill of Rights, thought it was a communist document, and thus rejected parts of it. Ignorance of our basic democratic tenets requires a serious, massive, educational campaign at all age levels, through all mediums of communication."

1992 The Department of Defense and a group of self-selected media executives agreed on nine out of ten ground rules for press coverage of America's next military engagement. The contested and unresolved issue concerned prior restraint on the part of the military. The policy, which apparently supplements the First Amendment, evolved from the pool concept of censorship developed by the Reagan administration for the Granada War, subsequently refined by the Bush administration for the Panama War and given a full-scale test during the Gulf War where it failed.

1992 Volume 1, Number 1, of *America's CENSORED Newsletter* was published in April. The premiere issue revealed how the U.S. media dwell on foreign censorship while ignoring it in the U.S., warned about a classified Department of Defense document proposing the U.S. assume the role of a benevolent worldwide authority in the post-Cold War era, and noted how the press ignored the apparent impact of Halcion, a reportedly dangerous sleeping pill, on President George Bush.

1992 The Center for the Study of Commercialism (CSC) invited 200 media outlets to a press conference to be held on March 11 in Washington, DC. The purpose was to reveal how advertisers, one of the nation's most powerful media voices, influence, corrupt and censor a free press. Not a single radio or television station or network sent a reporter; and only two newspapers, the *Washington Post* and the *Washington Times*, bothered to attend. The *Post* didn't run a story on the press conference while the *Times* (also known as the Capitol's Moonie Paper, since it is owned by Sun Yung Moon) ran one but didn't name the advertisers cited in the CSC study. The well-documented study, which has been seen by few Americans, was titled "Dictating Content: How Advertising Pressure Can Corrupt a Free Press."

1992 In the June introduction to "Less Access to Less Information By and About the U.S. Government: XVIII," the American Library Association, Washington Office, reflected on how the Reagan/Bush administrations have significantly limited access to public documents and statistics and warned that it might get worse, given the increasing commercialization of what was once public information. It noted that since 1982, one of every four of the government's 16,000 publications has been eliminated. For the future it warned of "... the growing tendency of federal agencies to utilize computer and telecommunications technologies for data collection, storage, retrieval, and dissemination. This trend has resulted in the increased emergence of contractual arrangements with commercial firms to disseminate information collected at taxpayer expense, higher user charges for government information, and the proliferation of government information available in electronic form only."

1993 A final chronologically censored word. In his latest update on the increasing monopolization of the media, Ben Bagdikian reports that fewer than 23 corporations now own and control the majority of the media in America.

> ### The Writer and the Asterisk
> *A writer owned an Asterisk,*
> *And kept it in his den,*
> *Where he wrote tales (which had large sales)*
> *Of frail and erring men;*
> *And always, when he reached the point*
> *Where carping censors lurk,*
> *He call upon the Asterisk*
> *To do his dirty work.*
>
> *—Stoddard King (1889-1933)*

Index

A

B

J

Japan
 effect of bomb on 220
 media 95
Jeremiah 198
John (King of England) 199
Johnson, Nicholas 10–11, 223
Johnston Island 72–73
Journalists. *See* Media
Joyce, James 211

K

Kaltenborn, H.V. 206–7
Karpatkin, Rhoda H. 11
Kellogg's 29, 121–22
Kemper, Vicki 30, 124
Kennedy, John F. 217–18, 218–19
Kent State University, students killed by National Guard at 222
Kerner Commission 104
King John (of England) 199
Kinsey reports 215
Kistner, William 82
Kline, David 9–10
Knaus, Holley 76, 77
Kruschev, Nikita 217
Kuwait, war involving 102–3

L

Labor 207
Lady Chatterly's Lover 217
Lawrence, D.H. 217
Laxalt, Paul 228–29
Leo, Katherine 124
Lewis, Damien 79–80
Lewis, Sinclair 210
Libel 218
Library and reference sources 189–90
Licensing Act 200, 201
Lippman, Walter 209
Literature, censorship of 210, 211, 217
Logging 78–70
Long–Scott, Ethel 67, 68–70
Los Angeles, riots in 104
Luling, Virginia 78, 80
Luther, Martin 200
Lutz, William 21

M

Publications. *See* Media
Public Media Center 23
Pulitzer, Joseph 2

Q

Quayle, Dan 23, 91, 92. *See also* Bush, George

R

Radiation
    electromagnetic 107
    microwave 94
    nuclear. *See* Nuclear power; Nuclear waste; Nuclear weapons
Radio. *See* Broadcast media
Rainforests, clearcutting 78–80
Rathaus, Jennifer 85, 87–88
Reagan, Ronald
    censorship under 228, 229, 233
    drug war under 42–44, 153–54
    Iran/contra affair and 98, 99
    media sell–out under 25–28, 110–14
    1992 top censored stories and 15–16, 18
    Paul Laxalt and 228–29
Reference sources 189–90
Regulation
    Bush interference with 44–46, 155–57. *See also* Bush,
        George, 1992 election
    weakening of EPA 55–57
    See also Competitiveness, Council on
Religion, censorship and 7
Republic, The 198
Research, dearth of 93
Right to Know, The 232
Right–to–know publications and organizations 183–85
Riots 104
Rogers, Linda 34–35
Rome, ancient 198, 199
Rowse, Arthur E. 30, 32, 44, 46
Royko, Mike 30, 193
Russell, Bertrand 210
Russia
    arms build–up 104
    logging in 78–80
    See also Communism

S

T

U

V

Sign Up Today
for Next Year's  News!

If the real issues and stories behind the stories are important to you, be among
the first readers of *CENSORED: The 1994 Project Censored Yearbook*.
By returning the form below, you'll be added to "the CENSORED list" to
receive a sneak preview of news you didn't see or read about this year.
Plus, an updated resource guide, 1993's "Junk Food News" and more!

To receive a pre-publication announcement and a special discount offer on next
year's edition, please complete the form below and return it to Shelburne Press,
P.O. Box 2468, Chapel Hill, NC 27515. FAX: 919/942-1140.

Yes! Please add me to the 1994 CENSORED list. I would like
to receive information and a special offer on next year's
edition of *CENSORED: The News That Didn't Make the News—and Why.*

Name _____

Address_____

City _____ State _____Zip _____

Country_____Phone_____

Return to: CENSORED 1994, Shelburne Press,
P.O. Box 2468, Chapel Hill, NC 27515.
FAX: 919/942-1140.

CAN'T WAIT?

If you'd like to stay up-to-date on the latest CENSORED news, junk food stories and more, sign up below to receive *America's CENSORED Newsletter*. Published monthly, the Project Censored newsletter includes

- ☞ Information on the latest Censored nominations.
- ☞ Reports on censored books and films.
- ☞ Profiles of censored investigative journalists.
- ☞ Tips on learning more about censorship and censored issues.

To stay informed and in touch with important issues and events that you need to know about, subscribe to *America's CENSORED Newsletter*. Please complete the form below and return it with your payment ($30 in the U.S. or $45 for international subscriptions) to America's CENSORED Newsletter, P.O. Box 310, Cotati, CA 94931 USA.

Yes! I'd like to subscribe to *America's CENSORED Newsletter*. I have enclosed my payment ($30 in the U.S. or $45 for international subscriptions).

Name _____

Address _____

City_____State_____Zip_____

Country_____Telephone _____

Please return this form with payment to:
America's CENSORED Newsletter
P.O. Box 310
Cotati, CA 94931 USA